On War on Board

ON WAR ON BOARD

Archaeological and historical perspectives on early modern maritime violence and warfare

Edited by
Johan Rönnby

Södertörns högskola

Södertörns högskola
Biblioteket
SE-141 89 Huddinge

www.sh.se/publications

Cover image: *Skirmish between Amsterdam and English warships, 20 April 1605*,
detail of a painting, by Hendrick Cornelisz Vroom (1566–1640), 1614 (A.0002)
The National Maritime Museum, Amsterdam
Het Scheepvaartmuseum, Amsterdam (HSM)

Cover: Jonathan Robson
Graphic form: Per Lindblom & Jonathan Robson
Stockholm 2020

Södertörn Archaeological Studies 15
ISSN 1652-2559

Södertörn Academic Studies 78
ISSN 1650-433X

ISBN 978-91-88663-86-3 (print)
ISBN 978-91-88663-87-0 (digital)

Contents

On War on Board
– Introduction

JOHAN RÖNNBY

A sunken battlefield

On May 31, 1564, the Swedish king Erik XIV's newly built flagship *Mars* sank to the northeast of the island of Öland in the southern Baltic Sea having taken part in a naval battle against a joint fleet of ships from Denmark and the town of Lubeck. Named after the Roman god of war, this huge warship was constructed with high fighting castles to the fore and aft and was armed with around 120 guns. During the battle, *Mars* became surrounded by two enemy ships and was subsequently boarded. During the hand-to-hand fighting on deck, the ship started to burn and exploded violently after a while. A witness' testimony by the captured Swedish admiral Jakob Bagge describes how the foremast flew high up in the air, and the ship then quickly sank to the bottom, leaving just a large ghostly cloud of yellow-brown smoke and steam above the water.

Today, the remains of Erik XIV's great warship lie in the dark of the sea bottom at a depth of 70 metres. More than 450 years have passed since the ship sank dramatically, but evidence of the violent battle is clearly distinguishable in the light of the dive lamps. The large oak timbers that held together the heavy hull are sooty and marked by fire. Between the gaping gun ports in the side, the damage from projectiles is visible. Most of the front section is missing due to an explosion that occurred when the fire reached the powder store causing the foremast to shoot up in the air.

Among the burned timber and objects are many guns of various sizes. A few of them are made of iron, rusted and corroded, but most are of bronze. Some have a serial number and the royal Vasa monogram engraved on the barrel. Several of the large guns are broken and appear to have exploded from the heat of the fire. There are also bone remnants of the approximately 800 sailors and soldiers who died in the battle. Their last hour at sea was clearly turbulent with overwhelming noise, smoke and flying splinters, besides the heat and fire (see Eriksson & Rönnby 2015).

The sight of the material traces gives rise to questions and reflections about warfare. In a battle situation such as this, how can people be motivated to work and function practically? Why do the gunners remain at their posts in the smoke and the noise and continue to systematically handle the guns instead of running away to protect themselves? What is it that makes it possible for humans to jump aboard a burning enemy ship while the crew of that ship armed with knives, pikes and axes are doing their best to kill them? Why do these kinds of events seem to have followed us through history and keep on repeating themselves?

The ambition of this volume is to investigate questions that the encounter with sites like *Mars* creates. It concerns specific topics directly connected to battlefield situations. The anthology is perhaps most of all, however, about the human organization of and attitudes towards systematic violence and warfare. How to describe, analyse and understand the human experience of war?

The book is a cooperation between archaeologists and historians from several countries. The starting point for the study was a research project "Ships at War" financed by the Foundation for Baltic and East European Studies based at Södertörn University. Besides archaeological investigations of a handful of shipwrecks, the aim of the project was to raise some more general historical and humanistic questions related to old warships. Furthermore, a workshop with this theme was held at Västervik Museum during the spring of 2017 where the project research group was augmented by external researchers with similar interests.

The authors of the articles in this volume have selected different ways to discuss and explore subjects connected to warfare, based on their expertise and research interests. A common denomination in the papers is however the nautical context, the historical perspective and the time period in focus, the early modern period.

Why a historical perspective?

Using a historical and archaeological perspective for approach questions related to war in general, human behaviour on a battlefield or the ability to kill other humans, is truly not the easiest or most obvious way. Direct observations or talking to people with first-hand experience of conflict and violence, give insights and details that no historical document or archaeological remains can ever provide. In addition, if one wants to study the tools, the technology of war and the material conditions involved, there is certainly no lack of examples in our contemporary world.

However, what a historical perspective possibly can bring is an opportunity to compare our contemporary knowledge of systematic violence with war equipment, behaviour and events from a completely different cultural context in history. Such a perspective allows both the specific and the general aspects of warfare to emerge more clearly. Cultural and social aspects can be made visible (compare so called thick descriptions in anthropology, Geertz 1991).

A well-known problem in social sciences and humanities is that it is difficult to understand, or even recognise, behaviours and events just when they are part of our contemporary world. It is only afterwards that they can emerge and be understood as parts of more general structures and patterns. The Russian author Leo Tolstoy uses this argument in 1865, half a century after the Napoleonic Wars, when he analyses the mechanisms of war in his epilogue to *War and Peace* (Tolstoy 1959:80ff, 1968, see also Tingsten 1958:11–26, von Wright 1994:240ff). Tolstoy's viewpoint on warfare is expressed in the novel by the Russian general Kutuzov's fatalistic attitude to his own personal importance for the outcome of the bloody battle at Borodino 1812. Wars and battles are unpredictable for the people involved, including emperors, and are instead described to be determined by very complex historical circumstances. Also, according to Tolstoy, the further back in history we examine an event, the wider our perspective is, the less important single actors or "great men" turn out to be.

The specific historical perspective in this book, the early modern period, was also a time when there were unusually large dramatic changes in power structure, shipbuilding and war technology. The Renaissance led to new thoughts concerning many aspects of war, especially regarding societal organization and the importance of the individual. During this period, the Reformation changed the roll of Christian religion, and all over Europe there was a strong state-building process taking place. As far as naval ship development is concerned, this was also an unrivalled period. The warships at the end of the 15th century became bigger and more powerful and started to sail long distances all around the globe. During the 16th and 17th centuries the navies and the warships developed into the leading tool for most of the new states in Europe, used for exploration, conquest and power domination (see Glete 2000, 2002, but also for example Parker 1988). Therefore, the preconditions for discussing the role of maritime material culture and new naval technology in relation to power, ideology, war and violence is unusually good in relation to the early modern period, especially in a perspective where one considers the "social" to consist of a dialectical web of acting humans and material "pre-consequences" (see Adams & Rönnby this volume).

Although, of course, we cannot today understand and reach all aspects of a past society, but we have from our 21st century perspective an opportunity to position both maritime battlefields, expressions of power and old ideological structures. We can put ships, weapons, clothes and various human attitudes associated with warfare during the early modern period in a wider historical as well as in a more general context. For example, regarding the wrecking of *Mars* the 31 May 1564, we can view the specific occasion in the past from our perspective in the present. We then know not only the historical context of the events, but we also know now how these events relate to King Erik's ambition in general and not least what happened later.

On the study of war

War as a field of study is enormous and of course impossible to summarize in a just way. There are also various possible perspectives. War can be analysed from a strategic, historical, sociological, moral or other point of view. This makes the study of war a subject where one can find strict military theory but also anthropological conclusions and philosophic thoughts. This possible variation of perspectives is in fact also demonstrated in this book and the different authors' choice of subject.

The interest in the topic of war is very old. An early example of a systematic analysis of warfare is found in texts which are usually interpreted as belonging to the Chinese general Sun Zi. His book "The Art of War" was probably written around 500 BC (Cleary 2005). The general's almost rational analysis of the structure and the different aspects of war, to be used for practical warfare and strategy, have been a common way of dealing with the subject, used at military academies and by military thinkers throughout history (Widén & Ångström 2005:19ff).

Almost contemporary with Sun Zi, the Greek historian Herodotus's (484–425 BC) work on the Persian War is another well-known example of early writing on warfare. It is from Herodotus that we best know the famous battles at Marathon in 490 BC, at Thermopylae in 480 BC and the sea battle of Salamis the same year. Herodotus claims that 300–400 Persians ships were lost in the battle of Salamis. Another classic, ancient study of historical war is by Thucydides (460–397 BC); his book is about the Peloponnesian War between Sparta and Athens during the late 4th century BC.

In addition, more specific theoretical ideas regarding naval warfare have a long story going back to these ancient Chinese and Greek authors. A central theme regarding maritime warfare has been the concept of "sea power". This is mentioned by the Athens commander at Salamis, Themistocles (527–460 BC), but also later by Francis Bacon (1561–1626) and the famous naval historian Julian Corbett during the early 20th century. In brief, the doctrine can be said to stress the importance of controlling the sea. In that way one does not control just transport routes and the economy, but also the war as such (Widén & Ångström 2005:211–242, Speller 2014:1–11, Widen 2012).

The concept of having power over the sea and the actual state formed as a *thallasokrati* ("Sea based state") is also highly relevant when discussing the roll of the fleet and the warships in the Baltic area during the early modern period. Just as the Romans once regarded the Mediterranean as an important arena of dominion, so did the early states of Denmark and Sweden, by formulating their ambitions as *"Dominium maris baltici"*. This was also one of the reasons why Erik XIV, with his desire to expand the country, was building the great new ship *Mars Makalös* ("Matchless") in 1563. During the 17th century and Sweden's "Great Power Era," the control of the Baltic was essential for keeping the empire together (see, for example, Glete 2000, Asker 2005).

The most well-known study regarding warfare of all time may, however be the Prussian, general Carl von Clausewitz's (1780–1831) work, *On War*, (*Vom Kriege*). Clausewitz's work is complex and deals systematically with many aspects connected to warfare, combining philosophical, historical and strategic arguments. Perhaps his most widely known conclusion is that war is just a continuation of politics (von Clausewitz 1997, Johansson 1988:24–48).

Clausewitz was however, not the first to link war to politics. One of the most important political philosophers in the beginning of the early modern period was Niccole Machiavelli (1468–1527), and war is a central theme in his production. In his famous book *The Prince* written in 1513, he argues that a successful ruler's first and most important mission is warfare and its organization (1993:73). How early modern warfare best should be organized is also discussed in his "Dell´arte della Guerra" (Art of War) from 1520 (2014).

Living in renaissance Florence it is not surprising that Machiavelli connected to practices in the prosperous old Roman legions both regarding organization and tactics. Machiavelli's suggestion for the ruler is to organize a state militia and trust armed citizens instead of just paid mercenaries. This form of military organization can be seen in Sweden for example, in the recruitment of soldiers and seaman for King Gustav Vasa's new army and fleet in the 1530s but also later, in the wars of the 17th century, in the young country's development of an organized system for enlisting new soldiers in the armed forces. To get this new system to work, however, was rather complicated and required negotiations and agreements with the public and their leaders (see Hallenberg & Holmberg 2017, Neudin Skoog 2019).

In a post-medieval Europe with growing armies and navy fleets which gathered men from very different strata, training, drilling and classification was becoming more and more necessary (see Sjöblom 2016). Kings and military innovators during this time could find theoretical arguments and justifications for their efforts and demands in Machiavelli's work.

The face of battle

For people directly involved in battles or on-board ships involved in fighting, war of course is very different from military and political strategy, theoretical modelling and philosophical reflections about the nature of war.

From later warfare there are rather many books written by people who have personally taken part in the fighting. For example, in Erik Maria Remarque's famous descriptions of being a soldier in the muddy trenches on the western front during WWI, and in Veinnö Linna's novel about fighting in east Finland during the winter war of 1942, we meet the reflections, feelings and everyday life of war from a participant soldier's perspective (Remarque 1972, Linna 1955). Historians, of course, are also able to collect stories from people involved and then organize and analyse them. Peter Englund, in *The Beauty and the Sorrow of War*, has sampled different short stories and destinies and edited them together. In this way he can give both an individual and a collective description of the Great War from 1913 to 1917 (Englund 2011).

The special insight that can emerge when this kind of individual experience is presented as part of larger collective is demonstrated in Nobel prize winner Svetlana Aleksijevitj's books about World War II and the Soviet war in Afghanistan, *The Unwomanly Face of War* (2012) and *Boys in Zink* (2014). The first book also gives a unique presentation of the experiences of female soldiers on the front and in the Red army during 1939–1945. Their personal stories show that the bravery, fear and sorrow connected to fighting and killing were the same for them as for their male colleagues. The difference for the women soldiers was the attitudes and structures in the society around them. This was something they seem to have had in common with women taking part in other wars earlier in history (see also Larsdotter 2016, Bourke 2016 and last chapter this book).

An interesting exception regarding older, first-hand sources from the early modern period is the mercenary Peter Hagendof's diary from the 30

Years' War. During more than two decades, 1625–1649, he served as a soldier, mostly in the Emperor's army but also in the Swedish army for a period. His book describes marchers and field camps, but also how he got married, how new-born children died, how cities were plundered and, rather occasionally, also how some battles were fought. In comparison to Remarrque and Linna, Peter Hagendorf is, however surprisingly short and neutral in his tone. It is hard to believe that this tone mirrors a totally different attitude to the horrors of war; most likely it is a result of another tradition of writing (Petters 2006).

Written descriptions about naval battles from the early modern period are in most cases rather short reports without any ambition to recount details from the actual fighting on board. One exception is however from Oliwa 1627, when the Admiral Nils Stiernsköld's ship *Tigern* was boarded by Polish soldiers. The source describes how the Admiral himself was hit by several small shots, one in his back and one in his neck, and how after that a gunshot ripped his left arm from his body. A similar thing also happened to his servant Mats, whose arm bones were smashed by a shot, so his arm was just hanging on his body by the skin.

During the first half of the 17th century there is a transformation regarding the tactics of fighting on board. The old tactic of boarding the enemy ships is replaced by the tactic of firing the guns from a distance and sailing in a line formation. A description of the horror one could meet on board during such a fight exists from the battle of Hogland in 1788, related by Friedrich Hjerta Larssons. The battle lasted for hours. There is noise, smoke and confusion, and some of the iron shots kill several people, one after another, when they flee over the deck. The crew steps in blood and brain tissue and parts of skull bones are stuck in the sides of the ship. The bodies of the dead are continually thrown over the side (see Höglund forthcoming).

Visiting the battlefield

It is a challenge for a historian or archaeologist to make credible depictions of how people really experience war. There is, despite that, however several attempts to use a participant perspective when writing about historical warfare and battles. A work that is often mentioned in this context is John Keegan's book *Face of Battle* (1978). He describes in this book three different battles, Somme in 1916, Waterloo in 1815 and Agincourt in 1415.

George Duby's *Legend of Bouvines* (1990) is a similar study of a single event, even though the focus is on how the 1214 battle of Bouvines has been used in

French national ideology. In his book about the knight and nobleman Wilhelm Marshal, the same author gives an interesting insight into the world and mentality of 13th century power and warrior culture (Duby 1987). The Swedish Army's marches, rallies and hardships during the 17th century's great continent wars have also been portrayed in close detail several times by Peter Englund (1993, 2000, 2011, 2013).

A skilled researcher and author can use his general knowledge and his own experience as a human being to understand and describe the situation on a historic battlefield. Nevertheless, this kind of work needs to rely on detailed written source material, to prevent them from turning into pure fiction (which, like visual art, can also have a great value for understanding humans in war, but is different from the one gained through historical research).

An additional way to enrich descriptions and the "hermeneutic interpretation" is to use archaeological methods. When doing battlefield archaeology, one can investigate the place where something happened and the remains that may be left. This work can shed light on details during a particular battle but can also be seen as a more general study of the materialization of war (for an overview regarding battlefield archaeology, see Sutherland 2005, Scott et al. 2000). Experimental archaeology, technical analyses and even re-enactment can also fill in details and give new insights (see Hocker this volume).

A special opportunity for a deeper understanding additionally emerges when written sources describing the battle can be combined with archaeological material from the place. A well-known study of this kind has been conducted at Little Big Horn in Montana. The field archaeological investigations have given a new, detailed perspective of General Custer's defeat in 1878, known in traditional American history as Custer's last stand (Scott 2000). A similar kind of critical battlefield study has been done by the archaeologist Tomas Englund at the inlet to Stockholm at Stäket. He has been able to tell a new story regarding the fight here between Swedish defenders and amphibian Russian troops 1719 (Englund 1995).

On the sunken battlefield of Mars (1564), there is a possibility to combine sources for a closer and greater human understanding. In the documents there is sometimes information of an individual's fate on board in the battle. One such example is the *arklimästaren* ("gun master") Esbjörn Svensson. The stress and the horror on the deck seemed to have been too much for this officer, and he commits suicide by blowing himself up with the powder from a gun (Smirnov 2009:103). Esbjörn's situation and fear is for us underlined and easier to understand when we meet the heavily burned timbers on the bottom, pieces of guns which have exploded from the heat and burned human bones spread out over the timbers. The face of the battle then meets us rather unmasked, 70 metres down in the Baltic Sea.

The content of the book

The fact that the authors in this anthology have relatively freely chosen different perspectives regarding maritime warfare means that the articles vary in scope and ambition. Some are more general, and some have the form of more specific case studies.

This short introduction on how to describe, present and study the very large field of battles, war and organized killings are followed by two articles by Kekke Stadin and Patrik Höglund which both deal with material attributes communicating the status and power of the officers on board early modern warships. Stadin discusses the admiral Jakob Bagges and other highly ranked noblemen's self-fashioning as naval heroes.

Heroes and courage, but especially fear on board 17th century ships, are also discussed in the next text by AnnaSara Hammar. Her starting point is old court documents which she analyses with the aim to better understand the emotions and feelings of seamen in the past. The next article by Niklas Eriksson is about shipwrecks of the Scanian War between 1676–1679 raises general questions regarding the making of history and why certain stories, persons and shipwrecks get attention and others not.

The Rolf Warming chapter concerns the actual praxis of fighting aboard. By combining written sources describing strategy during battle and archaeological examples of actual weapons, he can give new insight into the process of naval hand-to-hand battle.

The "tools of warfare" is also the subject in Fred Hocker's contribution, about the guns on board early modern warships. Experimental archaeology has given new understanding about the function and efficacy of these guns and the sort of impact they really had on the people on board. Mathilda Fredriksson and Sabine Sten's text describes how information about the effect of weapon technology, but also more general conditions oaboard, can be investigated by digital osteological analyses.

Jon Adams and Johan Rönnby's contribution summarizes a mutual long experience of archaeological investigations and studies concerning different early modern warships. The new ships of the period, and the new way to fight at sea, are here interpreted as an active part in the state driven societal change during the 15th and 16th century. However, the roll of material agency and human agents in history are argued as clearly different things.

The last tree chapters of the book are all studies focusing on specific cases. Ingvar Sjöblom analyses the crew aboard the warship *Mars* (1564) and gives a detailed insight into the organization on board. Art Cohn writes about naval warfare during the American revolution 1776 at Lake Champlain, and the memories of individual people connected to this fighting, and Carlo Beltrame discusses aspects of the archaeological results of the investigation of *Mercurio* (1812) which sank during the Napoleon wars in the Adriatic Sea. A warship with a surprisingly big variation of artefacts.

The book *On War on Board* ends with a short reflection where the concept of war on board, and issues raised in the different articles, are discussed more generally and linked both to our interest in this subject and to the general humanistic question about the origin of war and violence.

Figure 1: A sunken battlefield, photomosaic *Mars* (1564) (Tomaz Stachura: Ocean Discovery)

References

Aleksijevitj, S., 2012 [1985]. *Kriget har inget kvinnligt ansikte: utopins röster*. Stockholm: Ersatz.

Aleksijevitj, S., 2014 [1991]. *Zinkpojkar*. Stockholm: Ersatz.

Asker, B. (red.), 2005. *Stormakten som sjömakt: marina bilder från karolinsk tid*. Lund: Historiska media.

Cleart, T., 2005. *The Art of War. Sun Tzu*. Boston & London: Shambhala.

Clausewitz, Carl von, 1997. *On war*. Ware: Wordsworth.

Duby, G., 1990. *Söndagen vid Bouvines: den 27 juli 1214*. Stockholm: Atlantis.

Duby, G., 1987 [1985]. *William Marshal: the flower of chivalry*. New York: Pantheon Books.

Geertz, C., 1991. Tjock beskrivning för en tolkande kulturteori. *Häften för kritiska studier*. 1991:3, s. 13–33.

Glete, J., 2002. *War and the state in early modern Europe: Spain, the Dutch Republic and Sweden as fiscal-military states, 1500–1600*. London: Routledge.

Glete, J., 2000. *Warfare at sea: 1500–1650. Maritime conflicts and the transformation of Europe*. London: Routledge.

Glete, J., 2010. *Swedish naval administration, 1521–1721: resource flows and organisational capabilities*. Leiden: Brill.

Englund, P., 1993. *Ofredsår: om den svenska stormaktstiden och en man i dess mitt*. Stockholm: Atlantis.

Englund, P., 2000. *Den oövervinnerlige: om den svenska stormaktstiden och en man i dess mitt*. Stockholm: Atlantis.

Englund, P., 2011. *The beauty and the sorrow: an intimate history of the first world war*. London: Profile books.

Englund, P., 2013[1992]. *The battle that shook Europe: Poltava and the birth of the Russian Empire*. London: I. B. Tauris.

Englund, T., 2015. *Baggensstäket, 1719*. Nacka: HAMN.

Ericson Wolke, L., 2007. *Krigets ideer: svenska tankar om krigföring 1320–1920*. Stockholm: Medström.

Ericson Wolke, L., & Hårdstedt, M., 2009. *Svenska sjöslag*. Stockholm: Medström.

Ericson Wolke, L., 2012. *Sjöslag och rysshärjningar: kampen om Östersjön under stora nordiska kriget 1700–1721*. Stockholm: Norstedt.

Fox Jr, R. A., 1993. Archaeology, History, and Custer's Last Battle: The Little Big Horn Re-examined. University of Oklahoma Press: Norman.

Hallenberg, M. & Holm, J., 2016. *Man ur huse: hur krig, upplopp och förhandlingar påverkade svensk statsbildning under tidigmodern tid*. Lund: Nordic Academic Press.

Herodotos. 2000. *Herodotos historia*. [Ny utg.] Stockholm: Norstedt.

Höglund, P. In Prep. *Skeppssamhället. Befattningar och status på örlogsskepp under 1600-talet*. Diss Södertörns högskola.

Jünger, E., 2008. *I stålstormen*. Stockholm: Atlantis.

Junger, S., 2011. *War*. London: Fourth Estate.

Larsdotter, A., 2016. *Kvinnor i strid*. Lund: Historiska media.

Linna, V., 1955. *Okänd soldat*. Stockholm: Wahlström & Widstrand.

Lybeck, O. (red.), 1945. *Svenska flottans historia: örlogsflottan i ord och bild från dess grundläggning under Gustav Vasa fram till våra dagar. Bd 3, [1815–1945]*. Malmö: Allhem.

Keegan, J., 1978. *The face of battle: A study of Agincourt, Waterloo and the Somme.* [New ed.] Harmondsworth: Penguin.

Keegan, J., 2004 [1993]. *A history of warfare.* 2.ed. London: Pimlico.

Machiavelli, N., 2014. *The art of war. Translated by Henry Neville.* New York: Dover Publications Inc.

Machiavelli, N., 1993. *Fursten.* Stockholm: Natur och kultur.

Mouwitz, L., 2012. *Filosofi: en lärobok.* 2. uppl. Malmö: Gleerup.

Neuding Skoog, M., 2018. I rikets tjänst: krig, stat och samhälle i Sverige 1450–1550. Diss. Stockholm : Stockholms universitet, 2018

Nordland, H., 2015. *Känslor i krig: sensibilitet och emotionella strategier bland svenska officerare 1788–1814.* Diss. Lund: Lunds universitet, 2015.

Parker, G., 1988. The Military Revolution: Military innovation and the rise of the West 1500–1800. Cambridge.

Peters, J. (ed.), 2006. *Sedan stack vi staden i brand: en legoknekts dagbok från trettioåriga kriget.* Stockholm: Ordfront.

Panzeri, P. & Katcher, P. R. N. (red.), 2010. *Little Bighorn 1876: general Custers väg mot katastrofen.* Stockholm: Svenskt militärhistoriskt bibliotek.

Remarque, E. M., 1972. *På västfronten intet nytt.* 5. uppl. Stockholm: Aldus/ Bonnier.

Scott, D. D. et al., 2000. Archaeological Perspectives on the Battle of the Little Bighorn. University of Oklahoma Press: Norman.

Scott, D. D., Babits, L. E. & Haecker, C. M. (ed.). 2006. *Fields of conflict: battlefield archaeology from the Roman Empire to the Korean War. Vol. 2, Nineteenth and twentieth century fields of conflict.* Westport, Ct.: Praeger Security International.

Sjöblom, I., 2016. *Svenska sjöofficerare under 1500-talet.* Diss. Stockholm: Stockholms universitet, 2017.

Sjöström, O., 2008. *Fraustadt 1706: ett fält färgat rött.* Lund: Historiska media.

Smirnov, A., 2009. *Det första stora kriget.* Stockholm: Medström.

Speller, I., 2014. *Understanding naval warfare.* Milton Park, Abingdon, Oxon: Routledge.

Syse, B. (red.), 2003. *Långfredagsslaget: en arkeologisk historia.* Uppsala: Upplandsmuseet.

Sutherland, T., 2005. Battlefield Archaeology – A guide to the archaeology of conflict. *British Archaeological Jobs Reports.* Bradford: University of Bradford.

Tolstoj, L., 1959. *Den andra epilogen till Krig och fred.* Stockholm: Bonnier.

Tolstoj, L., 1968. *Krig och fred. Del 1–3.* Stockholm: Forum.

Tingsten, H., 1958. *På marknadstorget.* Stockholm: Wahlström & Widstrand.

Widén, J. & Ångström, J., 2005. *Militärteorins grunder.* Stockholm: Försvarsmakten.

Villstrand, N. E. & Westerlund, K. (red.), 2015. *Stor seger – ett litet nederlag? Perspektiv på sjöslaget vid Rilax 1714.* Åbo: Sjöhistoriska institutet vid Åbo Akademi.

Widén, J., 2012. *Theorist of maritime strategy: Sir Julian Corbett and his contribution to military and naval thought.* Burlington, VT: Ashgate Pub. Ltd.

Wright, G. H. von., 1995. *Att förstå sin samtid: tanke och förkunnelse och andra försök: 1945–1994.* [Ny utg.] Stockholm.

The Performance of a Naval Hero
Admirals in the Nordic Seven Years' War 1563–1570

KEKKE STADIN

In a biography written by a naval commander in 1899, Jakob Thordsson Bagge, the Swedish High Admiral in 1563–1564, is described as the first well-known Swedish naval hero since the Viking age (Munthe 1899, 32). This nationalistic description, typical for its time, was repeated nine years later in a popular book called "Swedish feats and great achievements" *(Svenska bragder och stordåd,* 1908). Bagge's successor as high admiral, Klas Kristersson Horn, was also portrayed in these books and described as a naval hero. The late 19th century has been called "the age of hero worship" (Segal 2000, 3). This focus could explain the biographies, but these admirals were described as heroes long before the 19th century.

The Nordic Seven Years' War in the 1560s was complicated, because Sweden fought against Denmark-Norway, Poland-Lithuania and Lübeck (Sjöblom 2016, 317). Sweden's foremost enemy at sea was Denmark, allied with Lübeck. In the first volume of Danish-Norwegian hero stories *(*Larsen Liljefalk, *1893)* no fewer than three of the Danish high admirals in the Nordic Seven-Years'-war were presented as naval heroes: Peder Skram, Herluf Trolle and Otte Rud (Larsen Liljefalk 1893). The most famous of them was Herluf Trolle, still remembered as a famous Danish admiral. This war produced remarkably many naval heroes, celebrated in their lifetime and remembered in Scandinavia hundreds of years later (Briand de Crévecoeur 1959, *Humanitas Cristiana* 1990, Olden-Jørgensen 2016).

In this essay I will argue that Scandinavian admirals of the 1560s were performing themselves as naval heroes and that the kings' ambitions to become European renaissance princes made that possible. Centuries before military uniforms were introduced in the European navies, the admirals could create a long-lasting image of themselves, reminiscent of the manner of Louis XIV, as Peter Burke had shown (Burke 1996). In speeches, portraits, ritualized entrances and other media of the time, they made themselves recognizable as admirals and naval heroes.

The easiest way to find out a person's rank in the military is to look at the uniform. Historically 'officers' uniforms differed from the plain soldiers' uniforms. Stripes, stars and other signs showed the specific rank of the officer. In a distinctive hierarchal society as early modern Sweden, order was connected to hierarchy. The legitimacy of the hierarchal order depended on the visibility of the hierarchy, what we call "the discourse of recognition". (Runefelt 2015, 32) To be recognized as a king you had to perform as a king, likewise, a peasant should look and behave like a peasant, and not dress up (Stadin 2010, 50–54). But what about the admirals? What types of actions or performances were necessary for them to attain the recognition of their contemporaries and to be remembered as naval heroes decades after their death?

In the Swedish army, military uniforms, as in most western European armies, were introduced during the Thirty Years' War. In 1687, the whole Swedish army should have similar dark blue uniforms (Mollo 1972, 23). The fundamentals of hierarchical uniformity were established in Denmark between 1675 and 1685 (Lind 2010, 51). Military uniforms represented the country but also order in society and within the military organization. Moreover, they created uniformity, discipline and affinity amongst those men who wore the same uniform. Finally, in the battlefield, the uniforms made it easier to distinguish between an enemy and an ally. The Danish soldier in a red coat could not be mistaken for a Swede, dressed in blue. In that respect the uniforms contributed to the formation of a national identity.

At sea, not only did the soldiers represent their country, but foremost the ships with their decorations and flags. Uniforms were introduced much later to navies than armies. The British navy uniforms were introduced in 1748, the Swedish in 1778 (Miller 2007, 7; Melinder 2003, 27). Even though the admirals did not wear uniforms, they made themselves recognizable on deck, as well as when they came home to celebrate a victory and in media of the time.

Theoretical perspectives

One theoretical starting point for my study is that our appearance and our overall performance play an important part in communication. Mostly we are not aware of that, nor do we even desire it, but still, our appearance always communicates something about ourselves. Dress is an important part of this non-verbal communication. It is not an innocent or neutral way of communication, quite the opposite. It is important when power positions and relations are established and reproduced, usually involving both ideology and power (Barnard 2002, 5, 46).

The theoretical perspective is inspired by Erving Goffman's concept *performance*. Goffman defines the concept *performance* as everything a person does, consciously and unconsciously, to influence another person's impression of him or her and the impression of the situation (Goffman 2009, 22–23). In this essay I will use the concept performance to find out if they are meaningful in the study of the admirals in the Nordic Seven Years' War and what made them recognized as naval heroes.

The myth of a naval hero

In May 1563, Jakob Bagge won a battle at Bornholm over the Danes under admiral Brockenhuus. Back in Stockholm one month later, the victory was celebrated and Bagge was honoured as a hero. Even though he was defeated in a later battle, the memory of him is that of a naval hero, or rather what I would call a heroic myth. When Robert Segal, in his book *Hero Myths*, presents different kinds of hero myths, the warrior hero comes first, represented by the Norse hero Sigurd, the dragon slayer, known in all of Scandinavia. Hero myths transform humans into virtual gods by conferring on them. The heroic qualities must, according to Segal, be magnified to the point of divinity, and some types of heroes fit certain periods. (Segal 2000, 7–9) In Scandinavia the naval hero seems to fit the early modern period.

In early modern Sweden, a man described as a hero already in his life time and at his funeral was, with few exceptions, a victorious warrior (Stadin 2001). One person described in his life-time as a hero was the Swedish king Gustavus II Adolphus, also called the "Lion from the North", in connection with the myth of the Lion (Åkerman 1996, 23–25). After his death on the battle-field in the Thirty Years' War he became, for generations of Swedes, *the* symbol of a hero. Representations of him give the image of a brave warrior giving his life for the sake of the common good, his native country and the protestant cause. He was described as the most heroic example of them all, a hero-king (Stadin 2001, 95).

The admirals Jakob Tordsson Bagge and Klas Kristersson Horn, were celebrated as naval heroes in their lifetime for their victories in the Nordic Seven Years' War in the 1560s. In Denmark admiral Herulf Trolle was honoured as a hero. All these admirals had won sea battles, which was the first criteria for a naval hero.

The second criteria to be recognized as a warrior hero was high rank. Only high-ranking officers could be described and remembered as heroes, plain soldiers could not. Normally, only men in the nobility had the highest military positions (Sjöblom 2016, 367–368, 408–413). Bagge, Trolle and Horn all belonged to the Scandinavian high nobility. Bagge was originally a

Norwegian (then under Danish rule) noble family, but his father moved to Sweden in the 1520s and in 1556 Jakob Bagge was also ennobled in Sweden (Westling). Trolle was a family belonging to both the Swedish and the Danish nobility and their estates were found on both sides of the border. That also meant that the Danish admiral Herluf Trolle and his first cousin Arvid Trolle, who was vice admiral in the Swedish navy, were fighting against each other in the sea battles in this war (Olden-Jørgensen 2016, 20–25). Horn was a noble family in Sweden, and they had most of their estates in the eastern half of the Swedish realm, in what is now Finland (Broomé).

Thirdly, to be celebrated as a hero, the warrior had to be considered virtuous. The reputation, true or not, was very important. As Segal states, heroism permits and even requires make-believe. This reputation was established in one of the more widespread media of the time, namely in congratulatory poems and in funeral orations, held orally during funerals or memorizing ceremonies. Those who could afford this had these speeches printed and they were read as edifying literature (Stadin 1997, 225–226).

A definition of virtue given by Aristotle is: "A virtue is a deliberated and permanent disposition, based on a standard applied to ourselves and defined by the reason displayed by the man of good sense" (Aristoteles 1967, 22–22, 57, 59. In its greatest generality, the virtuous disposition presents itself as the aspiration to goodness (Beacher 1992, 41). For an admiral in early modern Scandinavia, this aspiration to goodness should be used serving the native country and the king.

Ever since classical antiquity, some virtues were understood as universal dispositions, important for every person, or at least every man, while others were more or less specific for each social rank, estate, gender and profession. The four universal virtues are Prudence, also described as wisdom, Justice or fairness, Temperance, also known as restraint, the practice of self-control, discretion and moderation and finally Courage, also called fortitude. In the middle Ages these Cardinal virtues, as they were called, were completed with the three Christian virtues; faith, hope and love. "*Pietas*" was the comprehensive term for these Christian virtues. (Stadin 2007, 229). The naval heroes of the Nordic Seven Years' War were described as men with all these seven virtues, making them almost divine. I will argue that the myths about them as naval heroes were connected to their performances.

Portraits of naval heroes

In a funeral oration for Jacob Bagge, he is described as pious man. The oration first praised him for his faithfulness and fidelity to Sweden and to no less than three kings. He was praised for his justice, he separated good from evil. He was also described as "highly wise" and "prudent" (Ludvigsson 1577). Prudence gave the ability to oversee all the circumstances and factors in a given case and to give "good advice", settling the prosperity of a country in peace and in war (Schefferus 1671, 33). Finally, and foremost, a prudent man had foresight and stayed calm in the battle, he was not a daredevil (Ludvigsson 1577).

As a warrior he was described as loyal and what was described as *"manlig"* (Ludvigsson 1577). Today, the English words manliness, masculinity and manhood, are all used to express this word. This is, however, old Swedish, a language very different from modern Swedish, and many words had a different meaning. In the 16th and 17th centuries *manlig* meant courage in the battlefield, that and nothing else (Stadin 2001, 115). Bagge's courage was further emphasized saying he was fearless (Ludvigsson 1577). There is no doubt, Bagge had all the virtues worthy a hero. The main question is, how did he perform to be recognized as a naval hero by the contemporaries and posterities?

After the victory over den Danish fleet under Jakob Brockenhuus at Bornholm in May 1563, Bagge went back to Stockholm where the ships arrived one month later. The entrance into the Swedish capital was arranged as a celebration of the glorious victory, but moreover as Bagge's personal triumph. Bagge lead a procession from the ship and up to the royal castle (Munthe 1899, 30). The entrance also gave admiral Bagge the opportunity to perform his image in front of the king and the people in Stockholm and to influence how he was perceived and remembered.

The annals describing Bagge during his triumphant walk are short: "he had a golden chain around his neck" (Stockholm… 1842, 128). The description in the biography from around 1900, not only mentions his golden necklace, but also his splendid dress. That is what made him recognized as a naval hero. (Munthe 1899, 32) We do not know if the author added the dress because he had seen a portrait of Bagge. It is hard to know whether the visual media such as portraits and rituals illustrated the words and the texts or if it was the other way around. However, we do know that these medias influenced and strengthened each other and were used in the king's and the aristocracy's performance (Burke 1996, 31).

To analyse the admirals' performance in the portraits, I use Roland Barthes' semiotic analysis of social values connected to materiality. He describes how the cultural sign contributes to constructing and maintaining social status for certain groups in society (Barthes 2007). Clothes are both historical and sociological objects and they could in any historical moment be seen on two levels: the first level is what you see, for example, hat. That level is *denotation,* the black hat, *the signifier.* The second level, *the connotation,* is our interpretation of what we see, connected to the general beliefs, conceptual frameworks and value systems in society, for example "elegance", the *signified* (Barthes 1977, 33–35). As these cultural values constantly change the meaning of clothes, hairstyles or any other *sign* in our appearance are constantly negotiated and changed.

This analytical system could be used to study a myth. In myths there is the same theme, signifiers, the signified and signs. According to Barthes, the myth consists of a semiotic chain where the sign is linked to a second set of signifiers on a broader ideological meaning (Barthes 2007, 206–223). Elegance becomes a signifier signifying for example aristocracy. This might help us to find out how the myths of the naval heroes in the Nordic Seven Years' War were formed.

A painted portrait is always a result of a negotiation between conventions, the artist and the portrayed. Within the conventions, the artist and the person portrayed negotiated several aspects, if the portrait should be *en face* or in profile, in half- or whole figure, the background and symbolic details. During the Renaissance and the Baroque rhetorical means were often used and the person portrayed communicated the viewer through gestures and expressions (Cavalli-Björkman 2001, 9). An admiral could by the choice of dress, symbols and gestures influence the view of himself, his masculinity and how his deed should be perceived by contemporary viewers and even more by posterity. The nobility had portraits painted as signs of the continuity of their dynasties, but also as signs justifying their position (*Visage du grand siècle* 1997, 75).

Figure 2: Jakob Bagge

Figure 3 (top) and 4 (above): Nils Sture and Erik Sture (detail)

Figure 5: Peder Skram

Above is a half-length portrait of Bagge with a plain black background. There are no obvious signs making direct connotations to the navy or his military rank in his personal appearance or in the background. However, no one in the 16th century would have expected that. Being an admiral was not an office in our modern meaning. Like other military and civil offices, it was considered as a mission and the admirals were appointed for each mission. It was the nobility's duty to help the king to rule the country as an officer or a civil servant, and the high-ranked missions were of course the most honourable. These missions were usually given as rewards to diligent and zealous noblemen from the right families, faithful to the king (Stadin 2001, 116–117). Missions in the army, civil offices and missions in the navy were often mixed in a way seemingly random for us today. Professionalism was not yet invented in the 1560s, neither in the Scandinavian military nor in the civil service (Asker 1983, 100–102; Arteus 1986, 69, 119–120).

The portrait shows a middle-aged man, whose beard is greyish. His gaze is fixed far away. A little selvage of the white shirt's collar is shown, but the rest of his dress is black. Black was the most fashionable colour in the 16th century. It was not possible to dye cloth totally black until the 1360s which is when it became exclusive. By and by it became a popular colour among wealthy men. The Italian official and diplomat Baldassare Castiglione recommended in his famous book *The courtier* from 1528 all men "with ambitions" to dress in black (Castiglione 2003, 160–161). When the Spanish court in the mid-16th century imposed its codes and customs upon the whole of Europe, black was a part of that. Furthermore, when the Spanish kings Charles V and Philip II of Habsburg demonstrated their personal taste for this colour, it became popular among mighty men all over Europe (Harvey 1995, 72–73; Pastoureau 2008, 103). That was true in the Scandinavian countries too. Because a vestimentary system is either regional or international, but not national (Barthes 2006, 5), the black dress showed that he was a diligent man, loyal to the king, prepared to give his life for the native country.

The fur collar gives the connotations of prosperity and dignity. His black hat, probably in velvet is not only elegant, it shows his authority. This discourse of recognition seems highly relevant looking at the portrait of Jakob Bagge.

The hat is a beret, a kind of soft hat very popular among the upper classes all over Europe in the 16th century. The beret has been described as an imitation of the magnificence of the royal crown, but still it could take different shapes. The decoration, hatbands, jewels, pearls and embroidery, were important, displaying status (Amphlett 2003, 89–93; McDowell 1992, 9–10). Bagge's hat is decorated with a golden ribbon and a white feather, also giving connotations to rank, dignity and prosperity. It showed he belonged to nobility and allowed him to receive what in early modern Europe was known as "hat honour". As the king expected his courtiers and all his subjects to respect his crown by uncovering their heads in his presence, officers and other nobility expected the same respect be shown to their hat by their inferiors. Hats proclaimed the man and was bound by etiquette (McDowell 1992 9–10, 34, 97).

The admiral's hat was very important in the navy and in sea battles. If an admiral surrendered, he signalled that by lowering the top sail and the admiral's flag on his ship. Moreover, he lifted his hat up high and gave the order to the officers to do the same. This was sign for surrender and that he wanted to give himself up as a prisoner of war. That is, for example, what the Danish high admiral Jakob Borkhuusen did in May 1564 when defeated by Jakob Bagge in a battle at Bornholm. The Danish admiral, officers and some 600 soldiers were moved to Swedish ships and taken as prisoners of war. According to the instruction for the Swedish high admiral Klas Kristersson Horn from 1565, those enemies who gave up voluntarily would not be killed but taken as prisoners of war (*Instruktion och befallning... 1565*). In that way, lifting the hat could save the admiral's and the officers' lives.

The most striking thing in Jakob Bagge's appearance, however, are the heavy golden chains hanging around his neck, also mentioned in the annals. There is also a charm hanging from one of the chains. When Bagge posed for the artist, his splendid dress and necklace were important. They signified how Bagge wanted to be perceived and remembered.

It is evident from the portraits that golden necklaces were high fashion among aristocratic men in Sweden and Denmark in the 1560s. Portraits of the time show men wearing necklaces over their black high-necked waistcoats. Good examples of this are the three brothers of the Sture family, which was at that time the topmost noble family in Sweden. Two of the brothers, Erik and Nils, together with their father, were put to death by order of the king in 1567. The portraits of the older two sons were painted some time before that, and that of the third son a couple of years later. In these portraits all wear thin golden necklaces, worn over their black waistcoats in the stiff, high-necked "Spanish fashion".

Bagge's chain was, however, more than a necklace. The chain was a gift from the king with a charm that appears to be a medal, but was it? Royal medals had been issued in the antiquity but subsequently the practice was forgotten. In the 15th century, medals were re-invented in the Italian states and spread to the rest of Europe. They should be related to the Renaissance princes and their political aspirations and fulfil their desire for fame and immortality. According to Stephen Scher, the medals were thereby signifying alliances and friendship (Scher 1994, 13). In Sweden, Erik XIV (1560–1568) was the first Swedish king to issue a medal. This was in connection with the funeral for his father, Gustav Vasa in 1560. The charm on Bagge's chain is not that medal, or any other known royal medal from this time (Hildebrand, 1975, 21–22).

Following the defeat of the Danish fleet in 1563, the already retired Peder Skram was recalled as the Danish high admiral for a short period of time (Larsen-Liljefalk 1893, 12–13). The portrait from 1571 shows the sixty-nine-year-old former Danish admiral, Peder Skram, called "the daredevil". He wears a necklace with three thin chains and a small charm, probably a medal.

In May 1564, the Swedish fleet led by Jakob Bagge once again met the Danish fleet in battle, this time off the northern cap of Öland. By then, Skram was dismissed and Herluf Trolle was appointed high admiral over the Danish fleet. This time the allied fleets from Denmark and Lübeck were victorious. *Mars*, the Swedish admiral's ship, was stuck in fire, exploded and sank. Admiral Bagge, his vice-admiral and some officers had given themselves up as prisoners of war before moving to the Lübeck admiral's ship (Sjöblom 2016, 332).

One year later, their luck changed once again. Trolle was wounded in a battle and died after some time. In one of the descriptions of this battle, it is mentioned that the Swedes could easily recognize the Danish admiral standing on the deck. He was dressed in armour and a big hat with feathers, showing himself to be the most important person on the ship (Munthe 1902, 60–61). An elegant hat was a sign of authority and made it possible to recognize the admiral, both among his own men, but also by the enemy. The hat proclaimed a man's authority and honour; therefore, it could also be his undoing.

In the funeral oration for Trolle held by the vice chancellor at the University of Copenhagen, Niels Hemmingsøn, and a in a memorial speech held by professor Christian Machabæus one year later, Trolle's virtues were praised. In both speeches the Danish high admiral was described as a true hero. Hemmingsøn praised his justice and his loyalty to the king and his native country, and of course his piety (Hemmingsøn 1565). Machabæus argued that Trolle's virtues honoured him in his lifetime and brought him admiration after his death. His justice, courage and valour were mentioned in particular, but also his prudence. Machabæus underlined that Trolle had never acted hastily, allowing reason and prudence rule (Machabæus 1566). Similar to Bagge, Trolle was praised for all the Christian and natural virtues required by a hero.

In describing Trolle's personality, Hemmingsøn referred to some words Trolle had said himself, which would later often said about him: "as I am wearing golden chains, have large estates and am more esteemed than others…" it was his duty to risk his life for his king and country (Hemmingsøn 1565). In a poem written in honour of Trolle, his heroic deeds were closely connected to his honour and wealth, but most of all to his golden chains. (*Epitafium* I) It was described as a prerequisite for his heroic deeds, not as a reward for them.

The quoted words about the golden chains are underpinned by the images of Herluf Trolle, for example, an etching showing him in his final year wearing armour and performing as a military officer (Figure 6). Around his neck and over the armour, he is wearing a golden chain with a charm in the form of an elephant, the symbol of the Danish Elephant order. He was conferred upon this order in 1559, when the Danish king Fredrik II was coronated. Later the same year, Trolle was appointed admiral. That means that the badge was given to him before any sea battle. The king had given him the golden chain, the order, then appointed him an admiral. The chain signified allegiance and Trolle carried out his duty.

But Trolle had been wearing golden chains long before he was appointed admiral. In a painted portrait from 1551, he has a forked beard, the latest fashion, is wearing a black dress and over that a coat with a fur collar and a beret hat with a jewel. In his left hand he is holding a pair of gloves. Under the coat he is wearing a necklace of gold. The connotations are prosperity aristocracy and a gentleman *à la mode*.

In an engraving from the same period, Trolle is wearing the chain over armour, as in the late etching, but here it is not the elephant order badge, it seems to be the same necklace as in the painted portrait. If a man wears a golden necklace over armour, it is not because it is useful when fighting. I suggest that it is because it is an important aspect of his performance as a warrior and a hero. Later on, when he was presented with the elephant-order badge, this was recognized by the king.

When the Swedish admiral ship *Mars* had been destroyed in the summer of 1564, Jakob Bagge became a prisoner of war in Denmark. The Swedish fleet needed a new high admiral and for a short period and Klas Eriksson Fleming was appointed. he was soon dismissed by the king, however, for neglect (Sjöblom 2016, 334). Klas Kristerson Horn was then appointed as the new high admiral over the Swedish fleet. He was involved in several sea battles against the allied fleet until his death due to the pestilence in September 1566. In 1787, a medal was made in memory of Horn and his heroic deeds. On the medal, he is described as the one who deliberated the Baltic Sea from enemies. In Swedish nationalistic writings from around 1900, Horn was dubbed a "patriotic hero".

Horn's biographies mention that he was conferred upon the Swedish Salvator order. This was a Swedish knightly order founded by Erik XIV.

According to an old notation, some men belonging to the high nobility working for the king were conferred upon this order when Erik XIV was coronated. If this is true, it is possible that Klas Horn was one of them, but there is no evidence at all that anyone else, other than the king himself, was conferred upon this order (Braunstein 2007, 6). In the painted portrait of Horn, he is adorned with two golden chains, one with a charm. This is not, however, the Salvator order or any other Swedish order or known royal medal (Dahlberg 1694, 1–9; *Antikvarisk tidskrift för Sverige*, 75; Hildebrand 1875, 21–22). Perhaps the charm is a gift from the king, but it could just as well be something he added to the chains himself. If he wanted it to look like a medal, he succeeded.

The portrait of Klas Horn shows a man in half profile with reddish hair and a short beard. He looks back at the observer, observably. He is wearing a black silk dress and over that a black coat. The coat has a fur collar and several broad golden ribbons. On his head he wears a velvet beret, also with golden decorations. In his left hand he is holding a pair of gloves and on one of his fingers he is wearing a ring with a large jewel. In his right hand he is holding a white silk scarf. Around his neck, Horn is wearing two golden chains, one with a large charm. The background is dark, and to the left there is a dark green drapery with a golden fringe. The denotations resemble the portraits of Bagge and Trolle, yet they are a little more splendid. His dress is *à la mode* and would have been considered suitable for ambitious men in the high nobility, working for the king and the state. The connotations are prosperity, high position, status and aristocracy.

Figure 6: Herluf Trolle in his final year

Figure 7: The Danish Elephant order

Figure 8: Herluf Trolle

Figure 9: Klas Horn (detail)

Let's look at the gloves! Like Herluf Trolle he did not wear them on, he is holding them in his left hand. Holding gloves was symbolic. In the Middle Ages, those who were dubbed a knight, installed a bishop or another high position besides receiving the insignia, they also got a pair of gloves as a sign of their privilege. Holding gloves was to demonstrate position and status. The gloves were, together with the sword, a sign of nobility. There were also a lot of rituals connected to the gloves, used in early modern Europe. For example, to throw the glove in front somebody was to challenge them to a duel, and to put a stake on one's own honour.

The admirals showed their gloves in their portraits, but not their swords. Considering the importance of the sword as a sign of nobility and dignity, this is remarkable. There are, however, representations of them where swords are shown, namely their gravestones. On the gravestone of Klas Horn and his wife, he is wearing armour and a customary sidearm. In Herluf Trolle's grave monument, a sword is lying beside him. This gravestone resembles the one made for the Swedish vice-admiral Nils Karlsson Gyllenstierna, who died in 1564. In both cases the swords are very long, probably two-handed swords. These swords were too long and too heavy to be used in a fight. They were ceremonial swords, carried over the shoulder, and used as a sign of dignity. In the army they were carried by special carriers, who also acted as guards for the officer. In the navy they were connected to the commander. Herbert Seitz finds that in Sweden, the flowering season for this ceremonial sword, was the second half of the 16th century (Seitz 1955). These ceremonial swords were shown on gravestones from the 1560s, but they do not appear in the admirals' self-fashioning performances in paintings and other media in their life-time.

The triumph and the golden chain

Erik XIV was king of Sweden up to the autumn of 1568. He was a true Renaissance prince, acting like the monarchs in France, England and other European states. One aspect of his princely rule was to arrange triumphal processions celebrating military victories. The processions were ritualized to make them appear special and they were arranged like a theatre. In ritualizing an action, different kinds of techniques were used, for example formalizing, dramatizing, repetition, and connection to traditions (Bell 1992, 74, 197). Like coronations, royal weddings and other ceremonies, the processions were multimedia events, where words, acting, music and pictures created a total effect. Afterwards, the processions were memorized through engravings, coins, and not least portraits of those involved. The ritualized ceremonies not only manifested power, in early modern Europe the pomp was a goal in itself (Burke 1996, 26–27, 32–33).

In at least two of the ritualized triumphs arranged by Erik XIV, the king himself lead magnificent processions riding on a horse. Another procession was the previously mentioned procession celebrating Bagge's first victory. After a Swedish victory of a naval battle in 1565, Klas Horn came back to Stockholm in July. The celebrations were carefully prepared to give glory to Sweden and to Horn. For his entry, a triumphal arch was built across the procession street. The king was not in Stockholm at the time, but he wrote instructions to the governor in Stockholm telling him how to arrange the procession (*brev från Erik XIV till ståthållaren i Stockholm 30 juli 1565*).

An important part of the triumphs was to show up trophies. The defeated admirals' flags and other flags conquered from the enemy were carried in the processions as proof of victory. The very triumphant trophies were, however, the defeated admiral and the other prisoners of war. Representing their navy and their country the defeated admirals were treated as living trophies by the victors. In the triumph procession for Bagge, the Swedish officers came just behind him. Then the flags were carried and after that came the prisoners of war, the Danish admiral, Jacob Brockenhuus, and some of his officers. All the Danes had their hair shaved off and, in their hands, they held striped canes. A court jester was playing the violin and was dancing around them. The officers were followed by some ordinary Danish soldiers, all of them chained together (Munthe 1899, 2).

The triumph procession celebrating Klas Horn one year later was arranged in a similar way to Bagge's triumph. The most important trophy was Danish high admiral Otte Knudsen Rud and some officers. There was a farmer playing bagpipes leading the prisoners. (Larsen Liljefalk 1893, 102–103.) This was alluding in a Danish song saying that "now the Swedes have to dance after our tune (originally pipe)", implying that it was the other way around. In the description of the procession, it is emphasized that the admiral and the officers, as well as the soldiers, had all got their hair shaved off (Munthe 1902, 83–84).

Shaving someone's hair off was, at least since Delila had cut Samson's hair, a symbolic act of humiliation. As for Samson the shaved hair deprived a man, his masculine strength, his dignity and symbolically his ability to win a victory. A bald man was, by definition, a weak man (Book of Judges16:17–22). There are a lot of European stories and tales about the connection between a man's hair and his dignity and/or physical strength. For the kings of Franks, long hair was a sign of wealth, rank and dignity. Other men were required to have their hair shorter than the king, as a sign of subservience. Among medieval Germans, short hair, especially shaved hair, was a sign of ignominy (Corson, 1980 91–95). This symbolic meaning of the shaved hair seems to have been topical in the 1560s. The importance of shaving the hair of the prisoners of war was further demonstrated in an instruction to those who were responsible for imprisoning the Danish officers and soldiers. They had orders to shave the prisoners' heads at least once a week (Munthe 2002, 81).

In the procession to the royal castle, the act of ignominy of the defeated admirals was highlighted by the jester, respectively the farmer mocking them and making fools of them. It appears the humiliation of the prisoners of war was meant to make the show more entertaining and the victorious Swedish admirals' triumph even greater.

The most interesting information in the king's instruction to the governor in Stockholm was that the captains who had boarded the enemy ships should be honoured with golden chains. The governor was instructed to give them all the golden chains he could find. Other brave captains and officers were to be decorated with silver necklaces and bracelets (*Brev från Erik XIV…*; Sjöblom 2016, 346). The important thing was that they were chains of gold, not how they looked or that they were of a specific kind. Badges of merit were not introduced in Sweden until the early 17th century. This clearly shows that in the second half of the 16th century not only medals, but also necklaces and bracelets were used as symbols of honour, signifying naval heroes.

The performance of naval heroes

Both Swedish and Danish admirals, fighting each other in Nordic Seven Years' War, have been remembered as naval heroes. This only applied, of course, to those who had won at least one great sea battle. In funeral orations and complimentary poems, after their death they were celebrated as true heroes. Around 1900, they continued to be described as naval heroes.

Both the Danish and the Swedish kings honoured these admirals in different ways, but most of all by giving them orders and golden chains. The Danish admiral Trolle was conferred upon the Elephant order. The Swedish king Erik arranged ritualized processions and ceremonies, celebrating the victories, giving, in particular, Bagge and Horn the opportunity to perform as heroes. An important part of that was to decorate the admirals with golden chains. When there were no military uniforms, no military orders and no badges of merit, these golden necklaces were used as signs of honour.

The kings' homage made the honour visible for their contemporaries. The admirals performed in a way that made their heroic deeds remembered a long time after their death, dressed and in other ways self-fashioned as sophisticated aristocrats in powerful positions and adorned in golden chains. This is remarkable, especially as portraits were unusual outside the royal family in the Scandinavian countries. Their performance, seen in the ritualized celebrations and in the portraits, promoted the myths of naval heroes.

References

Unprinted sources

Riksarkivet, Stockholm (RA)
Riksregistratur (RR)
Instruktion och befallning… för den ädle välborne herr Klas Kristersson… 29 aprilis 1565.
Brev från kung Erik till ståthållaren i Stockholm 30 juli 1565.

Printed sources

Epitafium I., in *Humanitas christiana. In Mindetaler over Herulf Trolle*, København 1990: Herulfsholms Skole og Gods.

Hemmingsøn, N., "En Predikan som bleff predicket… femtinde Julij Anno Dominj 1565", in *Humanitas christiana. Mindetaler over Herulf Trolle*, København 1990: Herulfsholms Skole og Gods.

Ludvigsson, R., "Gravskrift över Jakob Bagge", 1577, i *Handlingar rörande Skandinaviens historia* XII, Stockholm 1837: Kungliga Samfundet för utgivande av handlingar rörande Skandinaviens historia.

Machabæus, C., "Oratio funebris. Mindetale over den berømte mand Herluf Trolle… 1566" in *Humanitas christiana: Mindetaler over Herulf Trolle*, København 1990: Herulfsholms Skole og Gods.

Internet

Alvin. Platform for digital collections. http://www.alvin- Sverige, *Medalj till minne av Gustav Vasa 1560* (2018-02-06)

Antikvarisk tidskrift för Sverige, nr 7 http://runeberg.org/antiqtid/7/0081.html (2016-10-16)

Broomé, B., "Klas Kristersson Horn", http://sok.riksarkivet.se/sbl/artikel/13829, *Svenskt biografiskt lexikon*, urn:sbl:13829 (2016-07-13)

Dahlberg, E., *Suecia antiqua et hodierna*, 1694, http://www.kb.se/samlingarna/Kartor-bilder/Suecia-antiqua/forsta-bandet/ (2016-07-05)

Hildebrand, B. E., *Minnespenningar öfver enskilda*, 1860, https://sv.wikisource.org/wiki/Sida:B_E_Hildebrand,_Minnespenningar_%C3%B6fver_enskilda (1860).djvu/26 (2016-08-31)

Hårhistoria, http://www.shenet.se/ravaror/harhistoria.html (2016-06-30)

Venge, M., *Herluf Trolle*, http://denstoredanske.dk/Danmarks_geografi_og_historie/Danmarks_historie/Danmark_1536-1849/Herluf_Trolle (2016-06-10)

Westling, F., "Jakob Bagge", http://sok.riksarkivet.se/sbl/artikel/18993, *Svenskt biografiskt lexikon* (urn:sbl:18993), (2016-04-13)

Literature

Alm, J., 1932. *Blanka vapen och skyddsvapen från och med 1500-talet till våra dagar.* Stockholm: Militärlitteraturföreningens förlag.

Amphlett, H., 2003. *Hats. A History of Fashion in Headwear.* New York: Dover publications.

Aristoteles. 1967. *Den nikomachiska etiken.* Helsingfors: Schildt.

Artéus, G., 1986. *Till militärstatens förhistoria. Krig, professionalisering och social förändring under vasasönerna regering.* Stockholm: Militärhistoriska studier.

Asker, B., 1983. *Officerarna och det svenska samhället 1650–1700.* Uppsala: Studia Historica Upsaliensia.

Barthes, R., 1977. *Image – Music – Text.* Essays selected and translated by Stephen Heath, New York: Hill and Wang.

Barthes, R., 2007. *Mytologier.* Lund: Arkiv.

Barthes, R., 2006. *The Language of Fashion.* Oxford & New York: Berg.

Barnard, M., 2002. *Fashion as communication.* 2nd ed. London & New York: Routledge.

Beacher, J., 1992. "Virtue, its Nature, Exigency and Acquisition". in *Virtue* eds. New York: Chapman & Galstone.

Bell, C., 1992. *Ritual theory, Ritual practice.* New York & Oxford: Oxford University Press.

Bohrn, E., 1942. "Claes Christerson Horns gravvård i Uppsala domkyrka." *Fornvännen, Journal of Swedish antiquarian research* 1942:1.

Braunstein, C., 2007. *Militära utmärkelsetecken på militära uniformer.* Stockholm: Statens försvarshistoriska museer.

Briand de Crévecoeur, E., 1959. *Herluf Trolle. Kongens Admiral og herlufsholm Skoles Stifter.* København: Herulfsholm Skole og Gods.

Burke, P., 1996. *En kung blir till. Myter och propaganda kring Ludvig XIV (The Fabrication of Louis XIV).* Tiden/Athena, Stockholm.

Catiglione, B., 2003 (1528). *Boken om hovmannen,* [*Il libro del Cortegiano*] Stockholm: Atlantis.

Cavalli-Björkman, G., 2001. *Ansikte mot Ansikte. Porträtt från fem sekel.* Stockholm: Nationalmuseums förlag.

Corson, R., 1980. *Fashions in Hair. The first five thousand years.* London: Peter Owen.

"Domarboken", *Bibeln.*

Goffman, E., 2009. *Jaget och maskerna. En studie i vardagslivets dynamik. (The presentation of the self in Everyday Life).* Stockholm: Norstedts.

Göransson, G., 1990. *Virtus militaris. Officersideal i Sverige 1560–1718.* Lund: Lund University Press.

Harvey, J., 1995. *Men in Black.* London: Reaktion.

Hildebrand, B. E., 1875. *Sveriges och svenska konungahusets minnespenningar, praktmynt och belöningsmedaljer.* I Stockholm: Kongl. vitterhets historie och antiqvitets akademiens förlag.

Humanitas christiana. 1990. *Mindetaler over Herulf Trolle.* København: Herulfsholm Skole og Gods.

Kuylenstierna, A., 1908. *Svenska bragder och stordåd. Ute och hemma, i krig och fred.* Stockholm: Fröleen.

Kybalova, L., 1979. *Den stora modeboken.* 3: uppl. Stockholm: Folket i bild.

Larsen Liljefalk, A., 1893. *Dansk-norske heltehistorier.* København: Gyldendalske Boghandels Forlag.

Lind, G., 2001. "Uniform and Distinction: symbolic Aspects of Officer Dress and the Eighteenth-Century Danish State." *Textile History.* vol 41 Supplement.

McDowell, C., 1992. *Hats, Status, Style and Glamour.* London: Thames and Hudson.

Melinder, N.-E., 2003. *Flottans sjöofficersuniformer i Sjöhistoriska museets samlingar.* Stockholm: Statens maritima museer.

Miller, A., 2007. *Dressed to kill. British Naval Uniforms.* London: National Maritime Museum.

Mollo, J., 1972. *Military Fashion. A comparative history of uniforms of the great armies from the 17th century to the First World War.* London: Barrie & Jenkins.

Munthe, A., 1899. *Jakob Bagge, Svenska sjöhjältar II*. Stockholm: Norstedt.

Munthe, A., 1902. *Klas Kristersson Horn, Svenska sjöhjältar IV*. Stockholm Norstedt.

Olden-Jørgensen, S., 2016. *Herulf Trolle. Adelsmand, kriger og skolestifter*. København: Gyldendal.

Pastoureau, M., 2008. *Black. The history of a Colour*. Princeton: Princeton University Press.

Runefeldt, L., 2015. *Att hasta mot undergången. Anspråk, flyktighet, föreställning i debatten om konsumtion i Sverige 1730–1830*. Lund: Nordic Academic press.

Schefferus, J., 1671. *Memorabilium sueticæ gentis exemplorum liber singularis*. Amsterdam: Janssonius van Waesberge.

Scher, S., 1994. *The Currency of Fame: Portrait medals of the Renaissance*. New York: Thames and Hudson.

Segal, R. A., 2000. *Hero Myths*. Malden Massachusetts: Blackwell.

Seitz, H., 1955. *Svärdet och värjan som armévapen*. Stockholm: Kungl. Armémuseums handböcker.

Sjöblom, I., 2016. *Svenska sjöofficerare under 1500-talet*. Stockholm: Universus Academic Press.

Stadin, K., 1997. "Att vara god eller att göra sin plikt? Dygd och genus i 1600-talets Sverige." *Historiska etyder. En vänbok till Stellan Dahlgren*. Uppsala: Uppsala universitet.

Stadin, K., 2001. The Prince, the Hero and the Swedish Empire. In: *Society, Towns and Masculinity. Aspects on Early Modern Society in the Baltic Area*, Kekke Stadin (ed.). Huddinge: Södertörns högskola.

Stadin, K., 2010. "Gråkappan – en medveten modekung." In: Stadin, K. *Maktens män bär rött. Historiska studier av manlighet, manligt framträdande och kläder*. Stockholm: Carlssons förlag.

Stockholm, dess historia och topografi: en skildring af dess historia från äldsta tider till våra dagar samt en vägledare till de minnesvärdaste byggnader m. m. inom mälarstaden och dess omgifningar: med illustrationer och kartor. förra delen, 1842. Stockholm: Bonniers förlag.

Tunefalk, M., 2015. *Äreminnen. Personmedaljer och social status i Sverige cirka 1650–1900*. Lund: Nordic Academic Press.

Visage du grand siècle. Le portrait française sous le regne de Louis XIV 1660–1715. 1997. Coquery, Emmanuel, ed. Paris: Somogy & Musées des Augustins.

Åkerman, S., 1996. "The myth of the Lion from the North and its origins of Paul Grebner's visions". In *Cultura Baltica. Literary Culture around the Baltic 1600–1700* ed. Andersson & Schade. Uppsala: Studia Germanistica Upsaliensia.

Symbols of Power
– Attributes of Rank on Warships in the 17th Century

PATRIK HÖGLUND

On a warship in the 17th century, social difference could be shown in a variety of ways such as space, equipment and practices. This paper discusses various symbols and attributes that were used to show the officers' rank separating them from the non-commissioned officers, petty officers and sailors. The senior officer's role in battle in connection to these symbols is also discussed. Some of the attributes showed only rank, but some also had a practical function in the handling of a ship. The information concerning symbols of rank is very scarce and must be sought in various archaeological and historical source-material – in archives and museum collections as well as on paintings and wrecks.

In the 1600s a person's exterior appearance was of uttermost importance and an important way of showing status and position in society (cf. Englund, 1989; Stadin 2005; 2010). Due to the lack of uniforms, the only way to visually distinguish officers from common men was, well into the second half of the century, mainly through clothing and different attributes. There were also other ways for naval officers to distinguish themselves on a ship. The senior officers, who almost exclusively came from nobility, could be recognized by their symbolic and cultural capital as well as their embodied capital, what Pierre Bourdieu calls habitus (Bourdieu 1993). These were mannerisms, and behaviour codes learnt from childhood and in the case of a nobleman, the almost automatic ability to gain respect and to command.

In the Swedish army, uniforms became common and standardized in the second half of the 17th century. The officers' uniforms differed generally from the soldiers in that they were more lavish and ornamented. In the navy, however, not even the officers wore uniforms. The first evidence in Sweden of naval officer uniforms stems from the middle of the 18th century (Ekman 1943:446). This means that on warships at the end of the 17th century, army officers and soldiers on the ships had uniforms, but naval officers and sailors did not. Naval officers were thus, due to the absence of uniforms, more difficult to distinguish from the common sailors, but because of their elaborate costumes and attributes such as wigs, rapiers and hats, there was, after all, a visible difference (Miller 2007:7). However, this was a blunt tool and could lead to misunderstandings, especially in stressful situations.

Another difficulty was to distinguish the ally from the enemy. The problem of confusion with enemy soldiers was obviously not as great on a ship as on land. However, there were occasions when mistakes and misunderstandings were made. This is easy to comprehend considering the chaos of a boarding-battle, when the smoke blurred the vision, the thunder from the guns was deafening and the screaming from adrenaline rushed men frightening. When the combined Swedish/Dutch fleet was victorious against a Danish fleet at the battle of Femern in 1644, the Swedish *Riksamiral* (admiral of the realm, commander of the navy) Karl Gustaf Wrangel reported home to queen Christina that the Danish admiral Pros Mund, who had fallen aboard his flagship *Patientia*, had, unfortunately, been thrown into the sea with the other dead men, because he could not be distinguished from the common sailors and soldiers (Wrangel's journal, 1644).

The baton

The supreme commander of the fleet, usually *riksamiralen*, like the commander of an army, carried what is known as a *baton* (also *marshal's baton* or *command staff*). The baton was a strong symbol of high rank and military power. There are a number of paintings showing admirals with batons from various European navies, for example the Swedish *Riksamiral* Gustav Otto Stenbock (MM 10418). The baton can also be seen on portraits of Swedish kings as military commanders. One interesting image is a stern-decoration from the ship *Carolus XI* (1679, later renamed *Sverige*), a huge wooden carving in almost natural size showing the king on horseback with a baton in his hand (SM O 02519). There are no known Swedish sources that mentions whether the baton was actually used or was shown as an attribute in, for example, battles, in contrast to some of the other symbols in this article.

The great sword

One of the most symbol-laden attributes that were used by the highest officers was the *great sword* (also *broad sword* or *long sword*). The sword was two-handed and an exclusive sign of dignity, only to be worn by royals and high commanders on, for example, fortresses and ships (Lenk 1946:44–45).

The great sword is described in a few 17th century sources. At the start of the battle of Oliwa in 1627, between a Polish and a Swedish squadron, a Polish source describes how the Swedish admiral Klas Stiernskiöld could be seen wielding his great sword on board his flagship *Tigern* (Djerw 2002:26). During the Battle of Öland in 1676, the Admiral Lorentz Creutz stood on *Kronan* "with a broad sword upon the cabin in the stern" (Translation by the author) (Lundgren 2001:49). The great sword seems to have been used in several navies. The Danish ship *Stora Sofia* was, in 1644, equipped with two long and two short swords (Inventory/*inventarielista* 1644). Several Danish ships obtained swords in 1660 (Lenk 1946:52). The Danish admiral Pros Mund is reported to have carried a great sword on the quarterdeck of *Patientia* during the Battle of Femern in 1644 (Probst 1996:247). Likewise, the English admiral Deane was, in 1653, "struck down as he stood flourishing his sword" in the stern of his flagship (Capp 1989:195). Several Dutch paintings from the first half of the 1600s also show how the commander was on the quarter- or poop deck in the ship's stern carrying a sword during battle (e.g. RM SK-A-460).

Archaeological finds of great swords from ships are very rare. However, on *Vasa* (1628), a grip and a scabbard that had probably belonged to such a sword have been found. Furthermore, a couple of two-handed sword grips have been found on *Kronan* (1676). These items support the historical source above, mentioning a great sword on the ship (Draeseke 2009:49–50, 66–67). There are also several 17th and 18th century great swords from ships preserved in Swedish museums (e.g. MM 02489). The great sword phenomenon persisted for a long time in the Swedish navy. During the first half of the 1700s, it was decided that the largest ships would receive two swords and the smaller ships one (Lenk 1946:46). In 1750, several swords were made to celebrate the appointment of the only two-year-old duke Karl as *storamiral* (grand admiral) (Halldin 1949:103; Berg 1992:9–13).

Great swords could obviously be carried by more than one person on a ship. However, besides the senior naval officer aboard, who else carried them? Possibly the senior army officer or the second naval officer in command. The great sword had no real practical function and was more of a ceremonial character. However, the sword was carried in battle. When the commander stood with it in his hand, it was apparent to both friend and foe who was in charge on board.

The gorget

An attribute worn by the army-officers were *gorgets*, metal plates hanging on the chest. This symbol of rank had evolved from plate armour but had no longer any practical function. There are several portraits from the 1600s showing naval officers with gorgets in the form of breastplates that have emerged from armour. One example is the Dutch admiral Witte de With who, on a portrait from around 1650, is depicted wearing a gorget that covers his upper chest as well as his neck and part of his upper back (HSM 1991.0209). This type of gorget had been used in the Swedish army as a symbol of rank since at least the early 1600s (Brandt 1947:48). Later in the century, the gorgets became smaller, more crescent-shaped, simply to hang in a chain or ribbon on the chest. In Swedish museum collections, there are very few gorgets from the 17th century. All of them seem to stem from the army, in which regulations from the previous decades of the century established that all officers should wear gorgets (Brandt 1947:50). In Swedish sources from the 1600s, there are no references to gorgets being worn in the navy.

However, on the wreck of the flagship *Kronan* (1676), three gorgets have been found (Einarsson 1997:212–214; Einarsson 2016:88). Thus, it is possible that Swedish naval officers also used gorgets in the 17th century, but the evidence is fragile. *Kronan* had some 300 soldiers and army officers, as well as 500 sailors and naval officers on board. The circumstances of the finds do not clearly show who wore the gorgets. It is known that the gorgets were more richly ornamented the higher the rank the wearer had. All three gorgets from *Kronan* have different decorations, and one of them, made of gilded brass and decorated with banners, swords and guns, could have possibly belonged to the commander of the fleet, Lorentz Creutz (Einarsson 2016:88).

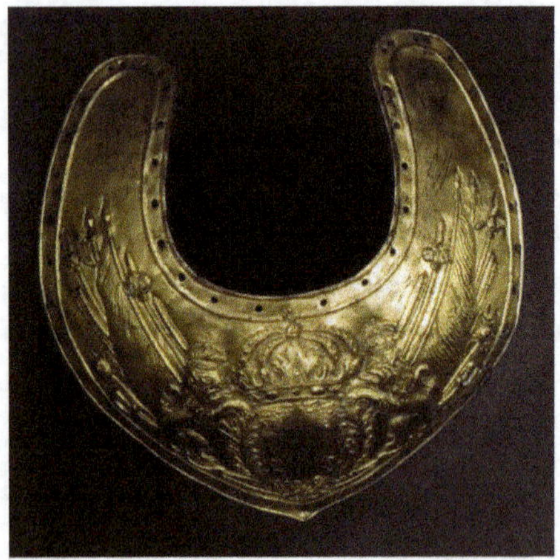

Figure 10: Gorget for an officer. Late 17th century.
AM.017981 Armémuseum, Stockholm

The speaking trumpet

Another sign of an officer was the funnel-shaped *speaking trumpet*, a kind of megaphone used to make oneself heard on board, or between ships. The trumpets were therefore of different sizes, depending on the intended use. The speaking trumpet was, in contrast to the baton, the great sword and the gorget, certainly a practical tool, used both at work and in battle. But it was also an object with symbolic value, only not as evident as the baton, the great sword or the gorget.

Information on speaking trumpets from the 1600s is very scarce. However, in the material from the trials after the Swedish defeat at Öland in 1676, when the navy's two most powerful ships *Kronan* and *Svärdet* were lost, we do have some information. Olof Nortman, one of 50 survivors of the 650 strong crew from *Svärdet*, mentions in the interrogation-protocol that when the commander, admiral Klas Uggla, was closing in on the enemy, he shouted to the other Swedish ships through an "instrument" made of tin, "…as it is usually done at sea, to be heard a long way" (Translation by the author) (Lundgren 2001:177).

There are no known depictions of a speaking trumpet in action on a ship from the 1600s. However, a painting of the Duke and Grand Admiral Karl on his flagship *Gustaf III* during the battle of Hogland in 1788, shows him leading his men, holding a speaking-trumpet made of pewter or silver in his right hand (NM MDrh 772).

There are a few speaking trumpets in Swedish museum collections. The oldest, and also the only one from the 17th century, is Karl Gustaf Wrangel's brass speaking trumpet. It stems from the mid-1600s and is over one and a half metres long (LSH 7134). The length indicates that it was probably put on the gunwale and used for communication with other ships. In the Swedish National Maritime Museum's collections, there are a few speaking trumpets from the late 18th century, one of which is a so-called "stormropare" (gale-trumpet) from the ship of the line *Dristigheten* (SM O 00362). As seen above, Swedish sources from the 17th and 18th centuries merely mention the speaking trumpet in connection to officers.

The boatswain's call

The *boatswain's call* (also *bosun's call*) was a metal whistle with a very shrill tone that could be heard far. Its practical function was to "pipe" seamen to different tasks. The call was comprised of a long narrow tube with a flat blade attached to it. At the end of the tube there was a hollow spherical end. A boatswain's call was usually worn in a lanyard or chain around the neck. The call has a very long history, deriving from at least the 14th century (Redknap 2005:284–285). In the 19th and 20th centuries, boatswain's calls are known to have been used by non-commissioned officers (Lundström 1989:182). However, they were earlier also worn and used by high rank officers. Mark Redknap, who has studied the boatswain's calls from the wreck of the English ship *Mary Rose* (1545), also discusses a number of mostly English finds and historical sources concerning calls from the 16th to the early 17th centuries (Redknap 2005).

Five boatswain's calls, all made of silver, have been found on the *Mary Rose*. The overall length varies from 4 centimetres to almost 16. They are interpreted to have belonged to both non-commissioned officers and officers such as the captain, master and boatswain. Redknap suggests that the size and material of the whistles show the status of the bearer. In England, the Lord High Admiral's personal insignia in the 16th century was a gold or silver (or both) boatswain's call, often worn on a golden chain around the neck. A portrait of Lord High Admiral Edward Clinton from 1562, shows him wearing a silver call around the neck (Redknap 2005:291). Vice Admiral Sir George Carew, commander of the fleet aboard the *Mary Rose* was given a gold whistle by Henry VIII just before the ship set sail. Similarly, French admirals wore boatswain's calls as a symbol of rank in the 1500s (Lundström 1989; Redknap 2005).

One of the few English historical sources from the 17th century that mentions a boatswain's call, does this in connection to the funeral of a boatswain. The funeral took place on land, and when the coffin was taken to the graveside, some items were put on it, among them a boatswain's call, (Davies 1991:95). The boatswain's call is mentioned in Danish sources from the middle of the 16th century. In the Danish King Kristian IV's articles of war from 1625, the punishments for the ones who ignored the pipe-call is listed (Garde 1832:110).

In Sweden, evidence of boatswain's calls from the 16th and 17th centuries is hard to find. The only known archaeological find is from the island of Gotland in the Baltic. In 1566, Sweden was at war with Denmark and the Hanseatic town of Lübeck. After a hard-fought battle, the allied fleet anchored on the Visby roadstead. The purpose was to bury the Danish Vice Admiral Kristoffer Mogensen who had died in the fight. A fierce storm suddenly struck the fleet, 14 ships were smashed to pieces and thousands of sailors lost their lives, among them both the Danish and the Lübeckian admirals. Today, not much remains of the ships but some interesting finds have been made in the shallow water, among them a boatswain's call. The call is made of silver, very richly ornamented and 18.5 centimetres long – longer than any of the finds from the *Mary Rose*. Redknap does not mention this call in his article and might not be aware of its existence as he refers to a pipe with a length of 16.9 centimetres as very large (Redknap 2005:292). The boatswain's call from Visby roadstead has been interpreted as possibly belonging to the Lübeckian Vice Admiral Johann Kampferbeck on *Josua*, who survived the disaster (Lundström 1989:183). So, the only known archaeological find in Sweden of a boatswain's call is actually of Lübeckian (or possibly Danish) origin. However, there are finds that might have functioned in a similar way as the boatswain's call. Two whistles have been found on *Kronan* (1676). Their area of use is not known, but they might have been used for some sort of signalling, in a similar way as a boatswain's call (Einarsson personal communication).

Death on the quarterdeck and the officer's Role in Battle

The officer's main task was to act as role models for the men and lead them with a firm, but fair hand. In battle, they had to be brave, give prudent orders and stoically endure cannon-shots, thunder, smoke, swirling splinters and the sight of mutilated crewmen. As shown above, the senior officers – admirals and captains – led the battle from the unprotected quarter- and poop decks in the stern. This is also evident in contemporary instructions (Fleming's instruction 1628; Cavallie 1976:138). In contrast, most military commanders on land had a protected position behind their armies (some of them, for example the Swedish King Gustavus Adolphus, sometimes chose to lead from the front). This was not the case with an admiral on a ship. The commander's place was high in the stern and nowhere else, where he could stand clearly visible to both his own men and the enemy. There he would swing his great sword and shout encouraging comments to the men and con-temptuous words to the enemy.

The commander was supposed to act boldly, but at the same time preserve his calm and keep control of the situation. The good commander, therefore, conducted himself with vigilance and patience, while awaiting the right opportunity to exploit advantageous situations. "...experience and conduct must accompany courage and braveness, otherwise there is confusion, like a body without a soul." as a contemporary admiral expressed it (translation by the author) (Cavallie 1976:161).

Figure 11: The commander with a great sword in the stern. Detail from a painting by Hendrik Cornelisz Vroom. A.0002, Scheepvaartmuseum (The National Maritime Museum), Amsterdam

The high decks in the stern were exposed locations, and the officers were just as vulnerable in battle, if not more, as the common crew. In their often colourful and sumptuous clothes, they were tempting targets for enemy snipers. Many high-ranking officers died aboard accordingly, most likely on the quarter- or poop decks. In the battle of Oliwa in 1627, both the Swedish Admiral Nils Stiernsköld and his Polish opponent Arndt Dickman died (Zettersten 1890:489–490; Djerw 2002:25–32). After the Swedish victory against the Danish fleet at Femern in 1644, Karl Gustaf Wrangel wrote in his journal that both the Danish admiral and vice admiral had fallen (Wrangel's journal 1644). In the bloody struggle at Öresund (the Sound) in 1658 between the Dutch and the Swedish fleets, the Dutch Admiral Witte de With and the Vice Admiral Pieter Floriszoon died (TiS 1900). In 1676, the two leading admirals in the Swedish navy – Lorentz Creutz and Klas Uggla, both died at the battle of Öland (Zettersten 1903:478–480). The three Anglo–Dutch wars in the second half of the 1600s took their toll on both the English and the Dutch. Several Dutch admirals were killed during the war and in the English fleet, 36 captains died in the brief period from 1649 to 1660, including the "general at sea" Deane (Capp 1989:195; Bruijn 1993:47, 51, 114). Perhaps the most well-known naval officer who died on the quarterdeck, was the British admiral lord Horatio Nelson at the Battle of Trafalgar in 1805.

Conclusion

In this article I have discussed five symbols of power and dignity that were used by Swedish officers on warships. I have also discussed the role of the senior officers in battle.

The *baton* and the *great sword* were used by high rank officers. Both objects showed the power and the symbolic capital that was entrusted in the hands of loyal servants by their state superior, usually the king. The baton and the great sword were pure symbols of authority and dignity and were used in a ceremonial way, even in battle. The great sword was swung as a sign of potency and force – an encouragement to the crew and a potential threat to the enemy, although it was not actually used in close combat. The fact that the sources rather often mention the admiral standing with a sword in the stern during battles, tells us that this was what he was expected to do, and in most cases, he probably did act as a role model to his men, a brave commander, always ready to die for king and country.

The *gorgets* were, from the end of the 1600s, officially established symbols of rank, used by officers of all ranks in the army. It is not clear if they were ever really introduced into the navy. However, archaeological evidence from *Kronan* (1676) shows that gorgets were worn by some, but it is not clear by whom. The *speaking trumpet* and the *boatswain's call* were officers' symbols that also had a practical function in the handling of the ship in contrast to batons, great swords and gorgets. In the 16th and early 17th century the boatswain's call, at least in some navies, was a symbol of high rank and worn by senior officers. It was also a sign of rank among non-commissioned officers, but their calls were generally of lower quality and made from cheaper materials. There is no evidence that boatswain's calls were used in Sweden in the 16th or 17th centuries, either as symbols of rank or practical tools. The substitute was speaking trumpets and possibly other whistles that were used for signalling. However, the speaking trumpet in Sweden and the boatswain's call in, for example England, both attributes of rank that had a practical function, gradually lost status as symbols of high rank. In the 19th century they became more associated with non-commissioned officers such as masters and boatswains than with admirals and captains.

The symbols and attributes worn by the officers, as well as the status and the privileges that came with them, meant nothing during a clash with the enemy. Nor did their symbolic capital as noblemen. A battle was therefore, in more than one sense a unique experience, when the differences in status temporary levelled out – ultimately everyone on the ship was just as vulnerable to the enemy fire and only God could decide who should die and who should not.

References

Printed sources

Fleming, H., 1937 (1628). Instruction för den flåtan som närvarande ligger på Dantzicher Redd, Actum eodem loco, Den 10 septemb: Anno 1628. Marinstaben. *Sveriges sjökrig:1611–1632*, s. 264–268. Stockholm.

Wrangel, C. G., 1900 (1644). Carl Gustaf Wrangels "journal" under expedition med stora flottan, hösten 1644: ur sjökrigsarkivet, benäget meddeladt genom kapten S. Natt och Dag. *Tidskrift i sjöväsendet*. 63:1900, s. 236–245. Karlskrona.

Tidskrift i Sjöväsendet (TiS) 1900. Slaget i Öresund 1658. Utdrag ur "Diariet" hållet "uppå siööresan 1658" å flaggskeppet Victoria, nr 2, s. 116–122. Karlskrona.

Cavallie, J., 1976. Werner von Rosenfeldts sjömansmemorial. *Karolinska Förbundets årsbok*. s. 100–166. Stockholm.

Stora Sofias inventarielista från 1644. Bergstrand, Thomas & Arbin, Staffan von (2003). *Stora Sofia: Dokumentation, skyddstäckning och kontroll: Vård av fartygslämning: Styrsö socken i Göteborgs kommun, Västra Götalands län, Västergötland*, bil. 2. Uddevalla.

Paintings and artefacts

Armémuseum (AM)
AM.017981. Ringkrage för officer. Karl XI:s tid.

Het Scheepvaartmuseum, Amsterdam (HSM)
A.0002. Schermutseling tussen Amsterdamse en Engelse oorlogsschepen, 20 april 1605. Painting by Hendrik Cornelisz Vroom 1614.

1991.0209. Portret van Witte Cornelisz. de With (1599–1658). Painting by Abraham van Westerveldt.

Marinmuseum, Karlskrona (MM)
MM 10418. Porträtt av riksamiral Gustav Otto Stenbock. Okänd konstnär.

MM 02489. Slagsvärd av år 1657.

Nationalmuseum, Stockholm (NM)
NMDrh 772. Hertig Karl (Karl XIII) i slaget vid Hogland. Målning av Per Krafft d.y. ca. 1810.

Rijksmuseum, Amsterdam (RM)
SK-A-460. Hollandse shepen overzeilen Spaanse galeien onder de Engelse kust, 3 oktober 1602. Målning av Hendrik Cornelisz Vroom, 1617.

Sjöhistoriska museet, Stockholm (SM)
O 00362. Ropare/stormropare.

O 02519. Akterspegelsornament till *Carolus XI*.

Skoklosters slott (LSH)
Inv.nr. 7134. Ropare som sannolikt tillhört Carl Gustaf Wrangel.

Literature

Berg, O. P., 1992. *Marinens blankvapen. Aktuellt 19th 92 Marinmuseum*, s. 5–68. Karlskrona.

Bourdieu, P., 1993. *Kultursociologiska texter*. Stockholm.

Brandt, T., 1947. Ringkragar. *Föreningen Armémusei Vänner Meddelanden VIII*, s. 48–60. Stockholm.

Bruijn, J. R., 1993. *The Dutch Navy of the Seventeenth and Eighteenth Centuries*. Columbia.

Capp, B., 1989. *Cromwells Navy, The Fleet and the English Revolution 1648–1660*. Oxford.

Davies, D. J., 1991. *Gentlemen and Tarpaulins. The Officers an Men of the Restoration Navy*. Oxford.

Djerw, U. (red.), 2002 (1627). Den hårda drabbningen. *Örlogsliv: röster ur svenska flottans historia 1632–2002*, s. 25–32, Stockholm.

Draeseke, T., 2009. *The sword aboard ship. The evolution of a weapon and naval identity*. Unpublished diss. Southampton university.

Einarsson, L., 1997. Artefacts from the *Kronan* (1676): categories, preservation and social structure. Redknap, Mark (ed.). *Artefacts from wrecks: dated assemblages from the late Middle Ages to the Industrial Revolution*. pp. 209–218. Oxford.

Einarsson, L., 2016. *Regalskeppet* Kronan: *historia och arkeologi ur djupet*. Lund.

Ekman, C., 1943. Livet ombord och i land. Sjöfolkets beklädnad och uniformer. Personalens klädsel. Lybeck, Otto (red.). *Svenska flottans historia vol. II*, s. 446–454. Malmö.

Englund, P., 1989. *Det hotade huset. Adliga föreställningar om samhället under stormaktstiden*. Stockholm.

Garde, H. G., 1832. *Efterretninger om den danske og norske Søemagt*, vol. 1. Köpenhamn.

Halldin, G., 1949. *Slagsvärdet i svenska flottan*. Sjöhistorik årsbok. Stockholm.

Lenk, T., 1946. *Om slagsvärdet som maktsymbol*, Svenska Vapenhistoriska Sällskapet, s. 41–54. Stockholm.

Lundström, P., 1989. Dolk och pipa från Brissund. *Gotländskt arkiv: meddelanden från Föreningen Gotlands fornvänner, s. 177–184. Gotlands fornsal*. Visby.

Lundgren, K., 2001. Sjöslaget vid Öland: vittnesmål – dokument 1676–1677. Kalmar.

Miller, A., 2007. *Dressed to kill*. British Naval Uniforms. London.

Probst, N. M., 1996. Christian 4.s flåde. Köpenhamn.

Redknap, M., 2005. Boatswain's calls. *Before the mast. Life and death aboard the Mary Rose*, Gardiner, J. & Allen, M. J. (ed.), pp. 284–292. Portsmouth.

Stadin, K., 2005. The masculine image of a great power: representations of Swedish imperial power c. 1630–1690. *Scandinavian journal of history* (Print). 2005(30):1, pp. [61]–82

Stadin, Kekke. 2010. *Maktens män bär rött: historiska studier av manlighet, manligt framträdande och kläder*. Stockholm.

Zettersten, Axel. 1890. *Svenska flottans historia: åren 1622–1634*. Stockholm.

Zettersten, Axel. 1903. *Svenska flottans historia: åren 1635–1680*. Norrtälje.

Personal communication

Einarsson, L., Kalmar läns museum. Project manager *Kronan*, nov. 2017.

Notions of Fear in a 17th Century Navy

ANNASARA HAMMAR

The questions

When the ordinary seaman Johan Matsson Lund was accused, in 1692, of deserting the naval ship *Gotland*, he claimed the reason to be a rumour that the sailors on *Gotland* were going to be transferred to a privateer in the North Sea. Therefore, he "took fear upon himself" [*tog fruchtan till sig*] and escaped the ship in the harbour of Gothenburg. (Admiralty court, protocol of August 20, 1692) The explanation was unusually straightforward since it was rare for sailors to refer to sentiments or feelings in the Admiralty court. Hence the mentioning of fear in this case raises some questions. Why did Johan Mattson Lund want the court to know he had been frightened? What did he mean with the expression "took fear upon himself"? The phrase is even more intriguing since there are other court cases where defendants spent a great deal of effort in denying even the hint of fear. Jonas Palmquist, captain of the convoy ship *Spes*, for example had his whole ship crew witness on his behalf that he had "always been fearless and never shown any fear" [*warit helt frijmodig, och wijst ingen räddhåga*] when he was on trial for lowering his main topsail in 1698 (Generalauditören, summary of the trial in December 8, 1698).

Why did captain Jonas Palmquist have to prove his courage in a long trial, when sailor Johan Mattson Lund could admit he had been affected by fear in a case that was only two sentences long? In this article I will try to answer these questions in order to understand the use of "fear" and its meanings in the 17th century Swedish naval court. I will thereby claim that "fear" is not a static, unchangeable emotion, but the opposite: its expressions and its meanings change, and these changes are precisely what makes it interesting.

Emotives in court

Court records, which will be the main sources for this investigation, are a special challenge, often rich in detail but also the result of a specific situation. The Swedish naval court consisted of 5–8 naval officers and, from 1674, also included a legal officer. The court required a way of talking and behaving and people did not always reveal their inner beliefs and opinions (Hammar 2014, pp. 89–92), which I consider to be an opportunity rather than an obstacle. It is because the court situation is so specific, I am interested in how fear is mentioning in context. Fear is of course not the only emotion visible in naval court minutes documentation from the 17th century; but when fear is mentioned it is always significant. At first glance the reason for that might seem self-explanatory: the presence of war, violence and death in an early modern war force would naturally arouse strong emotions like fear, which in turn, eventually would make its way into the interrogations and testimonies of the naval court.

However, emotions are not simply reactions to events, they are entangled within social relations, their system of communication and are thus dependent on the community where it appears. Therefore, in court the expressions of fear are not only descriptions of actions or reactions, they are a way to explain, to defend, to accuse or to argue in the courtroom. Yet, they are not merely rhetoric either, the reason fear is mentioned is because it is regarded as a reaction that mattered in real life. Thus, fear operates in two settings at the same time: firstly, as a reaction belonging to an event described in court by defendants or witnesses, and secondly as a device used in court for a reason. The concept "emotives", developed by the historian William Reddy, will function as a way to understand and analyse this. Speeches about emotions, Reddy claims, are not merely descriptions, but statements made to make things happen, either at an individual level, or at a relational level. Predicates such as "I am sad "or I am frightened" are utterances that "present themselves at first glance as semantically the same as 'I have red hair,' 'I am clean,' or 'I feel ill,' which are genuinely descriptive or constative. As descriptive statements, however, emotion claims do not admit independent verification" (Reddy 1999, p. 268.). Statements about emotions can be made to change relations or social scenarios. "To say 'I am afraid of you' may be a way of refusing to cooperate with someone or a request for a change in the relationship" (Reddy 1999, p. 268.). A statement about emotions can also be made in order to change the emotion itself, or to strengthen it. To say "I love you" might be a way of finding out if it is true or not (Reddy 1999, p. 269. See also Reddy 2001, pp. 63–111 and Reddy 2000, pp. 113–119 for a longer discussion of the concept of emotives).

Even if I, for various reasons, will not use the word emotives (see my discussion on the concept emotion below), I find that Reddy's perspective offers a useful tool for analysing historical sources since the only way a historian can investigate emotions, is through statements. To claim "I took fear upon myself" or "I have never been fainthearted" are therefore not simply descriptions, but actions that required a social context to make them meaningful. In order to analyse statements about emotion as emotives, there is a need for a careful examination of the particular words used in a particular situation and how these words corresponded to a context. There is a risk that nuances get lost in the translation from a source material in Swedish, which is why I have added the specific Swedish phrase or word in square brackets next to the quote form the sources.

Emotions as a subject of historical research

Reddy is one of many historians belonging to the vivid, expanding field of history of emotions. Even if emotions have been a subject of interest to historians for a long time (see for example Huizinga 1919 or Febvré 1941), it is not until quite recently emotions have become its own field of historical research and thus explored more systematically. (For a description of the establishment of the field see for example Rosenwein 2006, pp. 1–31 or Plamper & Keith 2015, pp. 40–74.) Researchers within the field have two things in common: they have been able to show the potential of using emotions as a way of exploring historical change, events and ideas, but they also acknowledge its difficulties. Because historians are a species who joyfully borrow concepts, theories, ideas and methods from other research fields; discussions about modern emotion research have been a significant part of the theoretical and methodological development.

The concept of "emotion" happens however to be a loose one. "We see emotions as based as biological processes, elaborated in our close relationships, and shaped by culture", say the writers in the introduction chapter of an ambitious modern textbook on the subject (Oatley et al. 2006, p. xxi). "Anything that is a passion with regard to one subject is an action with regard to something else", René Descartes writes in his Passions of the soul in 1649 (Descartes 2010, p. 1). It is almost 360 years between the two definitions, and if nothing else, it reminds us that there are different ways to speak about feelings and what they are, and thus there is no definition that could cover all possible meanings over time and space. There are two crucial disputes on how emotions are perceived and understood. First there is a disagreement between those who see emotions as a part of a cognitive operation, and those who see emotions as something else than cognition (see discussion in Reddy 2001, pp. 8–21). The other disagreement is between those researchers who believe emotions to be genetically hardwired, a sustainable part of our DNA and therefore always invariant in every time and every society, and those who believe emotions are socially constructed, a learned habit and therefore changeable (for a thorough discussion on this see Plamper & Keith 2015, chapter 2 and 3). While older historians such as Huizinga and Febvré might have agreed with the view that emotions, although used in different ways, remain essentially the same, today's historians generally have adopted the opinion that emotions are, at least in part, socially constructed (Rosenwein 2010, pp. 19–20. See also Rosenwein's discussions on an older view on the history of emotions in Rosenwein 2002, particularly about the contribution to the field made by Huizinga, Febvré and Norbert Elias and the problem with their use of a "grand narrative"). This might be a result of historians' habit of historicalizing everything possible, but it might also be a logical consequence of empirical data. Descartes' view on passions is indeed not the same as our contemporary textbook's definition of "emotions". This leads us to another difficulty, which is that the concept "emotion" is problematic.

The concept of emotion

The concept "emotion" is a modern one, an umbrella term that had no equivalency in early modern Europe. The historian Thomas Dixon argues that it is therefore misleading to use the concept "emotion" when trying to understand love, hate, anger, joy and fear before the 19th century (Dixon 2003, p.18). In early modern Europe other words were used: passions, appetites, desires, affections or sentiments. Their meaning partly overlaps what we today mean by "emotion" but not entirely and there is a prominent discussion about weather our different words for the reactions and expressions we today call emotions, also alter our way of thinking about them and how we feel them. Many historians studying emotions use the concept "emotion" in their research anyway (see Rosenwein 2006, Reddy 2001, Plamper 2015) and argue that the similarities are more significant than the differences (see for example Rosenwein 2006, pp. 3–4).

Thomas Dixon has adopted a different view: he means there are connotations and meanings lost when we replace the glossary of passions, affections, appetites and desires with the umbrella concept "emotion". He also points out, and this I believe is his most relevant argument, that we by using "emotions" imply the modern concept to be the right and final one, perhaps even the better one, while "passions" and "affections" are less useful or understandable (Dixon 2003, especially his discussion on presentism, pp. 6–15). Emotions are however many times less precise than the early modern concepts. Therefore, it is perhaps unjustified to try to force the nuances of passions, affections, appetites, desires and sentiments into the clumsy concept "emotion". By using the modern word, we lose a different way of thinking, what the early modern person might have described as, "movements of the soul" (Dixon 2012, p. 343). Hence, I chose to use the early modern concepts instead, and by doing so I make Reddy's theoretical concept "emotives" a little less adequate. However, the essence of the concept remains useful. To express or speak about fear is to enforce an action on a situation or a relation and not a mere description of a state of mind.

Fear in a world of passions and affections

In order to use a 17th century vocabulary, there is a need to explain it, hereby also adding desires, appetites, and motivations to the palette, phenomena we tend to see rather different from emotions. The society of the 17th century was a religious world, and therefore the understanding of passions, affections and appetites, were closely connected to the understanding of human beings as religious creatures, made by God, driven out from Eden and since then predestined to despair, pain and misery. The human soul was considered as broken, and it could only be redeemed by the grace of God. The two theologians Augustine (354–430) and Thomas Aquinas (1225–1274) had an enormous influence over the early modern period's understanding of body, mind, passions and soul. Both describe passions as unruly forces, which needed to be controlled by reason, will and virtue. Passions were a sign of the sickness of the fallen soul, the rebellion of the body against the mind and a punishment for Adam and Eve's disobedience to God (Dixon 2003, p. 29). For Augustine the soul was divided into two, an inner soul, where reason and will operated, and an "outer" soul, easily affected by the world and consequently also its passions. Aquinas took this thought further and made a fundamental difference between active and passive parts of the soul. The intellective soul and its higher appetites (also called the will) towards God, virtue, truth and goodness were active rather than passive. The sensitive soul in contrast, was in the hands of the lower appetite, the desires towards the material world, and reacted rather than acted. Hereby there emerged a difference between passions – the sinful, unruly forces that moved the sensitive part of the soul – and affections, the movements of the intellective soul that could be both voluntary and virtuous (Dixon 2003, p. 39).

In contemporary etiquette and educational literature of the 17th century, passions are seen mainly as a natural disorder: "They are winds that put the mind in tumult, sweeping us along like ships in a gale, and as storms disturb the harmony of nature, passions are discordant and jangling" (James 1997, p. 13). This negative view of passions as something unruly, disobedient, fuming forces has a direct consequence on how we today might interpret expressions of feelings in both official and personal sources from this period. Being overwhelmingly sensitive was not appropriate and therefore there are no endless dwellings on the number of tears or the thrill of joy in the surviving sources from the 17th century, which we find instead among certain social groups in the 18th century, "the sensitive era", or in the frequently used emoticons on today's social media. Passionate expressions were not used to "show off" socially, and social status was given to those who were patient, calm, controlled and mild, not the quick tempered, sentimental or enthusiastic person. This means that people only expressed or spoke about their passions when they were considered to have an important significance.

Even though passions were very often seen as unruly forces outside control, the understanding of how the soul, body and will worked in that period, made appetites, desires, passions and affections altogether more cognitive in its nature, than it did later in the 19th and 20th centuries. For Renée Descartes, who was heavily inspired by Aristotle, the passions were not merely a result of a sinful, broken soul, devastated by the world's misery and temptations. Passions had a clear function to him, which was to guide the will to make the right choice and protect the body from dangers (Descartes 2010, p. 17). This is quite close to a modern Darwinian view where emotions are basically a biological respond to things happening to us. However, a closer look at Descartes' arguments reveals that there is in fact a fundamental rift between his time and ours. Today fear is normally seen as one of our basic emotions (for a discussion on a scientific perceptive of fear, see Plamper & Lazier 2012). Descartes considered six passions to be what he called "basic passions": wonder, love, hatred, desire, joy and sadness (Descartes 2010, p. 23). Observe that "fear" is thus not listed among these, since Descartes along with many others in the early modern period viewed instead fear as a "mixed passion". Fear, according to Descartes, is a state of mind where wonder mingles with hope and an insecure anticipation of a future that could cause displeasure, pain, ruin and disaster. It is merely an excess of shrinking reluctance, wonder and anxiety – an excess that is always unvirtuous, just as boldness is an excess of courage that is always good (provided the end intended is good). Because the principal cause of fear is surprise, there's no better way to avoid it than to think ahead and prepare oneself for any eventuality that one might fear (Descartes 2010, p. 53).

Generally positive to passions, he dismisses fear as completely useless. "As for fear or terror, I don't see that it can ever be praiseworthy or useful"

(Descartes 2010, p. 53). Fear according to Descartes himself, is not an automatic response from body or "outer soul" on terrifying events. Fear requires the special ability to recognise the future and imagine its consequences. Fear is therefore something that separates us from other living creatures and makes us particularly and distinctively human (Weiss 2012 p. 2–3). Yet it is also something we should avoid, since it, according to Descartes, is a passion that prevents us from doing the virtuous.

Even for Spinoza fear requires an act of cognitive processing. Fear is to him is "an inconstant unpleasure, born of the idea of a future or past way of thinking, the outcome of which we are somewhat unsure of." Moreover, he adds the somewhat beautiful idea:" there is no hope without fear and no fear without hope" (Spinoza 2010, p. 81). In short, unruly as the passions may be, according to Descartes and Spinoza, you are stricken by fear because you allow yourself to be so.

Frightened seamen in court

What did Johan Mattson Lund mean then when he said, "he took fear upon himself"? It seems safe to assume his belief on what fear was might have differed from the articulated ideas of the intellectual elite.

There are other cases from the admiralty court, when seamen refer to "fear" as a reason for their actions. There are several occasions when seamen state they had escaped, stayed away or avoided their commander in fear of being punished (Admiralty Court, protocols from December 21, 1685, December 3, 1685, September 7, 1692, November 16, 1692). Although they never explicitly said it, it is clear from the context in all the cases, that "punishment" meant physical punishment, such as beatings from a superior commander or a gauntlet. In another case a witness explained why the young volunteer Wilhelm Mertz had carried two knives around with him (of which he had used one to stab another sailor in his chest) with the following phrase: "He had a quarrel with Berlingen [another volunteer] and he was afraid of him [*för honom war han rädd*], and therefore he took the knives with him" (Admiralty court, protocols from May 19, 1685.).

It seems as if seamen used the word fear when they had reasons to anticipate violence. Even Johan Mattson's statement relates to this: he had heard a rumour that he and the rest of the crew from *Gotland* would to be sent out at sea again to serve on a privateer – which meant military action. The threat of being exposed to violence was always present for a seaman in the navy, so it is not difficult to believe there was a harsh reality behind the speeches of fear (for more on violence in the navy, see Hammar 2015, pp. 706–707). There also seems to be a strong connection between physical pain and fear in the early modern society in general. This is a period where war, diseases, accidents, famine and hard work made the body particularly vulnerable. It is perhaps no coincidence that fear, in a more popular understanding of the concept, turned into bodily malformations in early modern Europe. Unnatural, disturbing and terrifying monsters illustrated war (Lederer 2012, pp. 18–35) and misshapen newborns or animals were interpreted as signs of disasters and catastrophes (Håkansson 2014, pp. 119–131). Fear was also a bodily experience, where muscles might freeze or tremble, the heart beats faster and so on. The seaman and the officers in the court were likely to have a mutual understanding of this, and Johan Mattson's explanation that he was frightened, is never questioned by anyone. On the other hand, that does not explain why he or any of the other seamen mention it. What was it those seamen wished to accomplish when they admitted in front of the naval court, that they had been frightened? We will come back to this question but let us first examine some other testimonies of frightened seamen.

Talking about frightened seamen: the sinking of *Kronan*

In a special court summoned after the (for the Swedish navy) two disastrous battles against the Danish navy in May and June 1676, three high ranked officers were accused of cowardice and traitorous behaviour. The trial lasted over a year and included over fifty testimonies, interrogations and confrontations, 259 folio pages of court records and a volume of letters from witnesses and defendants. In his first testimony, the witness admiral lieutenant Hans Wachtmeister described a navy in chaos and complained about the "common men" in the crew who were not only inexperienced but also "astonished and timid [*häpnade och försagde*] so they did not know what they were doing" (Kommissorialrätten, protocol from June 17, 1676). I use the word "astonished" here due to Descartes understanding of astonishment being a stronger variation of "wonder", causing the body to freeze in order to grasp the situation (Descartes 2010 p. 21.), which is what Wachtmeister seems to mean. To be astonished is not entirely the same thing as being frightened, nor is timid. However, the phrase comes back in different testimonies three more times. When *Kronan* capsized, captain Mats Mårtenson Dünkirch on board Hieronymus said, "this made everyone astonished and timid [*ther af blefwo wist alla häpne och försagde*]" (Kommissorialrätten, protocol from June 18,

1676). Gustaf Sparre, captain aboard *Draken* described his own reactions when *Kronan* capsized:

> [...] and when I looked for *Kronan* I saw with wonder [*förundran*] where she was, and at the same time I realized, not without much alteration and astonishment [*häpenheet*], that she lay on her side at the position where we were supposed to fight, and a short time after, I saw her explode (Kommissorialrätten, protocol from July 18, 1676).

Alteration here is also the word used in the Swedish original text and meant the same, a disturbing movement in the soul, making one dismayed or aghast. Sparre then continued by describing the difficulties he had aboard. His spritsail and topsail were shot to pieces and "thereto, the people were very astonished by the unfortunate shipwreck of *Kronan*, so I had to go down in the Ship and with my sword force them up on deck to fight" (Kommissorialrätten, protocol from July 18, 1676).

One notices that both Mats Mårtensson Dünkirch and Gustaf Sparre used the word "*häpen*" or astonished in one situation, when *Kronan* capsized, exploded and sank. Hence the word clearly refers to a reaction following a very dramatic, unexpected and presumably horrifying event. Admiral Klerck aboard *Solen* used the more direct word "terrified [stoor förskräckelse]" for the reactions among his crew when *Kronan* capsized (Kommissorialrätten, protocol from June 17, 1676).

None of the ordinary seamen were questioned in this trial so we have no confirmation from them that they indeed had been frightened and timid. Nevertheless, perhaps the officers' descriptions were not meant to be accurate descriptions of a battle scene, but an explanation and an excuse for their own actions. They wanted to highlight that the men aboard were so scared that the officers could not fulfil their duties. Why was this a possible excuse? One explanation is of course that it might have been true. However, another explanation has to do with the officers' view on the behaviour of ordinary men. These men from the higher elite assumed that men of lower ranks were easily frightened. The fact that no seamen were ever accused of cowardice is an example of how it was perceived to be the natural order of things. The strongest word to indicate cowardice among the men was timidity (försagdhet), but this should be contrasted to the words used to described frightened officers who were called pultrons, rascals or traitors (pultroner och skälmar). Admiral Johan Bär made a long defence speech in court where he described his officer colleagues as chicken-hearted runaways. If the court only asked the right witness, Bär said:

> [...] he would tell them who sailed into Kalmarsund and left rear admiral Johan Klerck alone with the enemy, who ran away to Sandhamn, who threw their ballast overboard [to get away quicker], who ran into Västervik and the archipelago and who, by the fear of the enemy [räddhåga för fienden] took his flag down and wanted to leave his ship (Kommissorialrätten, protocol from May 29, 1677).

Admiral Claes Uggla, who died on board his ship in the battle, was reported to have had twisted his hands when he stood at the quarterdeck and said to those beside him: "See how those pussy bitches [hundsfottar el. hundfittor] run, see how they flee [ränner], they serve their King and Fatherland as rascals [skälmar] and pultrons [pultroner]" (Kommissorialrätten, protocol from February 28 1677). The Admiral perhaps did not express himself quite so bluntly, but nevertheless the testimony reflected a general view of disloyal and fainthearted officers. Thus, there is a clear line here between how frightened seamen and frightened officers are described, treated and examined.

A fainthearted officer and a wailing volunteer

Another example might highlight this a bit more. During her voyage from Karlskrona to southern France as a convoy ship, the naval vessel *Spes* came across all sorts of misfortunes.

The ship left Karlskrona October 4, 1696 and almost instantly ran aground. The obviously inexperienced navigation officer was dismissed and finally replaced by another, more than two months later. By then the ship had sailed no further than Gothenburg. In December, a severe leak in the hull was discovered and when the ship was hit by a storm, she lost her rudder and eventually was forced to seek harbour and shelter in Valmouth England, where she spent months being repaired. The ship reached its final destination in France March 3, 1697. In late spring the ship was on its journey back to Sweden but on 27th of June she encountered two British naval ships, and the meeting turned into a military and diplomatic conflict. Swedish ships were – as ships from many other nations – strictly forbidden to show unnecessary respect to foreign powers. This included the special signal of lowering the topsail, a diplomatic courtesy at sea, made to honour a foreign ship. Nevertheless, because naval ships were nothing else than extended symbols of Kings and Queens, showing this kind of respect towards another ship also meant acknowledging another regent's superiority over the sea. The two British naval ships tried to force *Spes* to lower her topsail, but her captain, Jonas Palmquist, refused, by referring to the orders of his king, Charles XII (strictly speaking his orders came from Charles XI, who had died in April 1697). However, the two British ships quickly got support from a fleet of warships and Palmquist was eventually forced to surrender. Once again, *Spes* ended up in a British harbour and did not set sail again until October 28, 1697. A few days later she ran aground outside Skagen, due to another miscalculation by the navigation officers and a false light on the shore, which the officers mistook for the lighthouse on Skagen. The crew was all saved, but the ship was lost (Generalauditören, Captain Palmquist's first account, in the protocols from May 30 and 31, June 1, 3 and 7, 1698). Back home in Karlskrona, Captain Palmquist was brought to court for all these events, but it was the lowering of the topsail that was his gravest fault. The king perceived it as cowardice and insisted he should have refused to lower the sail and instead chosen to fight. Palmquist was not the only officer on trial for this offence. The ongoing war had made naval strategy politics more intense, and British naval ships had started to terrorize all other ships entering the British channel. Sweden was an ally to Britain in the war, but British naval ships did not hesitate to fire at allied ships, should they refuse to show their respect to the British king. Thus, Palmquist and other officers had to make the impossible choice between fighting and risking both the ship and the lives of their crew or face a death sentence back home. Palmquist chose the latter. A part of Palmquist's defence in court was to convince the court he was a loyal officer by proving he had acted accordingly to his orders, not disobeying them. He argued he had no orders to go into a battle with a whole foreign fleet and no orders to put his ship and the whole convoy in danger by such an action (see Rationes Rei in Exceptione et Duplic, Generalauditören, protocol from December 8, 1698). But his disloyalty was also discussed through the concept of cowardice. His behaviour, not only concerning the specific encounter with the British ships, but on the whole voyage, was of uttermost importance. Events that had nothing to do with the encounter were therefore discussed in detail (see also Perlestam 2004). The storm when the ship had lost its rudder, became significant. The captain, reading from his ship's dairy, described in court how he, during the storm, found:

> A volunteer named Thomas Wolter, who he had seen in this danger, started to cry and wail, [gråta och jembra sig] which the Captain had fortunately discovered before this volunteer had infected other men with the same fear [slik klenmodighet]. The captain called him into the Great Cabin and with his

own cutlass, punished him righteously for his fear, [klenmodighet] in order to prevent anxiety [wijdare klenmodighet] spreading to the other men, and the men, as soon as they found this out, instead of being timid [försagd], showed more diligence and courage [flijt och courage] (Generalauditören, protocol from May 31, 1698).

The lieutenants on board repeated the story of Thomas Wolter two more times. Senior lieutenant Carl Mannerfelt confessed: "the Captain has not been timid [försagd] but always encouraged his subordinate men, and a volunteer he had found crying and wailing [*gråta och jembra sig*], he had himself punished" (Generalauditören, protocol from June 9, 1698). The junior lieutenant, Ambjörn Siöman, described the Captain as "always fearless and courageous, he also found a volunteer, named Wolter, crying and wailing [*gråta och jembra sig*] and punished him with his own cutlass" (Generalauditören, protocol from June 10, 1698). The volunteer Thomas Wolter was also questioned in court, along with several others from the ship's crew, but neither he nor any of the other ordinary seamen, mentioned the episode (Generalauditören, protocol from July 5, 1698).

The officers who mentioned the event were positive to the captain's action and particularly pointed out that the captain had chosen to punish the volunteer with his own hands. This indicated, from the officers' point of view, that Palmquist was a good officer who took responsibility for keeping every man aboard the ship in good spirit. Palmquist's statement that he was able to punish the volunteer before he had influenced anyone else and that the men had been encouraged when they heard about the punishment, gives us a glimpse of the officers' perspective on ordinary men. The men were vulnerable to passions and therefore best controlled by physical correction. Fear was like a virus that could quickly spread among members of the crew if the officer in command was unable to prevent it. One can compare this view with the testimonies from the naval court where seamen exposed their fear of physical punishment and violent officers. In this case it is notable that none of the ordinary seamen that were brought to court to witness, said a word about the punishment of Wolter. Either the episode had very little significance to them, or they did not approve of the captain's action but were wise enough to keep silent in a court full of other officers (for an analyse of rhetoric and silence in court, see Hammar 2012, pp. 137–138 and Hammar 2014, pp. 207–212.).

I would argue there is a notable pattern when it comes to how officers used expressions of "fear". Ordinary men are, in their view easily frightened, but that is not labelled "cowardice". Frightened officers on the other hand are always disloyal cowards. Where the officers, according to norms and ideals, needed to be brave and show courage, ordinary sailors did not. Thus, when officers used different ways of describing fear, they did not intend to highlight different ways of feeling fear, but to highlight different people feeling fear. This was particularly important in a court situation. The 17th century social life was more than anything else about honour: truth and falseness or trust and untrustworthiness. Almost every social action in the 17th century depends on whether it was an action carried out by an honourable person or not. Since persons of higher status were considered more trustworthy than people of lower status, people from the elite used passions to highlight this difference. Trustworthy people – themselves that is – could control their passions. Untrustworthy, or simple and subordinate people could not.

Passions in court

Passion hereby became a rhetoric tool in the courtroom, used to create social differences and uphold hierarchy, and to emphasize the speaker's honour. Other expressions of passion could be used in a similar way. When little babies suddenly died (what we today would call sudden infant death syndrome), the woman in charge of the baby's care, which was usually the mother, was brought to court and her actions investigated to make sure she had not intentionally killed the baby. She usually told a story about finding the baby dead in the bed in the morning, and she almost always told it with what the scriber expressed as "crying tears" [gråtande tårar in Swedish.] The phrase was formal and always the same, implying it was not there to portray different expressions of sad mothers, but to highlight the importance of her tears. The tears signalled that she was heartbroken and therefore she could not be guilty of murder. She must be speaking the truth, otherwise she had not been crying (for a more thorough discussion on tears and its meanings, see Liliequist, 2012, p. 182). In the court protocols from the Royal commission, there is another example of the importance of tears.

Admiral Johan Bär, did not only have his actions during the battle questioned in court, but his whole attitude towards his King and duties. He had in fact been overheard in an outburst of disappointment and anger to say he did not want to serve anymore, because "they treat us like rascals and thieves [dhe wela handtera oss som skälmar och tjuvar]" (Kommissorialrätten, protocol from July 22, 1676). Based on this outburst, the prosecutor tried to prove him disloyal to the King. Temporarily dismissed during the long trial, he did not serve in the navy during the summer of 1677. One of the members of the court, Johan Gyllenstierna, made the following statement about him in July 1677:

> [...] everyone knows he is the oldest surviving Admiral and understands the work better than anyone else; he should still be useful to His Majesty the King and the Kingdom if he is treated as an Admiral. I noticed tears in his eyes when the navy set sail, because he was not allowed to go with them (Kommissorialrätten, protocols of July 27, 1677).

Here the tears once again are used to point out innocence: the old Admiral was still loyal to his King and he had tears in his eyes because he was not allowed fulfil his duties as an officer.

Even anger could be important in court if it was controlled and very specific. If you had been unjustly accused of a crime, it was a good thing to show some anger in court because showing anger made you more reliable and trustworthy (Hammar 2012b pp. 80–82). But anger could be a dangerous thing too. In court cases concerning conflicts or failing command, it was used as proof of wrong or bad intentions (Collstedt 2007). Captain Werner von Rosenfeldt and his lieutenant Erik Hansson Husman had had a conflict aboard the ship *Danska Phoenix* in late autumn 1672. The captain was accused of having treated the lieutenant badly, and the lieutenant was accused of disobedience and mutinous behaviour towards his captain. In a testimonial by the boatswain, the lieutenant is said to have:

> threatened Captain Rosenfeldt he wanted to throw him down into the hold, and he used expressions like 'the liver is growing so big inside me, it will soon no longer have room', and he would have done it if he [the boatswain] had not advised him not to do it" (Admiralty court, protocol from January 11, 1673).

The liver was believed to be the cause of anger, and a growing liver was another expression for an increasing rage. Here the boatswain used the expression to underline the lieutenant's violent intentions. The lieutenant was furious and could only control himself because the boatswain persuaded him not to attack his captain. This was important for Rosenfeldt's defence, since he could use it to argue that his subordinate lieutenant was a violent, unpredictable man with difficulties of controlling his own passions and thus subordinate both in rank and in honourability.

Those eruptions of tears, anger, irritation and stubbornness in court sometimes have made historians describe early modern people as "uncontrolled", "childish", "headstrong", or "temperamental". However, the expressions were an intricate part of the social game, not uncontrolled outbursts. Tears and anger became marking points in court, keys to the truth, or to put it more precisely: cues separating honourable people from less honourable ones. Fear had the same ability. Simply put: fear was a litmus paper that exposed the coward, the traitor and the common man and separated them from the brave, the loyal and the socially superior officer. Hence, cowardice was not the mere opposite of bravery, it was also the opposite of self-government. A man unable to be master over his own passions could not be master of other men (James 1997, pp. 2–3). There is an interesting comparison to be made here, with another violent passion, namely anger. This passion was, in the beginning of the 17th century, a rather acceptable reaction towards insults and threats of one's honour, but later it became a passion that a true nobleman should be able to resist (Liliequist 2014). There seems to be a link here between status, power and how passions and affections were supposed to be expressed. It is about a change in "emotional regimes" in the words of William Reddy, a different way of using passions and affections in social communication (Reddy 2001, pp. 113–118). The officers used control over passions to distinguish themselves from the men who were to obey them. The king in turn demanded the very same ability of control by his officers as a sign of loyalty and obedience. The opposite of fear is in his eyes was therefore, not bravery but self-control and obedience.

Johan Mattson's use of fear

Let us then return to Johan Mattson's use of fear. He was not an officer and could not use the fear of others to prove himself more honourable. Instead he used his own fear as a tool of argumentation in court. According to the court records, Matsson Lund said: "He took fear upon himself". We cannot know if these were his exact words, but it was how the court scribe chose to interpret them. If this was his real expression, it means he had a clear idea of his own will as an acting subject in the matter. He chose to be frightened and chose to react on it too. One argument for that is that officers in court rarely acknowledge ordinary sailors to have any will or reason for their actions at all. They preferred to see sailors' behaviour as a result of random, unruly whims, not calculated responses to well defined situations (Hammar 2014, p. 210). Nevertheless, would it make more sense if Johan had tried to describe himself as a victim of forces outside his own control in order to make him less guilty of the crime? Perhaps yes, but the ship *Gotland* was not an ordinary ship and Johan Mattson Lund was not the only seaman escaping from it (Hammar 2012a). At least 45 other seamen had done the same on different occasions over a three-year long period (1690–1692). Like *Spes*, *Gotland* was a convoy ship and during the War of the grand alliance between 1688–1697, the ship sailed between Gothenburg and Portugal to protect Swedish merchant men from privateers. According to the naval court records in 1692, *Gotland* had not been a happy ship. One of the lieutenants was accused of having beaten a seaman to death when the ship was at anchor outside the coast of Spain. The lieutenant was released of all charges, but it is evident there was a sense of insecurity (Admiralty court, protocols from September 23, 1692). Some of the deserting seamen spoke of brutal officers, of being beaten and unreasonably punished (see testimonies from the seamen Peder Sigfridsson, Lars Berg, and Per Hillebard in Admiralty court, Protocol March 5, 1692) by the master and the boatswain aboard. One more seaman, Erich Jonsson Kåck, referred to the same rumour as Johan Mattson, admitting he took the fear upon himself (räddhågen till sig) and along with three other seamen deserted the ship (Admiralty court, protocol from June 8, 1692). It is, I believe, possible to see the statements by the two seamen as a very subtle critique of the existing order.

Firstly, it is a way to speak about criminal behaviour in a way that allowed them to have both a calculated mind while at the same time they could not be blamed for deliberate disobedience because there was a passion involved. And everyone knew how vulnerable ordinary men were to passions. Secondly, the statement was directed at the commanding officers aboard *Gotland*. They had failed to encourage their subordinate men, they had let a rumour run free aboard without being able to control it, and they had failed to keep their men to their duties. Thus, they were bad commanders. The seamen were, on their part, only ordinary men, easily influenced and ruled by unpredictable, forceful passions. So, Johan Mattson Lund could play with the stereotypes that defined him and his fellow seamen.

Fear in court – conclusions

The officers' view of their subordinates was that they were easy men to rouse, they often reacted violently or spontaneously to events and they were, for example easily frightened. The mention of fear in the naval court thus should be seen as speeches about the officers' social status rather than speeches about fear. Officers told the court about their crew's expressions of fear in order to prove themselves competent, brave and courageous officers. Thus, the expression of "fear" was used to highlight the officer's social status, especially their superior moral strength in comparison to the ordinary men's pre-destination for being ruled by passions. Ordinary seamen were never brave, they were merely obedient. On the other hand, this also meant that only officers could be accused of being cowards because only they had the inner capability of being courageous.

So, when Johan Mattson Lund claimed he "took fear upon himself" or Jonas Palmquist assured his fellow officers in the court he had been "fearless" they were not necessarily speaking about the same thing. The sailor and the captain were divided by hierarchy and belonged to different strata of the society and used fear accordingly. Palmquist tried to prove his lack of fear to convince the court he was a loyal officer. Johan Mattson Lund used the officers' view of him as someone easily afflicted by passions to speak more openly and perhaps even criticize naval order.

Figure 12: Frontispiece to 'The use of Passions', by showing the 'passions' or emotions personified

Figure 13: Charles LeBrun (1619–90) 'Passions'

Figure 14: 'Bellum symbolicum', 1632

References

Krigsarkivet (The Swedish War Archives)
Amiralitetskollegium med efterföljares kontor, rätter, kommissioner, Amiralitetsrätten A protokoll 1673, 1685 and 1692.

Riksarkivet (The National Archives)

Kommissorialrätt angående sjöstriderna 1676 (ÄK65), protokoll.
Justitierevisionen, Generalauditörens arkiv, handlingar i generalauditöresärenden, 1698, 8 december.

Literature

Collstedt, C., 2007. *Duellanten och rättvisan: duellbrott och synen på manlighet i stormaktsväldets slutskede*. Diss. Lund: Lunds Universitet.

Descartes, R. 2010. (1649) *Passions of the soul*, Electronic resource, January 31, 2017. http://www.earlymoderntexts.com/assets/pdfs/descartes1649part2.pdf

Dixon, T., 2012. Emotion: The History of a Keyword in Crisis, in: *Emotion Review*, no 4, pp. 338–344.

Dixon, T., 2003. *From passions to emotions*. Cambridge: Cambridge University Press.

Håkansson, H., 2014. *Vid tidens ände: om stormaktstidens vidunderliga drömvärld och en profet vid dess yttersta rand*. Göteborg: Makadam.

Hammar A., 2015. How to transform peasants into seamen: The manning of the Swedish navy and a double-faced, maritime culture. In: *International Journal of Maritime History*, no 4, pp. 696–707.

Hammar, A., 2012a. Strategic Silence and Rhetoric Lies. Common Seamen and their Explanations in the Swedish Admiralty Court. *In: Früneuzeit info. The Use of Court Records and Petitions as Historical Sources*. Vol 23, pp. 135–141.

Hammar, A., 2012b. Att fäkta som en ärlig man. Utredningarna kring sjöstriderna 1676 in *Karolinska förbundets årsbok*, pp. 49–83.

Hammar, A., 2014. *Mellan kaos och kontroll. Social ordning i svenska flottan 1670–1716*. Diss Umeå: Nordic Academic Press.

James, S., 1997. *Passion and Action. The emotions in seventeenth-century philosophy*. Oxford: Clarendon Press.

Huizinga, J., 1964 (1919). *Ur medeltidens höst: studier över 1300- och 1400-talens levnadsstil och tankeformer i Frankrike och Nederländerna*. Lund: Gleerup.

Lederer D., 2012. Fear of the thirty years war. In: Weiss, M., & Laffan, M. F. (ed.). *Facing Fear: The History of an Emotion in Global Perspective*. Princeton: University Press, pp. 10–30.

Liliequist, J., 2014. From honour to virtue: the shifting social logics of masculinity and honour in early modern Sweden. in: *Honour, violence and emotions in history*. pp. 45–67.

Liliequist, J., 2012. The political rhetoric of tears in early modern Sweden. In: Liliequist, J. (ed.), *A history of Emotions*, 1200–1800, London: Pickering & Chatto Ltd.

Febvré, L., 1941. La sensibilité et l'histoire. Comment reconstituer la vie affective d'autrefois. In: *Annales d'histoire sociale* 3, pp. 5–20.

Oatley K.; Kaltner D., & Jenkins J. M. 2006. *Understanding emotions*. 2 ed., Malden, Mass: Blackwell.

Perlestam, M., 2004. "Ringa prof av behjärtad soldat": mod, plikt och heder i en marin krigsrätt vid slutet av 1600-talet. In: *Forum navale*. No 60, pp. 15–81.

Plamper, J., & Tribe, K., 2015. *The history of emotions: an introduction*, 1. ed.

Plamper, J., & Lazier, B., 2012. *Fear: Across the Disciplines*, Pittsburgh: University of Pittsburgh Press, 2012.

Reddy W., 1999. Emotional Liberty: Politics and History in the Anthropology of Emotions. In: *Cultural Anthropology*, Vol. 14, No. 2., pp. 256–288.

Reddy W., 2000. Sentimentalism and Its Erasure: The Role of Emotions in the Era of the French Revolution. In: *The Journal of Modern History*. Vol. 72, No. 1. pp. 109–152.

Reddy, W., 2001. *The navigation of feeling: a framework for the history of emotions*. Cambridge: Cambridge University Press.

Rosenwein, B., 2010. "Problems and Methods in the History of Emotion", in: *Passions in context*, pp. 1–32.

Rosenwein, B., 2002. "Worrying about Emotions in History", in: *The American Historical Review*, No. 3, pp. 821–845.

Rosenwein, B., 2006. *Emotional communities in the early middle ages*. Ithaca, N.Y.: Cornell University Press.

Spinoza, B., 2010 (1665). *Ethics Demonstrated in Geometrical Order*. Electronic resource January 31, 2017, http://www.earlymoderntexts.com/assets/pdfs/spinoza1665.pdf.

Weiss, M., 2012. Introduction. Fear and its opposites in the history of Emotions: in Weiss, M., & Laffan, M. F., (ed.) *Facing Fear: The History of an Emotion in Global Perspective*. Princeton: Princeton University Press, pp. 1–9.

Heroes, Cowards and Their Shipwrecks
– Thoughts on the Maritime Archaeology
of the Scanian War (1675–1679)

NIKLAS ERIKSSON

In the 1660s the four largest ships in the Swedish navy were named after the royal regalia. They were called *Kronan* (The Crown), *Svärdet* (The Sword) *Riksäpplet* (The Orb) and *Nyckeln* (The Key). The four ships were similarly embellished with ornaments and carvings and two were built under supervision of the same Master Shipwright. They were equipped and manned in a similar way, they participated and fought side by side in two campaigns. Before that they were moored at the same base at Skeppsholmen in Stockholm. To summarize one could say they were parts of the same early modern society.

Within five days in June 1676 three of these ships sank. They came to rest on the seafloor of the Baltic where the conditions for preservation are favourable. As a result, substantial portions of these ships still survive today. But despite all that these ships have in common the wrecks have attracted very different attention from researchers and wreck-investigators through the years.

The wreck of the great ship *Kronan* has been the subject of maritime archaeological surveys for more than 35 years. *Svärdet* that sank farther from land and lies at more than twice the depth has been subject of extensive search expeditions. *Riksäpplet*, which sank in relatively shallow water in the Stockholm archipelago, has generated scarce interest among archaeologists and others, even though it can be easily reached without extensive resources, complicated techniques or advanced diving skills.

The objective of this paper is to establish why this wreck has never reached any prominent position within Swedish maritime archaeology.[1] In doing so, I will try to bring to light some driving forces behind the archaeology of large warships. I will argue that a focus on some specific wreck in favour of another is not necessarily determined by the *archaeological* potential of the wrecks. Rather, attention, is directed through other aspects than the study of

---

[1] The paper is based on the four first chapters of a book published in Swedish, see Eriksson 2017a.

shipwrecks as material culture. A wreck that receives attention should present at least one of the following qualities:

- It must be associated with a familiar historical course of events or a celebrated person, preferably a king or some other kind of national hero.
- It should be discovered under sensational conditions, which eventually creates another form of hero – the explorer.
- When found it should give the impression of being a 'time capsule', an object left untouched and unseen by humans for centuries.

If a wreck fails to fulfil these qualities, if the persons associated with the ship are unknown or described as cowards, or if the location of the wreck has been known since its foundering, or if the wreck has been damaged or affected in some way in later times, it is quite unlikely that anyone would bother paying attention to it. This is what happened to one of the ships mentioned above.

Narratives of ships

Ships that sail into history books usually carry a hero aboard. Think of Lord Nelson's *HMS Victory*, Columbus' *Santa Maria*, Michel De Ruyter's *Seven Provinces*, Thor Heyerdahl's *Kon-Tiki* or Noah's *Ark*. The glory of the hero spills over onto their ships, and the myth of the hero thus becomes a driving force in the archaeology of famous ships. So, before discussing the history writing and archaeology of each ship and wreck, it is necessary to sketch a brief historical background. A starting point is the period in between the wars of Karl X Gustav, which ended in 1660 and the outbreak of the so called Scanian War in 1675. During this period several new ships were built at Swedish shipyards (for an overview see Glete 2010:418–423). As mentioned, initially the largest of the new ships were named after the royal symbols. *Riksäpplet,* and *Svärdet* were both finished in 1663, *Nyckeln* in 1665, and *Kronan* in 1672. Until the outbreak of the war the ships mostly lay moored at the naval base Skeppsholmen in Stockholm, unless they were used for serving the navy's needs for various transports.

Through an alliance with France, Sweden had indirectly come into conflict with the Dutch Republic. In this situation Denmark, which was now allied with the Dutch, saw a chance to re-conquer territories that were lost to Sweden in 1658. In 1676 Lorentz Creutz (1615–76), a nobleman and bureaucrat, with no experience of war or the sea, became Admiral of the Realm (see biography in Lappalainen 2007). He was, however, a tough and experienced administrator. From a present-day vantage point some of his credentials might appear outlandish. Creutz, among others was head of a commission that served the death penalty to 15 women for witchcraft. His administrative skills came in useful when the navy was gathered and equipped for the fleet's campaign of 1676.

In May 1676 the Swedish fleet met the Danish between the islands of Bornholm and Rügen in the Southern Baltic. The Swedes were superior by number of ships but were not trained. The advantage slipped through their fingers and the Danes managed to escape to Öresund. The Swedish king Karl XI had witnessed the battle from a church tower and was very disappointed with the force of the Swedish navy. When he confronted the Admirals following the battle, they were all berated thoroughly. The Admiral who was accused of behaving in the most 'unmanly' and cowardly manner was Christer Boije who had command aboard *Riksäpplet*. The king immediately ordered him to lower his flag and removed him from command, although he was permitted to stay aboard and sail back to Stockholm. As I will return to below, this is where the first verdict falls with respect to *Riksäpplet*, as the characteristics of a ship's commander is intimately projected onto and entangled with their ships (cf. Tornqvist 1788; Zettersten 1903:476; Lundgren 1997:92; Hammar 2007:18; Einarsson 2016:71ff; Eriksson 2017a:23–52).

Meanwhile, whilst the Swedish Admirals were being lambasted by their king, the Danish navy received reinforcement in the shape of nine Dutch ships under the command of the legendary Dutch Admiral Cornelis Tromp. This considerably changed the balance of forces against the Swedes who found it best to sail north and return to the Stockholm archipelago. On the 1st of June, on reaching southern Öland, the allied navy had gained on them. Just as the first guns were fired, the great Swedish ship *Kronan*, under the newly recruited Admiral Lorentz Creutz's command, capsized and exploded (Figure 15). Approximately fifty of the 850 individuals aboard survived the disaster.

Figure 15: Ten years after the battle the Danish painter Claus Møincichen made a suite of the Danish–Dutch victories during the Scanian War. *Kronan* is exploding in the foreground and *Svärdet* is surrounded by enemy ships to the right (photo: Museum of National History, Hillerød, Denmark)

Figure 16: Anders Homman survived the *Svärdet* catastrophe. His epitaph in Kalmar church reveal the burning ship (photo by Patrik Höglund)

Figure 17: The Epitaph of Kapten Elias Johansson Garff in Hedvig Eleonora church in Stockholm. The central motif shows the drifting *Riksäpplet*, dragging its bow anchor in the seabed (photo by Niklas Eriksson)

Figure 18: Johan Tietrich Shoultz painted this picture in the 1770s. Note that *Svärdet* is the central motif and the exploding *Kronan* is in the background (after Brorsson 2004:170–171)

In the confusion that followed, the Swedish ships were dispersed and lost their formations. The vice-admiral ship *Svärdet*, under the experienced Admiral Clas Uggla was surrounded by enemy ships. This fight is one of the most famous in the history of the Swedish navy. For one and a half hours *Svärdet* was under constant bombardment from several enemy ships, including the largest in the allied fleet. The fight ended when a fireship attacked *Svärdet* (Figure 16). A fireship is a vessel filled with highly flammable material. After it is lit, it sails into its enemy in order to spread the fire. According to witnesses, admiral Uggla ordered the crew not to put out the fire as he did not want the ship with all its costly bronze guns, to fall into enemy hands. When the fire reached the gunpowder magazine there was a huge explosion and the ship sank immediately. Around fifty people survived and were brought to prison in Denmark, whereas 600 died, among them Admiral Claes Uggla.

The ships that were not taken by the allied fleet continued fleeing; the majority sailed to Dalarö in the Stockholm archipelago. Among these was the ship *Riksäpplet* with the deposed, former admiral Christer Boije aboard. Together with several other ships, *Riksäpplet* was moored outside Dalarö Sea fortress. After a few days there was a gale and the ropes that tied *Riksäpplet* to land parted. With one anchor dragging on the seabed the ship came adrift and was crashed against a rock and sank (Figure 17).

A long-drawn-out trial

The disastrous campaign rendered a trial to establish what went wrong and who should be blamed. The officers who had already been accused of being cowards after the battle at Bornholm and Rügen were the ones who were again blamed for the defeat. The process became long and complicated and has generated a lot of written testimonies (cf. Lundgren 1997; 2001; Hammar 2007; 2014: 116ff). It was difficult to establish what really happened not least as the most senior officers in charge of the campaign, the Admiral of Realm Lorentz Creutz and vice-Admiral Clas Uggla had been killed.

Two officers, Olof Nortmann and Anders Homman, had survived the *Svärdet* catastrophe. After release from Danish imprisonment they delivered compromising evidence that *Svärdet* had been left alone amongst the enemy outside Öland. According to them the trial would have taken a new turn if Clas Uggla had survived and could testify. In that case, they maintained, new gallows would have to have been built in Stockholm to execute all those who had acted in so unmanly a fashion. Their testimony cited Uggla on several occasions. For instance, he had said they '…should fight like men. It is better to die with the enemy than to get hanged in Stockholm' (…*kämpa manligen. Det är bättre att ärligen dö för sin fiende än att bliva hängd i Stockholm*, quotation from Lundgren 1997:108, author's translation. For a discussion on what it implied to fight like a man, see Hammar 2007; 2014: 116ff). Some 150 years later these famous last words were to become embedded in national-romantic history writing.

Anders Homman died in 1685 and his epitaph still hangs in the Cathedral in Kalmar. Its main motif shows the burning *Svärdet*. The event took place nine years before his death, and even though Homman was involved in several other battles during his life, *Svärdet*'s last battle appears as the zenith of his career. This is how he would like to appear in front of God and the congregation (cf. Eriksson 2017a; 2017c). One must look in the history books that were written during the following century to realize the reasons why he wanted to be associated with the event.

History writing

One of the first books on the history of the Swedish navy was written by Carl Nilsson Bechstadius (1690–1739), who was a priest in Karlskrona. Through practicing his profession in the town housing Sweden's naval base from 1680 onwards, he built up good insights in the genealogy of the Swedish naval officers. He thus published a book entitled 'Then adelige, och lärde swenske siö-man' (The noble and cultivated Swedish seamen) in 1734. The battles of 1676 appear in different contexts and chapters. The only hero in Bechstadius' account is Clas Uggla, who 'perished in the flames aboard *Svärdet* [...] and received the full of praise from the Dutch Admiral Tromp, that he did everything that a brave Sea-hero could do' (Bechstadius 1734:105, author's translation). One should remember that Tromp himself is one of the most well-known naval heroes of the 17th century (cf. Sigmond & Kloek 2007).

However, Bechstadius is also aware of the less heroic episodes. Aside from the drama with *Kronan* and *Svärdet* he describes the embarrassing chapter when 'the fine ship *Riksäpplet* with 80 guns, through the careless captain and unwise command, ran aground outside Dalarö and sank' (Bechstadius 1734:139, author's translation). Bechstadius, who was a careful writer, also revealed how exaggerated rumours have circulated around the loss of the ship. The chronicler Eberhard Werner Happelius (1647–1690) had declared that 'the captain [aboard *Riksäpplet*, author's comm.] was hanged for this from a nearby gallows' (*Ibid.* author's translation). Bechstadius says that he could not decide if the captain would have deserved such a measure, but he assures – in accordance with what really happened – that he was released. Happelius' chronicle, where it was argued that he got hanged, was printed the same year as the accident and thus provided an idea of the depth of emotions surrounding the event.

Slightly more than fifty years after Bechstadius' book, Carl Gustav Tornqvist published *Utkast till Swenska Flottans Sjö-tåg* (Outline of the Swedish Navy's campaigns) in two volumes (1788). As the title indicates it is an account of the navy's operations for each year. The descriptions of the persons involved as well as the losses of the ships *Kronan*, *Svärdet* and *Riksäpplet* are well grounded in written accounts, preserved in the National Archives. Standing on the shoulders of Bechstadius, to whom there are many references, Tornqvist has sketched an insolvent framework of events, persons, ships and battles. During the following centuries, his account was to be reproduced in several books describing the history of the Swedish navy. However, it was not cited literally word for word but surrounded and flavoured by an increasing degree of romanticizing expression.

Someone who was familiar with the history of the Swedish navy was the naval officer and marine painter Johan Tietrich Schoultz (1754–1807) who participated in the war against Russia 1788–1790. He is most well-known for his paintings from this war but also made several historical scenes of familiar heroic events such as the fight between Gustav Psilander, aboard the ship *Öland* against the English navy in 1704 or the battle and Femern in 1644 (compare Unger 1932:1–16).

A painting that generally has been called 'Battle between Swedish and Danish ships' (*Sjöslag mellan svenska och danska skepp*) undoubtedly depicts the battle outside Öland in 1676 (Brorson 2004:170–171). What is interesting is that it is painted with a nearly opposite perspective compared to Claus Møinichens famous painting (Figure 18). The burning *Svärdet* is the main motif in the foreground of the painting whereas the exploding *Kronan* appears in the background. This is not surprising at all. In the 19th century, the history of the Swedish navy was written, narrated and kept alive by officers in the navy. In this narrative, the loss of *Svärdet* was the important story. *Kronan* was lost by accident, with Lorentz Creutz a nobleman, bureaucrat and administrator in command. *Svärdet* on the other hand was lost after more than an hour of severe fighting, under the command of the experienced Admiral Clas Uggla, a hero in the most national-romantic sense of the word.

Figure 19: About two thirds of the portside is preserved at the *Kronan* wreck site (illus. by Lars Einarsson)

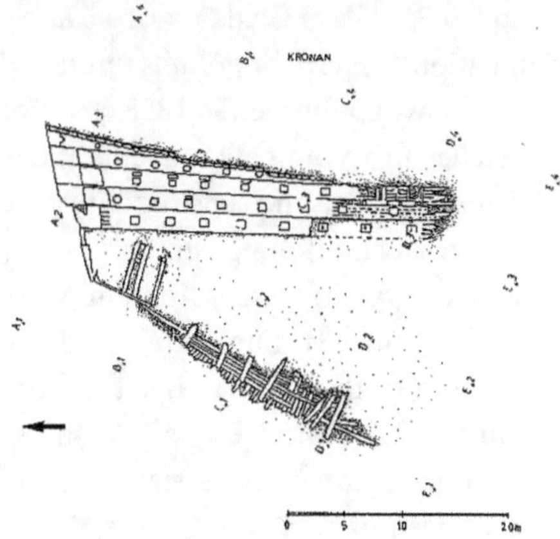

The books about the Swedish navy and its history written from the end of the 18th and well into the 20th century were to a large extent written in a moralizing spirit (see discussion in Cederlund 1997). This is far from the first time that nationalistic forces aim to build up confidence through examples from the past (for an overview, see Zander 2001, for a specific maritime archaeological example, see Arnstad 2009). This has had effect in the way the different admirals have been characterized. Creutz is more and more portrayed as a bad warrior, whose incompetence caused the *Kronan* catastrophe and the chaos that followed. This is a view which is expressed by lieutenant Henrik af Trolles' (1829–1886) book *Svenska Flottan, dess minnen och öden från äldre tider intill våra dagar*. In this book he reveals firm ideas about who was to blame for the defeat and who should have been in charge.

> With Uggla in overall command, the battle would likely have had a more pleasant end for the Swedes. When one also reflects that a restauranteur Haas was foolishly made commanding officer of the ship *Riksäpplet*, that because of a lack of due care and attention, came adrift and sank in Dalarö harbour, then one may wonder that the entire navy was not lost (af Trolle 1868:92–93, author's translation).

One who embraced the national-romantic history gaze towards naval history was prince Oscar Fredrik (1829–1907), who made a career in the Swedish navy and eventually ended up as vice-Admiral. His naval career later had to be set aside as he was made king of Sweden, under the name Oscar II, after the death of his older brothers. As well as being a sailor he also wrote poetry and among the many poems he wrote was one of the most fascinating expressions of the worship of the naval hero Claes Uggla, through the poem *Claes Uggla på*

Svärdet 1676 (Claes Uggla aboard *The Sword* 1676). The poem is part of the compilation *Ur svenska flottans minnen* (Out of the memories of the Swedish Navy) that was published in 1858. The poem consists of twelve verses in which he sketches an account of the events at the battle of Southern Öland, with focus on Uggla's courage and sense of duty (Oscar Fredrik 1858:19). I do not dare to try to translate it into English!

Another way in which different Marines honour their heroes is to name ships after them. In England several ships have been named after Admiral Nelson and in the Netherlands the situation is similar with De Ruyter and Tromp. That Admiral Uggla had the same status in Sweden is illustrated through the number of vessels bearing his name. As far as I know, no vessel has ever been named after Creutz, Boije, Bär, Borg or any other of the naval officers aboard *Kronan* or *Riksäpplet*. They simply did not form suitable examples or role models for the men in the Navy.

The statements as well as the archetypical distribution of the roles between the admirals were spread far outside the spheres of the navy's own history writing. Through the many books on Swedish history that were produced during the 19th century (and indeed later), the story about the brave Uggla, the noble administrator, but incompetent warrior Cruetz, and the coward Christer Boije, found its way into the bookshelves of many Swedish homes.

Anders Fryksells *Berättelser ur den svenska historien*, (Narratives from Swedish history, author's translation), were published in 49 volumes between 1828 and 1893 and holds a prominent position among these and is said to have influenced famous authors such as Zacharias Topelius, Victor Rydberg, Verner von Heidenstam, Carl Snoilsky, August Strindberg and others (cf. Hägg 1999:298). Fryksell describe the battle of southern Öland in some detail. His focus is on portraying the central characters and he describes the *Kronan*'s admiral Lorentz Creutz as choleric, hard and incompetent, in contrast to Claes Uggla aboard *Svärdet*, who 'in flames and waves (met) a hero's death' (Fryksell 1848:84–92, quotation: 91, author's translation). Fryksell's account thus contains a polarization of the two personalities.

In Fryksell's account, the only thing that alludes to *Riksäpplet* is that on the way home, one ship foundered outside Västervik and another through *"the captain's lack of skill"* in Dalarö harbour" (Fryksell 1848:92, author's translation and abbreviation). Thus, neither ship nor commander deserved to be mentioned by name.

To generalize, Swedish history writing in the 20th century may be polarized through, on the one hand the conservatives who romanticized national heroes and the kings of the Swedish empire, in contrast to the socialist-oriented writings that focused on 'ordinary people'. The books that were to replace Fryksell were Carl Grimberg's *Svenska folkets underbara öden* (The wonderful adventures of the Swedish people). Whereas Fryksell has received the posthumous reputation of being both pacifistic and critical towards the monarchy, Carl Grimberg has been regarded as the exact opposite (cf. Hägg 1999:298). Hjalmar Branting, the leader of the social democratic party criticized Grimberg's books for being nationalistic and glorifying war (Torbacke 1993, Matz 2001:42–45). Even if Grimberg's account of the battle of southern Öland is relatively short, it contains the by now so familiar components; that Lorentz Creutz's lack of experience and competence leads to the loss of *Kronan* and that it is Uggla's fight which is in focus (Grimberg 1922:158). The loss of *Riksäpplet* is not mentioned at all.

The authors of the standard works in history are of course far from the only persons to communicate narratives of the past. Many journalists certainly have the capacity to deliver historical drama. One interesting example among these is the daily paper writer Alexis Kuylenstiernas who wrote a book entitled *Svenska Bragder och stordåd* (Swedish achievements and great deeds) where he compiled several fascinating stories. Alongside familiar events such as Andrée's polar voyage, the battle of Brunkeberg, Gustav Vasa's rebellion against Denmark or the battle of Fraustadt, there is an entire chapter devoted to Admiral Claes Uggla aboard *Svärdet* (*Amiral Klas Johansson Uggla på Svärdet*). Again, Kuylenstierna concludes that the battle would have had a different course of events if Uggla had been in overall command, instead of Lorentz Creutz (1908:125).

According to Kuylenstierna

> Claes Johansson Uggla is one of the Swedish navy's most impressive, most attractive characters. For the misfortune of the Swedish navy, he never got the opportunity to carry the highest command during a battle, but through his heroic and hopeless fight aboard *Svärdet* he set an example of a true sailor's courage and devotion to the flag, an example of which the Swedish navy for all time may be proud (Kuylenstierna 1908:132, author's translation).

As is hopefully shown above, the admirals have been dressed in quite different but of course very simplified archetypical qualities. These posthumous reputations were created through the navy's own history writing and then transmitted to a general public through the means of widely-read history books, published in great numbers. In this narrative Uggla and *Svärdet* are the main characters, Creutz and *Kronan* come second, whereas Boije and *Riksäpplet* are supernumerary.

The question that arises is, how do these narratives spill over into the treatment of the material remains of these ships on the seabed? After all, *Kronan, Svärdet* and *Riksäpplet* still exist! Before dealing with the archaeology of these ships it is necessary to examine another kind of hero. These are not admirals or even warriors – they are wreck-hunters!

Wreck hunters

Steven Spielberg's film character Indiana Jones is probable world's most well-known archaeologist (cf. Holtorf 2007:62–83). The story in the four movies is built up around a similar plot, with Dr Jones being obsessed with finding a specific and renowned – but at the same time totally lost – historical object. This dramaturgy is in fact very similar to the mechanisms behind wreck-hunting (cf. Wijkander 2007:65–67) and the driving forces behind Sweden's most well-known wreck hunter, Anders Franzén (1918–1993). The Ark or the Grail, are like famous historical shipwrecks such as *Vasa, Kronan, Mars* or *Svärdet* in the sense that they had prominent positions in historical narratives long before their remains were rediscovered. Peculiar that Indiana Jones has never searched for historical shipwrecks!

The situation where an historical object is both famous and familiar, but totally lost at the same time, surely stimulates fantasy and lust for treasure and/or wreck-searching. Every expedition that leaves the harbour and returns empty-handed adds to the tension, mystery and excitement; something that makes a discovery – when it comes – even more releasing. This tension is also crucial for creating the wreck-hunter hero. Drawing on the discussions in Joseph Campbell's *The Hero with a thousand faces* (1949) archaeologist Carl Olof Cederlund argues that the hero goes through a series of phases, described as a journey, either real or abstract. The hero must withdraw from the world to a nearly spiritual existence where many troubles and obstacles occur and must be mastered and overcome. A hero is thus a person that manages to go beyond his or her personal limitations (cf. Cederlund 1997:49–51, after Campbell 1949).

When a team led by Anders Franzén relocated the remains of *Kronan* at the seabed outside Öland in 1981, he was already a famous person. His fame came from the rediscovery of *Vasa* in the murky water of Stockholm harbour in 1956 (even if most agree that the site was already known by then, see Cederlund 2006; 2012; Arnstad 2009). The discovery of the ship and the story of Anders Franzén's search for it, is a well-known story and has been reproduced by the Vasa museum and others ever since.

That he discovered another great warship was a sensation and became the starting point for a grand maritime archaeological excavation which is still ongoing (Figure 19). In the foreword of the latest magnificent volume about this ship, the author Lars Einarsson, who is also the project leader, mentions that the project holds an unofficial world record through the 35 field seasons out at the complicated wreck-site far out at sea. The project has been financed through sponsoring, which is a true achievement to say the least. The project has formed an amazing collection of objects of which a selection is shown in the exhibition at Kalmar county museum, which anyone with interest in maritime archaeology, should not miss. The discovery of the wreck, the archaeological excavation, the exhibition, the articles, books and TV documentary programs around *Kronan* has provided the ship, Lorentz Creutz and the catastrophe a prominent position in the common historical consciousness. My impression is that since the wreck was relocated in 1981, the story about *Kronan* has way surpassed that of *Svärdet* and Uggla. Now it is *Kronan* and Creutz that illustrate the narrative about the Swedish navy during the Scanian war rather than *Svärdet* and Uggla.

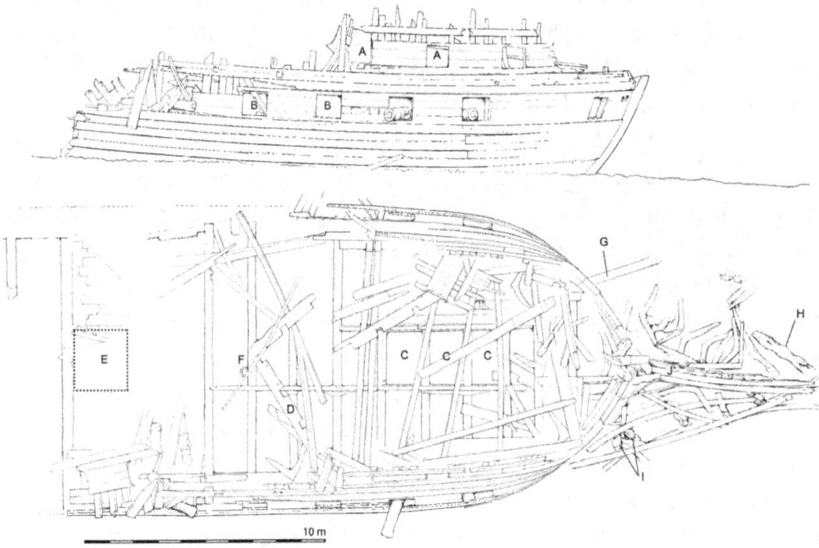

Figure 20: The tattered remains of *Svärdet* reveal several traces of the battle. A: ports from the upper gun deck, B: ports from the lower gun deck, C: place for gratings, D: shelf clamp for the uppermost deck, E: galley, F: bilge pump, G: cat head, H: lion figure head, I: loose sculptures, J: frieze (illustration by Niklas Eriksson)

When the discovery of *Svärdet*'s wreck site was announced in November 2011, there was a great public response, but it was not enormous. It appears as if the quotient of wrecks of large warships already was filled. Not only by *Kronan*, but the fact that the relocation of the wreck of *Mars* (1564) was announced in May the same year, may well have contributed to this (Eriksson 2016; Eriksson& Rönnby 2017).

The remains of *Svärdet* were relocated by a team led by Carl Douglas (who has led several wreck-hunting expeditions in the Baltic Sea and relocated many underwater sites. Perhaps the most well-known is the famous DC-3 aeroplane that was shot down during the cold war and rediscovered by Douglas team, cf. Hagberg 2004)). The stern of the ship blew up during the battle, but the forward half of the ship is surprisingly well preserved, with intact deck levels and cannons pointing out of the gun ports (Figure 20).

As I write this, nearly eight years have passed since the relocation of *Svärdet*. The archaeological research at the wreck, sprung out of scholarly curiosity was obstructed by the legal and bureaucratic situation as the wreck came to rest just outside the Swedish territorial waters. The archaeological efforts at the site have been limited to a few antiquarian attempts to monitor the site and protect it from looting (Hansson 2017). Admiral Uggla and his wreck, drowned in a discussion about laws, heritage Acts, and antiquarian management (for a summary of the archaeology of *Svärdet*, see Eriksson 2017c).

Kronan and *Svärdet* came to rest at the seabed, far out at sea and lost contact with the world above the water for several hundred years. The myths around their admirals were formulated in their absence, something that made the discoveries ever more spectacular.

A similar dramaturgy could never be created around *Riksäpplet*. Not only did the ship's admiral Christer Boije receive the posthumous reputation as a coward, not only did the ship sink as a result of clumsiness instead of being lost in battle, the wreck has been in continuous contact with the world above water since it sank. As if this was not enough, the wreck has received the reputation of being totally ruined as a result of careless blasting by a commercial salvage company. In order to nuance this, it is necessary to have a brief look at the antiquarian treatment of the remains of *Riksäpplet*.

Breaking the time-capsule

Some hundred metres east of Dalarö Sea fortress in the Stockholm archipelago, there is a small skerry named *Äpplet*. It is so named as it is the rock against which *Riksäpplet*'s planking were crushed. The remains of the ship rests on the seabed below. The wreck is so integrated in the landscape that most people do not reflect over its existence. What confronts a diver is a huge messy pile of ship-timbers caused by an older demolition process that began only days after the ship sank.

As the armament of a warship was often as expensive, sometimes even more so, than the rest of the ship (Glete 2010:566) salvage operations came to concentrate on recovering *Riksäpplet*'s rig and the guns. The majority of the 84 guns were expensive cast bronze and around seven were cast iron (Tornqvist 1788, appendix D; Lybeck 1942, appendix 7; Glete 2002:1; Eriksson 2017a:53–66).

Riksäpplet's hull came to rest with a list to starboard and in order to raise the guns on the lower decks and along the starboard side the hull was demolished. The work continued over several seasons and ended in 1684 when the wreck was blasted using black powder bombs (see Hafström 1958; 2006; Lundgren 1997:215–217, also Eriksson 2017a:53–66 with references). After this, the last bronze cannons were lifted out of the ship, further work at the site could not be economically justified.

In 1863 a new series of diving and salvage operations began at *Riksäpplet* (Cederlund 1983:39, 2012:12). It happened at this time due to the introduction of the 'standard' heavy diving equipment and nitroglycerine, which made underwater blasting much more efficient. A contributing factor was that wooden furniture made from the 'black oak' became popular. Everything from book-shelves and ash trays to doors and other details were made from material recovered from historical shipwrecks. A substantial portion of the hull was thus blasted apart, salvaged in pieces and sold (Cederlund 1983:39, 2012:18–19, Toijer 1958:65, Eriksson 2017a:67–88).

The iron guns left behind by 17th century divers were salvaged and sold as antiquities to Arthur Hazelius who later put them on display at the famous open-air museum Skansen in Stockholm (Cederlund 1983:39, Eriksson 2017a:67–71).

In 1919 the salvage company Olschanski had discovered the remains of the ship *Riksnyckeln*, sank in 1628, outside Viksten in the southern Stockholm archipelago. The Olschaniski family immigrated to Sweden in the 1870s. They founded a company for salvage of scrap metal from wrecks. Salvaging bronze cannons proved more lucrative and they were soon looking for other sunken warships to salvage guns from. At this time the salvage operations at *Riksäpplet* were forgotten and they thus went for the bronze guns at *Riksäpplet* in 1921. For several weeks they were looking in vain for cannons believed to be buried in the wreck. In order not to leave totally empty handed, they recovered the deck beams, as these could be sold as wood for carpentry (Cederlund 2006:126–136; 2012; Randall 2013; Eriksson 2017a, with references).

In the 1920s there was no general legislation to protect old shipwrecks. Sunken warships were argued to belong to the navy. When Olschanski applied for permission to salvage at *Riksäpplet*, it was under condition that the work was supervised by Commander Lenny Stackell, representing the navy and the conservator Erik Sörling from the National Heritage Board. Stackell (1875–1957) had a solid interest in naval history and carried out archival research on various naval historical topics. After the campaign on *Riksäpplet* he continued to collaborate with Olschanskis and together they came up with several wrecks that could possibly contain valuable bronze guns. Among these we find several familiar ships. Besides *Kronan* and *Svärdet* and the now famous *Vasa*, sank 1628 in Stockholm harbour, they mention *Resande mannen*, sank 1660 in Stockholm's southern archipelago *Nyckeln*, sank 1679 in Kalmarsund and *Rikswasa*, sank 1623 in Djurhamn. However, the failed expedition to *Riksäpplet* in 1921 had struck Olschanskis so hard that the company was declared bankrupt the following year (Randall 2013:40).

After the Second World War the diving activities on old naval shipwrecks were taken up by the above-mentioned Anders Franzén. In 1953, he launched what he later referred to as 'my wreck-programme which stimulated the development of diving and ship-archaeology in Sweden' (Franzén 1977:103, author's translation) consisting of twelve wrecks plotted on a map, which has been reproduced in different contexts (Figure 21). Despite most of the wrecks on the map being like the ones selected by Stackell and Olschanski in the 1920s, Franzén had no high thoughts about Olschanskis and even refers to them as "clowns" in a radio program in the early 1980s (Eriksson 2017a:71–82).

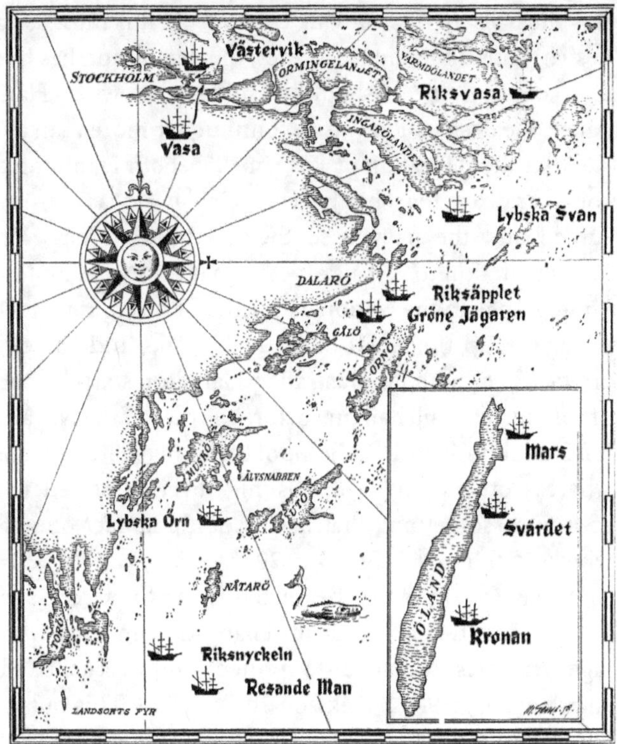

Figure 21: Anders Franzéns famous map, showing 12 wrecked ships that he was looking for. The majority of these are similar to those which diving company Olschanski and commanding officer Lenny Stackell were searching for (after Cederlund & Hocker 2006:174)

Franzén cooperated with commodore captain count Edward Hamilton (1895–1977), who after retiring from the Navy was made head of the naval department of the National Maritime Museum. Through his contacts within the marine, he and Franzén carried out several salvage expeditions to the *Riksäpplet* wreck site. Hamilton also wrote an article about their work entitled *En marinarkeologisk undersökning* (A Maritime Archaeological survey, 1957). In the article it is argued that the wreck is totally ruined.

> …the wreck would have provided us with a clear picture of the shipbuilding of the past, with all its constructional detail, as well as providing us with a lot of artefacts, that could have shed light on the equipment of warfare as well as the daily life aboard, if the wreck had not through careless blasting become so destroyed (Hamilton 1957:170, author's translation).

It is thus Olschanski's diving company that is most seriously accused for the destruction of the ship. However, the demolition has been going on since the 17th century. And it should be added that when Hamilton published the paper, the destruction was to continue for more than a decade.

After the relocation of *Vasa* in 1956, both Hamilton and Franzén came to concentrate on that ship instead. *Riksäpplet* was considered demolished and ruined and the navy used the site to train navy divers. There is little documentation to reveals exactly what they were up to at the wreck site, but photographs in the National Maritime Museum in Stockholm reveal a lot of salvaged ship timbers, cannon balls, casks and barrels, carvings and other artefacts. On a photo illustrating Hamilton's article, there is a large portion of *Riksäpplet*'s hull hanging before the bow of the Naval salvage steamer *Belos* (cf. Hamilton 1957:164). Some of the salvaged items ended up at the museum, whereas others vanished. Visiting divers received parts of the wreck as souvenirs, something that has made *Riksäpplet* one of the most dispersed wrecks in the world (Eriksson 2017a).

The navy continued their activities on the wreck-site until the end of the 1960s. The situation gradually changed from 1967 when the Swedish Heritage Act was extended to protect shipwrecks (Cederlund 1983:61–62; Arnshav 2011:39–44; Eriksson 2014:21–36). This put an end to the unregulated salvaging at the site but also the navy's monopoly of diving at *Riksäpplet* and other naval wrecks. These were now open for interested civilians. Eventually, this also meant that the wrecks were now also open for women, as diving training in the navy was exclusively reserved for men (cf. Eriksson 2017a:85–88).

In the 1970s diving amateur archaeologist made a survey of *Riksäpplet* and recovered sculptures among other artefacts. In contrast to previous work that was carried out by the navy, these divers compiled written reports revealing what they were doing (cf. Cederlund 1983:184–187; Eriksson 2017a).

Even though *Riksäpplet* has been continuously demolished during the past 340 years it is the diving company Olschanski that are condemned for this destruction. My opinion from working with the site and the scarce documentation that exists on it is that their contribution to the decay is limited. They salvaged timbers during some weeks in 1921, with a limited number of divers. The navy, on the other hand, continuously carried out their diving and salvage training at the site for more than fifteen years. That the naval divers have not received the same posthumous reputation as Olschanski's I think has to do with the fact that the navy may be argued to have what Bourdieu would refer to as 'cultural capital' (Bourdieu 1986). In order to salvage artefacts or to make statements regarding old warships or naval matters in the past, you preferably should belong to the navy rather than being a commercial company, like Olschanskis. Edward Hamilton's statement in the article from 1957, that Olchanskis had totally ruined the wreck, seems to have been taken literally ever since, despite the fact that he never dived at the wreck.

Three blown up ships

An important point I wish to make is that *Riksäpplet* is not as ruined as Hamilton and others have said. In 2014 and 2015, the author, together with several diving enthusiasts, carried out a minor, low-budget survey of *Riks-äpplet* in order to produce the first proper plan of the wreck site (see Eriksson 2017a; 2017b). (Figure 22). Compared to *Vasa* (1628) *Riksäpplet* is quite damaged. But compared to *Kronan* or *Svärdet* it is intact.

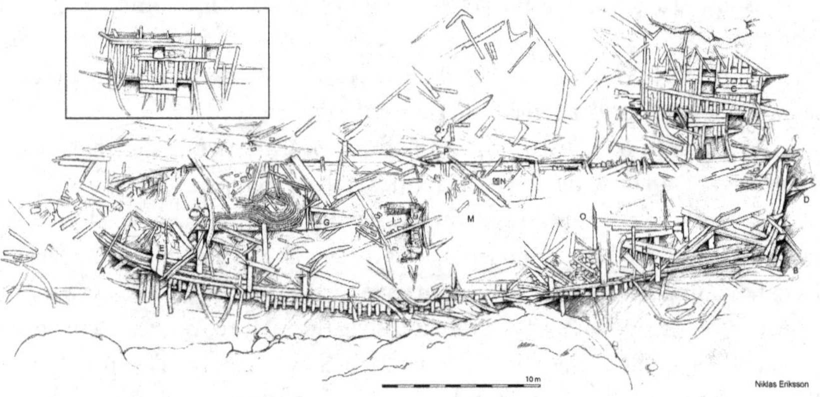

Figure 22: Plan of the *Riksäpplet* wreck site with the bow pointing to the left. The portion up to the left which is framed by a rectangle is located around 50m astern of the ship. A: stem, B: sternpost, C: starboard side preserved up to the upper gundeck, D: planking, which reveals the characteristic English 'round tuck', E: foremast step, F: stone ballast, G: orlop, H: remains of a platform on the orlop, I: galley, J: barrels containing tar stowed into the hold, K: anchor cable on the orlop, L: barrels on the orlop, M: area containing firewood, N: pump dale, O: pump tube, P: carlings, Q: gun carriage, R: mizzenmast step (illustration by Niklas Eriksson)

Is a ship that sank due to explosion necessarily more valuable than a ship that has been blown up after sinking? In order to understand this, we shall return to the phenomena of wreck-discoveries. The sudden relocation of the remains of a well-known ship, may be described as a release of tension. Such wrecks become unexpected visits of a familiar past into the present. The ghosts of the past send their regards from the bottom of the sea.

Wrecks are sometimes described as 'time-capsules' or 'frozen moments' (Adams 2003:21–23). The less contact the wreck has had with the world above water, the better. This gives the impression that the time that has passed since the ship sank and when it is discovered has never existed and provides a jump in time to the point when the ship was last seen by humans. Enthusiastic divers describe how they are the first ones in hundreds of years to witness a specific ship, like Howard Carter in the tomb of Tutankhamun.

To quantify the archaeological potential of shipwrecks or other remains from how hard they have suffered from the ravages of time, is of course misleading. The remains of the three large ships that were lost in the year 1676 makes an interesting comparison as they represent the entire scale, from 'frozen moments' to a vandalized pile of splintered planks. While *Kronan* is continuously described as the Pompeji of the Baltic Sea (Franzén 1985:9, Einarsson 2016:207), then *Riksäpplet* is described as totally ruined (compare Hamilton 1957:170). As if this was not enough, the fact that the *Riksäpplet* wreck-site has been known since the wreckage, deprives it of its capacity of being discovered under sensational conditions.

It is worth noting that both *Kronan* and *Svärdet* wreck sites have been damaged and affected by human activities since wrecking even if the location of the wrecks were forgotten. *Kronan*'s guns were salvaged by the same persons who raised the guns from *Riksäpplet*. The wreck has also been affected by mine sweeping. The remains of *Svärdet* is wrapped in trawlers nets which have torn down parts of the hull structure. Moreover, the deposits of marine debris and the pollution of the seabed in general makes it fallacy to think that a wreck can remain untouched and out of reach for humanity (cf. Arnshav 2014).

Towards a maritime archaeology of the Scanian War

Let us return to what was claimed in the beginning of this text, namely that *Kronan*, *Svärdet* and *Riksäpplet* were all somewhat equal ships and were part of the same 17th century society. That it was *Kronan* that capsized before exploding, *Svärdet* that was surrounded by enemies and set on fire, and *Riksäpplet* that came loose from its moorings and stranded were just circumstances and freak of fate. In the course of events any of these ships could have taken the others' place. The point I really want to make is that even the ships which have had an obscure role in the great narrative of the navy may all the same have a great *archaeological* potential. If we agree that archaeology is a humanistic academic discipline that deals with *material remains*, one would spontaneously assume that the potential of each wreck should be considered as similar – and – that each wreck would achieve similar attention. Looking at how they have been handled, it is quite obvious that this is not the case at all, with the *Kronan* survey proceeding for 35 years and *Riksäpplet* resting in shallow water, at a convenient distance from Stockholm, within a 45-minute car drive, and a five-minute boat ride from two universities and one maritime museum, has never been properly surveyed (until now that is, see Eriksson 2017a; 2017b).

In order to explore the archaeological potential of a wreck we must break loose from the familiar historical narratives of national heroes, from contemplating about the fascinating conditions of how wrecks appear 'frozen in time', and from worship of some wreck-hunters endurance and commitment to their task. We should address *archaeological* questions. Archaeology has been described as 'the discipline of things' (cf. Olsen et al. 2012). And a lot of these ships – as things – do survive. Two thirds of *Kronan*'s portside has survived and a lot of closed finds and well-preserved archaeological contexts have been recorded from the ship's interior (Einarsson 1997; 2016). Of course, there are similar contexts aboard *Svärdet* and *Riksäpplet*. The admiral's cabins, with the high-status objects may be lost on these ships, but there are other unexplored artefacts, spatial conditions and arrangements inside the bow of *Svärdet* and the hold of *Riksäpplet* that definitely could shed new light on the conditions aboard a large warship during the Scanian War (Figure 23).

Research questions that truly explore the archaeological potential of shipwrecks must thus be conceived from a discussion regarding humanity's constant entanglement with the material world. As such, there is no difference between *Kronan*, *Svärdet* or *Riksäpplet*. *Riksäpplet* does have great potential for such discussions (Eriksson 2015; 2017a; 2017b).

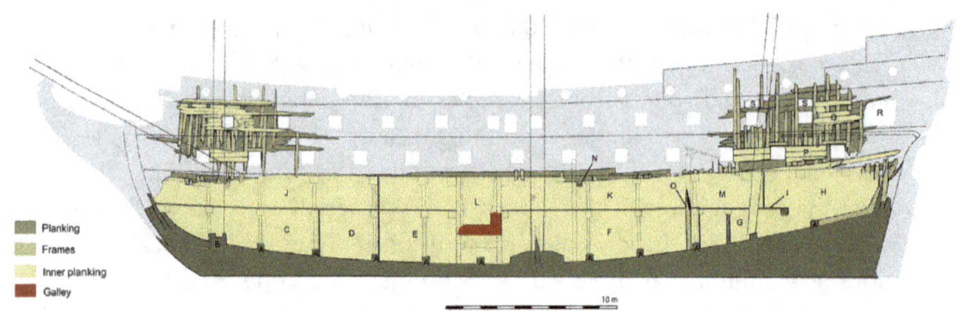

Figure 23: Reconstructed longitudinal section of *Riksäpplet*. The length and curvature of the stems as well as the height and sheer of the decks has been borrowed from the model Ö 3. A: rider, B: foremast step, C: storage department containing tar among other things, D-F: room in the hold, G: possible powder magazine, H: aft room, I: platform, J: room for anchor cable and possible lodging for the lower ranks, K: firewood store and lodging for lower ranks, L: galley, M: lodging for the lower commands and the 'cockpit' where the wounded were taken during action, N: pump dale, O: bilge pump, P: gunners store, Q: main cabin, R: opening towards quarter galleries, S: apertures above gun ports (illus. by Niklas Eriksson)

To summarize and to look forward, I think that the study of wrecks may draw on a recent trend within the humanities in general to 'turn to things' (compare Trentman 2009, Hicks 2010, Olsen 2010). The early modern wrecks of the Baltic Sea (and elsewhere for that matter) may be used to highlight aspects of early modern everyday life, not only particular events or great deeds (see also Eriksson 2014). But in order to do so it is necessary to let go of specific historical events, persons and ships, and look for the more general patterns in material culture. The ships themselves provide some insights into the material part of everyday life, which to paraphrase Fernand Braudel, sets 'The Limits of the Possible' (1981) from the dullest grain transport to the most spectacular and heroic naval battle. All three wrecks should thus be regarded to have a somewhat similar archaeological potential.

References

Adams, J., 2003. *Ships, Innovation and Social Change: Aspects of Carvel Shipbuilding in Northern Europe 1450–1850*. Stockholm Studies in Archaeology 24. Stockholm University.

Arnshav, M., 2011. "Yngre vrak – samtidsarkeologiska perspektiv på ett nytt kulturarv". Södertörn Archaeological Studies 8. Huddinge: Södertörns högskola.

Arnshav, M., 2014. The Freedom of the Seas: Untapping the Archaeological Potential of Marine Debris. *Journal of Maritime Archaeology*, Vol. 9:1, pp. 1–25.

Arnstad, H., 2009. *Varför bärgades Vasa: studie angående nätverk och historiekonstruktion under slutet av 1950-talet*. Kandidatuppsats. Stockholms universitet Historiska institutionen.

Bechstadius, C. N., 1734. *Then adelige, och lärde swenske siö-man*. Stockholm.

Bourdieu, P., 1986. The forms of capital. In J. Richardson (ed.) *Handbook of Theory and Research for the Sociology of Education* (New York, Greenwood), pp. 241–258.

Braudel, F., 1981. *Civilization and Capitalism 15th - Eighteenth Century, Vol. 1 The Structures of Everyday Life*. Berkley, Los Angeles: University of California Press.

Brorson, E., 2004. *Båtar på vägg: en bok om en samling marinmålningar*. Stockholm: M. Ullman.

Campbell, J., 1949. *The Hero with a thousand faces*, Cleveland.

Cederlund, C. O., 1983. *The Old Wrecks of the Baltic Sea*. Oxford: BAR (Intern. Ser. 186).

Cederlund, C. O., 1997. *Nationalism eller Vetenskap, svensk marinarkeologi i ideologisk belysning*. Stockholm: Carlssons förlag.

Cederlund, C. O., 2012. *Ett oskrivet kapitel i skeppet Vasas historia. Forum navale*. Vol. 86. pp. 9–63.

Cederlund, C. O. and Hocker, F. M., 2006. *Vasa 1: the archaeology of a Swedish warship of 1628*. Stockholm: SMTM.

Einarsson, L., 2016. *Regalskeppet Kronan: Historia och arkeologi ur djupet*. Lund: Historiska media.

Eriksson, N. 2014. *Urbanism under Sail: an archaeology of fluit ships in early modern everyday life*, Diss., Södertörns högskola.

Eriksson, N., 2015. Fragment av stormaktens försvarspolitik. skulpturerna från regalskeppet *Riksäpplet*, sjösatt 1661. *Finskt museum 2013–2015*, pp. 173–189.

Eriksson, N., 2016. The architecture of a great 16th century warship: results from the initial surveys of *Mars* (1564), *Proceedings from IKUWA V*, Carthagena, pp. 824–836

Eriksson, N., 2017a. *Riksäpplet: Arkeologiska perspektiv på ett bortglömt regalskepp*. Nordic Academic Press.

Eriksson, N., 2017b. The ship *Riksäpplet* and the introduction of English naval architecture in Sweden in the 17th century. *Post-Medieval Archaeology* 51/2 (2017), pp. 309–331

Eriksson, N., 2017c. *Svärdet* (1663–1676): ett regalskepp byggt på holländskt manér, *META: historiskarkeologisk tidskrift*, pp. 7–26.

Eriksson, N., & Rönnby, J. 2017. *Mars* (1564): the initial archaeological investigations of a great 16th-century Swedish warship, *International Journal of Nautical Archaeology*, vol 46:1, pp. 92–107.

Franzén, A., 1977. HMS Resande Man, *Tidskrift I Sjöväsendet*, nr 2, Kungliga örlogsmannasällskapet, pp. 96–103.

Franzén, A., 1981. *HMS Kronan The search for a great* seventeenth *century warship*. Stockholm: Royal Institute of Technology (Stockholm papers in history and philosophy of technology).

Franzén, A., 1985a. Kronan – Östersjöns Pompeji, In: Johansson, B. A. (ed.). *Regalskeppet Kronan*, Höganäs: Bra böcker.

Fryxell, A., 1848. *Berättelser ur svenska historien. D. 15, Karl den elftes historia, Afd. 1, ungdoms- och krigsåren.* Stockholm: Hjerta.

Glete, J., 2002. *Kronans artilleri. Kort genomgång av arkivmaterial och data om bärgade kanoner.* Opublicerat arbetspapper 2002-11-12, Stockholms universitet.

Glete, J., 2010. *Swedish Naval Administration 1521–1721, Resource Flows and Organisational Capabilities.* Lieden & Boston: BRILL.

Grimberg, C., 1922. *Svenska folkets underbara öden, Karl XI:s och Karl XII:s tid, t. o. m. år 1709.* Stockholm: P. A. Nordstedt & söners förlag.

Hafström, G., 1958. Äldre tiders bärgningsarbeten vid vraket efter skeppet Wasa, I. *Tidskrift i sjöväsendet.* Vol. 121, pp. 771–844.

Hafström, G., 2006. Salvage attempts 1628–1683, I Cederlund, C. O. & Hocker, F. (ed.) *Vasa 1: The Archaeology of a Swedish warship of 1628*, Oxford: Oxbow books, pp. 68–107.

Hagberg, B., 2004. *DC-3:an: på jakt efter sanningen.* Rimbo: Fischer & Co.

Hamilton, E., 1957. En marinarkeologisk undersökning utförd av Statens Sjöhistoriska museum, I Albe, G. (red.) *Sjöhistorisk årsbok 1955–1956.* Stockholm: Föreningen Sveriges Sjöfartsmuseum, pp. 163–183.

Hammar, A. 2007. *Att fäkta som en ärlig man: Den kungliga kommissorialrättens utredande av sjöstriderna i maj och juni 1676.* Magisteruppsats, Umeå.

Hammar, A. 2014. *Mellan kaos och kontroll: Social ordning i svenska flottan 1670–1716.* Diss. Lund: Nordic Academic Press.

Hansson, J. 2015. *Vård- och skyddsplan Svärdet.* Swedish National Maritime Museums.

Harpster, M. 2013. Shipwreck Identity, Methodology, and Nautical Archaeology, *Journal of Archaeological Method and Theory*, Vol. 20.4, pp. 588–622.

Hicks, D., 2010. The Material-Culture Turn: event and effect, In. Hicks, D. and Beadry, M. 2010 (eds.) *The Oxford Handbook of Material Culture Studies.* Oxford: Oxford University Press, pp. 25–98.

Holtorf, C., 2007. *Archaeology is a brand: the meaning of archaeology in contemporary popular culture*, Left Coast Press.

Hägg, G., 1999. *Den svenska litteraturhistorien* [Ny utg.]. Stockholm: Wahlström & Widstrand.

Kuylenstierna, A., 1908. *Svenska bragder och stordåd ute och hemma, i krig och fred: efter äldre och nyare källor skildrade.* Stockholm: Fröléen.

Lappalainen, M., 2007. *Släkten, makten, staten: Creutzarna i Sverige och Finland under 1600-talet.* Stockholm: Norstedt.

Lybeck, O. (red.), *Svenska flottans historia.* Bd 1, Malmö: Allhem.

Lundgren, K. 1997. *Stora Cronan: byggandet, slaget, plundringen av Öland: en genomgång av historiens källmaterial.* Färjestaden: Lenstad bok & bild.

Lundgren, K., 2001. *Sjöslaget vid Öland: vittnesmål - dokument 1676–1677.* 1. uppl. Kalmar: Lingstad bok & bild.

Matz, E., 2001. Grimberg: kungarnas och krigens uttolkare, *Populär historia*, nr 6, pp. 42–45.

Melins, G. H., 1845. *Lärobok i fäderneslandets historia*, Stockholm/Bokhandlare Looström.

Olsen, B., Shanks, M., Webmoor, T., Witmore, C. 2012. *Archaeology: The Discipline of Things.* Berkley, Los Angeles, London: University of Carlifornia Press.

Randall, L., 2013. Bärgningar – Regalskepp – Vasa: Olschanskis öden, Lorelei Randall.

Ransley, J., 2005. Boats are for Boys: Queering Maritime Archaeology, *World Archaeology*, Vol. 37.4, pp. 621–629.

Sigmond, P., & Kloek, W., 2007. Sea battles and naval heroes in the 17th-century Dutch Republic, Rijksmuseum: Amsterdam.

Stackell, L., 1929. Ur regalskeppet *Äpplets* historia: efter dokument i Riksarkivet och Flottans arkiv, stencil: Sjohistoriska museet: Stockholm.

Toijer, D., 1958. *Gustafsvik: historien om ett Värmlandsgods och dess ägare.* Kristinehamn.

Torbacke, J., 1993. *Carl Grimberg: ett underbart öde?* Stockholm: Norstedts.

Tornqvist, C. G., 1788. *Utkast till svenska flottans sjö-tåg.* Stockholm: C. G. Tornqvist.

Trentmann, F., 2009. Materiality in the Future of History: Things, Practices, and Politics. *Journal of British Studies,* Vol. 48.2, pp. 283–307.

Af Trolle, H., 1868. *Svenska Flottan: dess minnen och öden från äldre tider intill våra dagar, tecknade i sammandrag för Ungdomen och Folket,* Stockholm: Bonniers förlag.

Unger, G., 1932. Johan Tietrich Schoultz: En förbisedd marinmålare, *Meddelanden från marinstabens sjöhistoriska avdelning,* nr 3, pp. 167–175.

Wijkander, K., 2007. The role of the traditional museum. *In:* Satchell, J and Palma, P. (eds.) *Managing the Marine Cultural Heritage: Defining accessing and managing the resource.* Oxford: Council for British Archaeology (Research Report 153), pp. 65–68.

Zettersten, A., 1903. *Svenska flottans historia: åren 1635–1680.* Norrtelje: Norrtelje tidnings boktr.

An Introduction to Hand-to-Hand Combat at Sea – General Characteristics and Shipborne Technologies from c. 1210 BCE to 1600 CE

ROLF FABRICIUS WARMING

> Terrible is the battle of the sea for the eyes of man, and the senses refute and exalt it, for death is offered in it without any shelter from many troubles and torments. Either of these two things is enough to terrify humanity, let alone both together: the war and the sea.
>
> (Olivera 2008 [1555]:115, my translation)

While there has generally been a great commitment towards researching the use of naval power in European warfare in the past, surprisingly little focus has been centred on the subject of naval boarding and close quarter combat at sea in general. These aspects are largely attenuated in literature on war at sea (cf. Jesch 2001; Jesch 2002; Hildred 2011) and have to some extent sunken into oblivion under the enormous waves of literature on other naval subjects which have gained precedence in this research area, such as cannon fire, lines-of-battles and alike. Notwithstanding the significance of these other subjects, it is surprising that more attention is not given to naval hand-to-hand combat. It was, after all, not only the primary tactical means by which to achieve victory on the seas until the early modern period – and, for many forces, even beyond this date – but also the responsibility and habitude of a countless number of soldiers and mariners across the centuries. Indeed, for many of them, it was the path that led to their destruction. As such, the practice of naval hand-to-hand combat presents itself as an important but neglected aspect in literature on warfare at sea.

The question of how naval hand-to-hand combat practices were conducted aboard European warships of the past has become increasingly relevant with the recent archaeological discoveries of well-preserved Danish and Swedish warships in Scandinavian waters. These include *Gribshunden* (1495) and *Mars Makalös* (1564), both of which date to a period when naval hand-to-hand combat was at its zenith (discussed below; Warming 2015). Combined with historical sources, the state of preservation of these unique wrecks and their associated material culture provides an opportunity to address practical and social questions regarding the life and conduct of soldiers aboard in new ways.

To move towards a more developed understanding of naval hand-to-hand combat through such specialized studies, however, it is essential to address certain misleading but influential perspectives on this topic which have posed challenges for progress in this research area in the past. Predominantly, this involves abandoning the pervasive notion that such practices are necessarily characterized by impulsive violence and uncontrollable chaos rather than any sort of tactics or instrumental violence. Such viewpoints have been most powerfully propagated through the entertainment industry's creative displays of boarding actions, wherein elaborate fencing choreographies and highflying stunts are recurring action scenes. In actuality, however, the practice of hand-to-hand combat in naval warfare was far from a haphazard affair left to be ruled by unmanaged aggression.

The aim of this chapter is to clarify the general role and nature of hand-to-hand combat practices in European naval warfare before its decline in the early modern period. More specifically, this chapter seeks to establish the fact that the practice of naval hand-to-hand combat expresses itself in history conjointly with careful tactical considerations as well as an awareness of the principles that govern the proceedings of seaborne combat. To this end, the chapter will be divided into two parts. The first will consider the question of what characterizes naval hand-to-hand combat and discuss the environmental and cultural factors which influence such practices in general. With this background, the second part will offer a general introduction to a selection of shipborne technologies that can be considered significant developments in the history of naval hand-to-hand combat tactics. Rather than being any definite work on naval hand-to-hand combat, this chapter is an attempt at providing a general introduction and bringing attention to the value of this topic, thereby setting the stage for more thorough research projects in the future.

The nature of naval hand-to-hand combat

The overall trajectory of the development of warfare at sea is marked by great variation, both in terms of the manner by which fleets have been prepared before battle and the methods by which the fighting has been carried out in practice. Such variances aside, however, the practice of naval hand-to-hand combat can be said to be characterized by a set of distinctive properties. A number of historical naval treatises from across the centuries (treated below) offer valuable insight into these characteristics, highlighting how the hand-to-hand combat practices are greatly influenced by the maritime environment as well as by culture.

Generally, naval hand-to-hand combat has revolved around two over-arching concerns, namely boarding and anti-boarding. Within a combative context, boarding entails a forceful, non-consented entry aboard a ship which is carried out with the intention of defeating the crew or taking control of their vessel along with her cargo. Such an entry has ordinarily been carried out from another ship or by use of smaller, more manoeuvrable watercraft deployed from ships or harbours. Anti-boarding may thus involve an active participation on behalf of the defending crew but can also entail a more passive use of technologies designed to impede a successful entry, e.g. an anti-boarding net. Fighting between boarding and anti-boarding forces can occur in the process of entering the ship or aboard her. Typically, these close quarter encounters were preceded by an exchange of missile attacks which served to suppress and weaken the enemy before boarding.

Perhaps the most characteristic feature of the actual clash between boarding and anti-boarding forces is the high intensity of the fighting. This tendency has often been recognized by historical tacticians who in their military treatises advise the use of heavy armour in the context of seaborne hand-to-hand combat. In his *Epitoma rei militaris* (or *De re militari*), written sometime in the late 4th or early 5th century CE, Publius Flavius Vegetius Renatus emphasizes the importance of heavy armour for soldiers aboard ships:

> Land warfare requires many types of arms; but naval warfare demands more kinds of arms, including machines and torsion-engines as if the fighting were on walls and towers. What could be crueller than a naval battle, where men perish by water and by fire? Therefore, protective armour should be a particular concern, so that soldiers may be protected with cataphracts, cuirasses, helmets and also greaves. No one can complain about the weight of armour, who fights standing on board ships. Stronger and larger shields are also taken up against the impact of stones. (Vegetius in Milner 2001:149)

Here, as Milner (2001:149, note 6) rightfully observes, Vegetius addresses an alleged unpopularity of wearing heavy armour in seaborne combat. While such sentiments may be grounded in concerns about mobility or the fear of drowning, Vegetius makes the point that there is no place for light-armed troops on board ships, reflecting the intensity level of such combative scenarios. On Vegetius' account, moreover, hand-to-hand combat – or *commin-*

us dimicare, as he calls it – is the most dangerous aspect of naval warfare at close quarters (Milner 2001:150).

The need for heavy protective equipment in such encounters is likewise reflected in *Konungs Skuggsjá* (King's mirror), a Norwegian educational manuscript from ca. 1250 CE, in which the anonymous author advises that:

> Wide shields and chain mail of every sort are good defensive weapons on shipboard; the chief protection, however, is the gambison made of soft linen thoroughly blackened, good helmets, and low caps of steel (Anonymous 1917:217).

Interestingly, the above passage is the only section of the text where the author places such an emphasis on the protective equipment of the infantry-men, being comparable or surpassed only by the author's description of the armour for fighting on horseback.

The use of heavy infantry in naval hand-to-hand combat seems to have remained an important consideration even after the employment of firearm tactics at sea. In his *Espejo de Navegantes* from c. 1537 CE, Alonso de Chaves (who is the first to lay out naval instructions for the use of firearms at sea) describes the equipment necessary for carrying out boarding actions:

> Asimismo, si los nuestros saltaren en su nao, los primeros deben de llevar mon-tantes, que es mejor arma en tal caso, y los de coselete con espada y rodela.

> (Bauer Landauer 1921: 470, quoting de Chaves c. 1537)

> Likewise, if our people jump onto their ship, the first should carry **montantes** which are better weapons for such a case, and men of the **coselete** [should have with them] sword and shield." *(my translation and emphasis).*

I have left *montantes* and *coselete* unchanged in the above English translation since these are used as specialized generic terms in this context and require further explanation. *Montante* is a term referring to large, double-edged swords with hilts for two-handed use. Although sometimes used synonymously with *Zweihänder* or *Doppel-händer*, the *montante* should be considered as a narrower reference to similar swords with designs native to the Iberian region. Interestingly, two-handed swords seem to have been methodologically employed in naval encounters in Scotland already in the late 15th century (Melville 2018: 131ff.) while two later fencing treatises by Domingo Luiz Godinho (2015 [1599]: rule 2a-b) and Diogo Gomes de Figueyredo (2009 [1651]: rule 11) describe how the *montante* should be used on the gangway of a galley, reflecting its prolonged use as a weapon in naval warfare. In the context of seaborne formations armed with anti-boarding pikes (a typical feature of naval combat at this time), the *montante* would have been useful tool for crowd control and could have been used to hack to paths through the opposing formation, disrupting order by slashing and stabbing among the ranks. The second term in the above passage, *coselete*, translates as "cuirass." It is, however, also the generic name assigned to a class of heavily armoured pikemen who fought in the front ranks of pike-squares (*tercios*). In the above passage, *coselete* is seemingly used to describe the latter meaning. *Coselete* soldiers would wear full cuirass (hence their name) along with a morion, gorget, tassets, armour covering the upper and lower arms and metal-plated gauntlets (López & López 2012:36). Accordingly, de Chaves is assigning heavily armoured infantrymen to the task of undertaking boarding actions, thereby echoing the naval tacticians in their considerations regarding the use of protective equipment for shipboard hand-to-hand combat. As in terrestrial warfare, however, it is probable that the utility of heavy armour at sea gradually declined as firearms improved in the course of the 16th and 17th century CE.

The tactical emphasis on using heavy infantry forces in naval warfare throughout these centuries reflects a persistent awareness about the intensity of hand-to-hand combat at sea. The above sources illustrate that seaborne hand-to-hand combat forces were not selected at random or merely pulled from terrestrial ranks without considering the nature of fighting at sea. So, although terrestrial forces were commonly assigned shipborne duty, it is evident that specifically heavy infantry troops were preferred to carry out such tasks. The nature of fighting at sea also prompted the development of trained marine infantry and specialized arms for dealing with the many dangers of naval combat. An early example of this is the Byzantine *dorka*, which, as mentioned by Constantine VII in the 10th century CE, was a large iron shield used only in the navy because of its weight (*De Ceremoniis* 579 [II 15], 670 [II 45]; *De administrando imperio* 1:250 [51]); Grotowski 2010:213–214). Again, this suggests that seaborne combat was particularly intense, requiring sometimes different equipment than in terrestrial warfare. The apparent need for such heavy armour at sea is probably rooted in considerations regarding the dangers posed by missile exchanges as well as hand-to-hand combat scenarios. Heavy armour certainly would have been useful in all phases of the fight, given the overall intensity of seaborne combat that the historical tacticians seem to have stressed in their writings.

The overarching reason for this intensity of seaborne combat is chiefly to be found in the conditions brought about by the maritime environment. As illustrated in the quotation in the beginning of this chapter, shipborne soldiers were as much in danger of perishing at the hands of their enemies as by the natural environment. All ships are essentially floating sanctuaries which protect their crews from the seas. All ships can be understood as floating sanctuaries which protect their crews from the seas. A maritime battlefield can therefore be conceived as a sort of extreme island warfare, characterized by limited resources and a confined battlespace. Such maritime battlespaces, moreover, are typically severely lacking in safe entry and exit routes, although the fighting ships may be assisted by other ships. This has often been carefully exploited by the enemy, not least by friendly forces, as illustrated by a vivid first-hand account of a naval battle in the early 17th century by Alonso de Contreras (1582–1641):

> Our Captain then applied a refined stratagem: he allowed only a few people on deck, and had all the hatches carefully fastened down, so that people either had to fight or jump into the sea. It was a bloody confrontation.

> (Kirsch 1990: 67, quoting de Contreras 1961:84–86).

In hand-to-hand combat scenarios, where boarding and anti-boarding forces clash, the static conditions of maritime combat are amplified, especially in cases where the ships cling to one another by use of grapnels and alike. These circumstances render it difficult to disengage from the fight and offer little chance of escape. The two opposing forces are, quite literally, in the same boat, wherefore the mission becomes one of gaining ground and searching for a decisive victory.

As an inherent consequence, naval hand-to-hand combat scenarios are inclined to be fought out in the form of battles. Generally, battles can be distinguished from virtually all other forms of warfare- such as skirmishes, firefights and other minor engagements – by the desire or willingness to meet on a battlefield for a single, massive clash between armed men for the purpose of mass killing (perhaps, but not necessarily, with some other ultimate goal in mind). They are also said to be "one of the *most* organized, premeditated, regimented and patterned forms of human behaviour" (Staniforth et a. 2014: 77, my emphasis). As such, battles, however functional in appearance, are not simply pragmatically organized procedures contained within a social vacuum and devoid of a discursive history. They are inextricably bound up with cultural discourse and thus also a wide array of ideological assumptions and social considerations that guide warfare (Carman 2009:39). Hand-to-hand combat in naval battles is no exception to this general rule.

Following this mode of thought, naval hand-to-hand combat can also be understood as a cultural performance where social preferences influence the nature of combative practices. It is, in fact, often challenging to discuss the functional and cultural factors independently of each other. This is perhaps most poignantly demonstrated by one of the methods used in motivating a boarding party during battle in the 16th century:

> During the battle, the Drummer, Fifer, and trumpets must always play, un-ceasingly, with the greatest arrogance, and as bravely as they can, because beyond enlivening the friendly crew, they are apt to frighten the enemy."
>
> (de Palacio 1986 [1587]:154)

As on land, naval battles included highly cultural elements and practices which could influence the course and outcome of the conflict. These often served to intimidate the enemy as well as to reinforce and legitimize the combative setting itself. Musical instruments, as exemplified above, was not the only measure used to this end. The maritime battlespace was also filled with a massive array of subtle, ritualized behaviour and symbolism, such as flags, uniforms and ornamentation. The significance of such elements and practices in relation to boarding actions in late medieval naval warfare have recently been highlighted by the discovery of a monstrous figurehead from the wreck of *Gribshunden*, a Danish warship which sank in 1495 CE off the coast of Ronneby (south-east Sweden). The figurehead, which was probably painted with vivid colours, would have been positioned just afore the forecastle containing the offensive combat unit and was the first "face" with which the enemy crew made contact (Warming 2014; Warming 2017). Certainly, an initial encounter with such a spectacle would have been startling, if not frightful, to the enemy. A figurehead of this sort may therefore not only have served a symbolic role which, among other things, helped to identify the ship; it could also have given the infantry unit in the forecastle a brief tactical advantage in combat. Although such cultural elements and practices did not necessarily serve an explicit tactical purpose in naval warfare, they were nonetheless part of the maritime battlespace. As such, they had the potential to evoke certain emotions and sets of behaviour amongst the shipborne soldiers and others operating within such battlespaces.

A brief history boarding and anti-boarding technologies

While naval hand-to-hand combat can be characterized by a set of unique properties and understood in relation to both environmental and cultural influences, it is evident, too, that this practice has assumed many different forms in the course of history as a result of technological innovations.

Space does not permit a full review of the contest between boarding and anti-boarding technologies in this place; however, the following should suffice as a general overview of the history of close quarter combat at sea and the main developments therein until the zenith of naval hand-to-hand combat tactics. Such technological overviews often give the impression of an evolutionary or linear process, but it is important to note at the outset that new technologies do not necessarily replace the old. The naval technologies discussed here often existed alongside each other, especially as navies were commonly composed of different types of vessels serving different functions. At other times, new strategies and challenges demanded the revival of older technologies, such as the renewed emphasis on galley warfare in Baltic waters in the 18th century. The following overview is therefore not intended to provide a comprehensive insight into all the combative technologies used by European navies in each respective period. Instead, the advancements discussed in this section represent a selection of technologies which can be said to have greatly influenced the practice of naval hand-to-hand combat and the overall trajectory of the development of warfare at sea. The details presented here simultaneously illustrate the veritable importance of hand-to-hand combat in naval warfare since the inception of sea battles and well into the early modern period.

Given the ubiquitousness of warfare in both past and present, it is plausible to assume that both boarding and anti-boarding actions have been carried out in one form or another since the inception of naval warfare, i.e. since the employment of watercraft sufficiently stable for hosting hand-to-hand combat scenarios or for the launching of missile attacks. The inception of this is challenging to pinpoint precisely in time and space. Perhaps the oldest depiction of a boat more advanced in its design than a canoe is a pictograph on a granite pebble found in the Khartoum Mesolithic layer in Sudan (Usai & Salvatori 2007). The pictograph, however, is rather abstract and does not allow for an interpretation of the stability of the watercraft in question. Being the only one of its kind, it is also quite the exception. Several finds from Egypt, however, suggest that early naval warfare could have been conducted as early as the Late Neolithic/Early Bronze Age. These include Amratian ceramics from c. 3500 BCE which are decorated with depictions of what are considered the earliest convincing evidence for the emergence of more stable watercraft (McGrail 2001:17). Another important find is the flint knife with ivory handle from Gebel-el-Arak (Abydos, Egypt), dated to c. 3300–3200 BCE, on which two types of vessels are depicted in association with terrestrial battle scenes (ibid.: 19). In consideration of the tendency for large-scale violence to intensify with increased political complexity and the dating of the aforementioned finds, it is interesting to note in this place – although not wholly surprising – that the development of more stable watercrafts coincides with the emergence of early nation states. Stable watercrafts would not only have facilitated geographical expansion but almost certainly also the projection of power at sea.

Figure 24: Detail from the relief at Medinet Habu, Luxorm depicting the Battle of the Delta in c. 1175 BCE (Courtesy of the Oriental Institute of the University of Chicago)

Notwithstanding these vindications, the first secure evidence of sea battles comes in the form of historical evidence from the Late Bronze Age. Contained in one of the few surviving documents which detail the reign of the last Hittite king, Suppiluliumas II, is a mentioning of a Hittite *naval* victory in 1210 BCE (Gurney 1952:1–32; Bryce 2007:7). The account simply states that the Hittites were victorious on the sea against an enemy based in Alasiya (modern day Cyprus), offering no further details about the exact identity of the enemy or how victory was achieved. It is probable that the naval encounter was concluded by means of hand-to-hand combat, but the extant details are insufficient for drawing any decisive conclusion in this respect. Considerably more information is on the other hand available about the second battle in recorded history, namely the Battle of the Delta (c. 1175 BC) which was fought between the Egyptians and the Sea Peoples (Ermen & Ranke 1923: 648; Nelson 1943; Cornelius 1987). The proceedings of this battle are recorded on the reliefs of pharaoh Ramesses III's mortuary temple at Medinet Habu in Luxor, Egypt. The reliefs are composed of detailed battle scenes depicting both boarding and anti-boarding actions in which shipborne archers and hand-to-hand combat forces can be seen fully engaged in intense mêlée action (Figure 24). The belligerents are, among other things, using manned fighting tops, which probably functioned as observational posts in non-combative contexts, and grapnels which can be seen used to capsize enemy vessels. All in all, these scenes give the impression of a competent and well-established early naval institution. Specialized naval technologies and tactics, then, seem to have been in use at least as early as in the Late Bronze Age.

In Ancient Greece, naval warfare underwent several notable developments which came to have significant consequences for boarding actions. To avoid hand-to-hand combat encounters, Mediterranean navies developed ram-equipped warships which were deliberately used to collide with enemy ships in order to sink them. The earliest convincing evidence for a warship with a ram appears on the bronze fibula from a burial in Athens dating to around 850 BCE (Casson 1991: 76–77; Fawcett 1994: 84; cf. Mark 2008). By at least the 5th century BCE, frontal ramming – the deliberate head-on collision between two ships equipped with bronze rams – had become a common procedure (Murray 2012:17 ff.). This required that the bronze-casting technology had advanced to a point where bronze rams would survive repetitive ramming, a development that probably should not predate the latter half of the 6th century BCE (ibid.: 17, note 11).

Another early development in Greek naval combat was the so-called dolphin, a massive weight of led or iron which could be flung or dropped from a ship's yardarm onto an enemy vessel with enough force to sink it or damage its hull. As such, the dolphin, like the ram, should be understood as a technological device intended to counter boarding actions. While the exact origin of the dolphin remains unknown, several written sources (e.g. Thucydides 7.41 and 62; Aristophanes *Equit.* 762; Lucan's *Phars.* 3.635) attest that the device was in frequent use aboard ships as early as the 5th century BCE. In 2016, the Hellenic Ministry of Culture and Sports and the Woods Hole Oceanographic Institution recovered an artefact from the Antikythera shipwreck (dated to c. 65 BCE) which has tentatively been identified as a dolphin (Mazza 2016). If correctly identified, the artefact recovered from Antikythera is the only extant example of such a device. The artefact in question is teardrop-shaped lead weight tipped with an iron spike, certainly capable of causing severe damage to the hull of enemy ships if dropped from a ship's yardarm.

By the early 4th century BCE, the Greeks had constructed siege engines called catapults (also known as ballistae in their more developed form) and began mounting them on the bows of some of their warships towards the end of the same century (Murray 2012:146–8; Marsden 1969; Marsden 1971). The catapult underwent a series of considerable developments during the 4th century BCE. Around the time of their first attested shipborne use (the Battle of Salamis in 306 BCE), engineers had worked out two basic design formulas for the catapult: one which shot stones; another for bolts (Murray 2012: 146–8). These two designs allowed fleets to attack enemy ships and personnel at greater distances with a variety of round ball shot and bolts, including incendiary devices. As such, catapults greatly complemented ramming and dolphin tactics, which sought to lessen the risk of being successfully boarded but could also be used in tandem with boarding tactics, depending upon the situation and range (Wallinga 1956: 29–50; Murray 2012: 162–70).

Another two significant technological devices designed to facilitate boarding actions emerged during the time of the Roman Republic. The first of these, the *corvus*, was a boarding ramp with an iron spike on its underside which was used to penetrate the decks of ships when lowered. The *corvus* thus allowed the renowned Roman land army to effectively engage in regular, terrestrial battles at sea. The first attested use of this device was in the Battle of Mylae in 260 BCE (Polybius' *Histories* 1.22), where the Roman navy used it against the Carthaginian navy with considerable success (Pitassi 2011: 41ff.). Another important Roman development was the *harpax* or *harpago* which was assumedly first employed at the Battle of Naulochos in 36 BCE (Murray 2012: 148). The device essentially consisted of a grappling hook on a wooden shaft which was attached to a long rope and could be shot onto an enemy ship by a heavy catapult. Using the trailing line, the crew could then haul the enemy ship alongside for boarding. Commanders could consequently not only force enemy ships to engage in close quarter battles but, to a certain extent, also control the manoeuvring of the enemy ship and thereby exploit more favourable positions for boarding actions.

While the above inventions all developed into new and improved varieties, and continued in use over the next few centuries, naval warfare did seemingly not undergo any considerable change in terms of new boarding and anti-boarding technologies until the Early Middle Ages. This change came with the development of Greek fire, which was famously employed by the Byzantine navy after its invention in c. 672 CE (Luttwak 2009:324). Greek fire was an incendiary weapon composed of a flammable liquid (probably based on petroleum) which could be ejected onto enemy ships and personnel from tubular projectors known as *siphons* (ibid: 325; Figure 25). The *siphons* could be mounted on protected platforms at the bow and, later, amidships and even at the stern of warships. Greek fire could also be weaponized and projected by other means, such as handheld *siphons* and earthen closed pots which could be thrown either by hand or catapults (Stanton 2015:15). The invention of Greek fire and the production of new warships, which were designed to better accommodate the weapon, made Byzantium less dependent on boarding than other contemporary powers. The weapon was nonetheless far from a universal solution and certainly had its limitations. In particular, the combination of the need for favourable weather conditions and precise sailing manoeuvres (whereby the ship could make use of its projectile weaponry but stay out of boarding range) as well as the short range of the *siphons* rendered Greek fire primarily useful as a defensive weapon in calmer waters (Luttwak 2009:325–326). Boarding actions therefore remained a common procedure even as Greek fire came to constitute an important anti-boarding measure in the Byzantine navy and in the fleets of rivalling powers – such as the Arabs – who later adopted the weapon.

Figure 25: Depiction of Greek Fire in the Madrid Skyltizes, an illuminated manuscript from the 12th century (Codex Skylitzes Matritensis, Bibliteca Nacional de Madrid, Vitr. 26-2, folio 34v. Courtesy of Bibliteca Nacional de Madrid)

Later in the Early Middle Ages, the renowned Scandinavian fleets of the Viking Age made use of relatively simple tactics to transform a naval battle into one with properties more reminiscent of terrestrial battles. When fighting at sea, the Scandinavians occasionally lashed a large body of their ships together in order to provide a more stable platform for fighting and boarding (Rodgers 1967:79–86; Jesch 2001:203–215; Jesch 2002). In doing so, they facilitated the manoeuvring of reserve troops which could be inserted from lighter vessels at points where the main struggle needed support (Figure 26). The lighter vessels could simultaneously be used to harass enemy flanks and for protection of their own, which was naturally the most favourable point of attack. The forces comprising the main formation could be arrayed in different ranks and assigned different roles depending on the range of their weapons. As described in the *Saga of Magnus the Good* (Sturluson's *Heimskringla* VIII), discussing the proceedings in the Battle of Aarhus (1044 CE), warriors could only use their hand-to-hand weapons at the bow; those farther off would fight with projectile weapons, including light javelins, arrows, stones, etc. (Rodgers 1967: 80 ff.). Abaft the mast, the warriors would be required to use bows and arrows. Shelter from these projectiles would be sought behind the high stem and stern posts as well as the rows of shields placed along the gunwhale. One such shield-rack can be observed along the upper edge of the sheer strake on the Skuldelev 5 ship-find, a small long ship excavated in Denmark along with four other ship-finds, all dating to the first half of the 11th century (Crumlin-Pedersen 2002:262–264). On another of these ship-finds, Skuldelev 1 (a medium-sized cargo ship), a conical, pointed object (probably an arrowhead) has seemingly pierced the top strake from the outside, suggesting how cargo ships of the period could also serve certain martial functions, either as logistical support or fighting platforms (ibid. 108; Ravn 2016:110–114). The reliance on infantry weapons and the general renunciation of anti-ship technology (apart from fire-ships) in seaborne combat in the Viking Age is a peculiar feature in galley warfare, clearly illustrating the importance of cultural choices and the non-linear development of boarding and anti-boarding tactics.

Figure 26: Viking Age fleets lashed together to provide a more stable fighting platforms at sea (adopted from Hjardar & Vike 2013: 86, artist: Anders Kvåle Rue)

Another major development in warfare at sea in the Early to High Middle Ages was the emergence of ship types with high freeboards and large elevated fighting platforms which allowed soldiers to obtain the height advantage in combative encounters. An early use of such a type in naval warfare was the cog, which could be constructed with both fore and aft castles for defence. It should be mentioned that towers had already been constructed aboard seagoing warships at least since the beginning of the First Punic War (261–241 BCE) on Roman quinqueremes and that the Byzantines were known to have built shipborne castles into some of their larger *dromons* (Luttwak 2009:326 ff.; Pitassi 2011:46). The cog can nonetheless be said to represent a new technological development in this regard since it successfully integrated relatively large fore and aft castles as well as high freeboards into a sturdy seagoing design which relied on sailing propulsion instead of rowing. The design entailed that the ship had good seakeeping and was not reliant on many rowers for successful tactical manoeuvring; instead it could deploy a relatively large infantry force to carry out the fighting. Though mentioned in literary works as early as the 9th century CE, the archaeological and historical evidence suggests that the cog was not fully integrated into naval warfare in the form of the floating fortress that gained a near hegemony over the northern seas until the 13th or 14th century CE (Bill 2002; Bill 2003:41–43).

The Norwegian *Konungs skuggsjá*, written in c. 1250 CE, indicates an early Scandinavian use of martial cogs which were equipped with castles in both bow and stern as well as crow nests in the mast tops (Bill 2003: 45). In England, the cog accounted for about 57% of the 1300 ships attested for military service during the years 1337–1360 CE, proving itself as an effective engine of war in several major naval battles, including the Battle of Sluys in 1340 CE (ibid: 43). The castles facilitated boarding actions but also made it easier to repel attacks, especially since their height provided a better overview of the mêlée and much wider angles of attack for projectile firing. It is evident, too, that the enemy (should they be positioned at a lower height) would be at a disadvantage at close quarters owing to the challenges brought about by gravitational force. Other successful warship designs – such as the carrack and carvel – were later built with the same considerations in mind, although these were considerably more stable and spacious than the cog.

Notwithstanding the significance of the above developments, there can be no doubt that the employment of gunpowder weapons aboard ships was a particularly meaningful advancement in naval warfare, influencing both boarding as well as anti-boarding tactics to a considerable extent (cf. Friel 2003: 79). Ships were probably first equipped with guns during the first half of the 14th century, judging from the first mentioning of a gun bought for an English royal ship, the *All Hallows Cog*, in 1337 or 1338 CE. This is likewise supported by the first recorded instances of the employment of guns in naval battles in the first half of the 14th century, such as the Battle of Arnemuiden (1338) and Battle of Sluys (1340) (Friel 2003:72f.; Hildred 2011:12–3). Guns nevertheless seem to have remained relatively unimportant during the 14th century, serving only a minor role in battles (Friel 2003: 72ff.). The 15th century, however, witnessed a dramatic increase in the appreciation for gunpowder weapons at sea, these chiefly being comprised of light ordnance, small bombards and breech-loading swivel guns which were carried high in the hull, i.e. on the upper deck and in the shipborne castles (Barfod 1990:131; Friel 1995:152f.; De Vries 1998:390; Friel 2003: Guilmartin 2011:130f.; Hildred 2011:13). Such early guns were light, anti-personnel guns and not intended for the sinking of ships. Instead, they mainly offered support for hand-to-hand combat forces in repelling or carrying out boarding actions (Mortensen 1999: 225ff.; Warming 2014). The recently identified wreck of *Gribshunden* (1495), Danish King John I's flagship, is possibly the most well-preserved Late Medieval warship (Einarsson 2008; Rönnby 2015; Eriksson 2016), representing the final historical stage of naval warfare where guns only played a minor role and served as support for infantry forces. The ship was a carrack carrying small wrought-iron guns, as evidenced by the discovery of several gun carriages and small shot. According to Caspar Weinrich's chronicle (p. 309), some 150 men perished with the ship when it sank, most of whom were assumedly soldiers (see Sjöblom 2015). Granting that the crew numbers listed in an earlier record from 1487 accurately represents the number of mariners aboard *Gribshunden* (30 men) at the time of her sinking, the soldiers may have totalled some 120 men, these constituting the main fighting force of the ship (see Barfod 1990:72). Several finds of mail confirm the presence of infantry forces and the general martial nature of the ship (Rönnby 2015). That they were also well-equipped for battling at long-range is evidenced by the recent excavation of 2019 (led by Södertörn University, Lunds University and Blekinge Museum) which un-covered, among other things, a crossbow, crossbow bolt and an early arquebus (Figure 27). Future experimental trials with replicas of these artefacts are currently being planned by Lunds University in collaboration with the current author in order to better illuminate the fighting capacities of the *Gribshunden* warship. Being the oldest carvel-built ship discovered in Nordic waters, the wreck simultaneously reflects a design that would come to facilitate the impending construction of gun ports and employment of heavier ordnance in wars at sea.

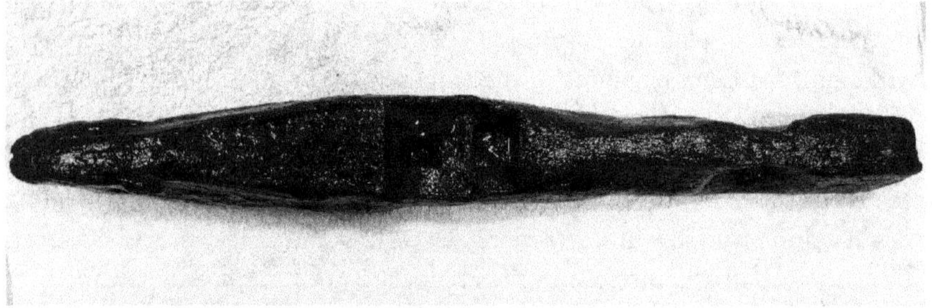

Figure 27: The crossbow stock recovered from the wreck of the *Gribshunden* (1495) during the 2019 excavation. The cut out for the trigger system can be seen in the middle. The original crossbow was probably equipped with a composite bow and spanned with a goat's foot lever. The remains of the stock measures 39 cm in length, 5 cm in width and 4.5 cm in depth (photo: Christoffer Sandahl, Blekinge Museum)

Ships capable of carrying enough heavy ordnance to sink other vessels did not appear until the late 15th or early 16th century. This advancement within naval warfare predominantly emerged as a result of improvements within gun, gun carriage and ammunition manufacture as well as a change in shipbuilding technique which allowed lidded gun ports to be placed close to the waterline (Konstam 1988; DeVries 1997; DeVries 1998; Hildred 2011:13;

Warming 2014). The latter not only entailed an increase in ship stability and the ship's capacity for carrying heavy ordnance; it also allowed guns to be fired closer to the waterline. Mediterranean galleys circumvented some of the challenges involved in using heavy shipborne artillery and initially mounted a single large gun forward of the bow, thus becoming the first ships to take advantage of the use of heavy ordnance at sea (Sicking 2010:241). The first recorded sinking of an enemy vessel by use of shipboard gunpowder weapons can probably be accredited to the French galleys in the Anglo-French naval engagement off the coast of Brest, France, in 1513 CE (Spont 1897:146, 153). Some of the French galleys involved in this engagement were equipped with three Venetian basilisks; one shot from these, according to the 16th century historian Peter Martyr (1457–1526), could "strike through any ship" (ibid.:51).

Heavy ordnance also seems to have played a significant role in the forerunner to this engagement the previous year, the Battle of St Mathieu (1512), where the *Mary Rose* (1545) shot away the main mast of *La Grande Louise*, the admiral ship of France. The design and armaments of *Mary Rose* herself, a carrack built in 1510–1511, also signal that heavy ordnance began to play a significant role in naval warfare around this time. Having been submitted to extensive archaeological and historical studies after the rediscovery and excavation of the wreck in 1971–1978, it has become clear that the *Mary Rose* reflects an early attempt to introduce a higher number of heavier weapons lower down in the hull of warships. The transitional design of the *Mary Rose* is particularly evident as a result of her rebuilding in 1536, when a lower tier of gun ports was added, and further emphasis placed on the use and upgrade of heavy ordnance to the detriment of anti-personnel armaments (Hildred 2011:856 ff.).

However, a successful and dependable use of ordnance for long-distance battling was not only a matter of ordnance types or numbers; there was also a need for carefully planned tactics which were construed to inflict maximum damage to the enemy's ship whilst avoiding hand-to-hand combat engagements. The first "modern" naval battles, wherein artillery not only played a crucial role but was deliberately used as a tactical measure to defeat and sink large warships at a distance without engaging in hand-to-hand combat, did therefore not take place before the second half of the 16th century (Warming 2014). The proceedings of the Battle of Öland (1564) between the Swedish and Dano-Lübeckian fleets provide the first clear indication that heavy ordnance began to take the foreground over naval hand-to-hand combat tactics in this sense. During this battle, the Swedish warship *Mars* (1564) successfully sank the Lübeckian *Alte Barke* (1564) by use of its superior heavy ordnance, following the orders of King Erik XIV who had instructed that *Mars* was to use its guns to sink enemy vessels from a distance (Ekman 1946: 64; Höglund 2012:146; Sjöblom 2016:329). This is possibly the first recorded incident of planned long-range tactics which were successfully carried out in practice at sea. Eventually, however, *Mars* was successfully boarded and defeated by the Dano-Lübeckian fleet, after which it exploded and sank. The newly discovered wreck of the *Mars* (Rönnby 2012; Rönnby 2013) provides an important arena of research for investigations into naval hand-to-hand combat practices, not only because of its pivotal role in naval history but also since the wreck site is essentially a 16th century battlefield capsulated in time. The most recent investigations of this wreck site (season 2019) has underscored the research value of the site and its potential for understanding the life of the crew and soldiers aboard as well as the battle itself. Some of the recent findings include the only surviving example of a large boarding grapnel, a femur with sharp-edge trauma around the knee region (see Frederiksson & Sten, this volume) and several artefacts which have been tentatively identified as hand-held weaponry, including a grenade. *Mars* and the Battle of Öland (1564), together with the decisive defeat of the Spanish Armada in 1588 CE, marked the beginning of the successful and dependable use of long-range guns as primary weapons in naval warfare, effectively ending the era of sea battles dominated by boarding (Probst 1992; Mortensen 1999:364; Parker 1988:92 ff.; Warming 2014). The potential of heavy ordnance fire in naval battles, however, was not fully realized until the 17th century when gun technology and tactics had developed even further (Friel 2003:79).

Accordingly, the 15th to 16th century can rightfully be regarded as the zenith of naval hand-to-hand combat in European naval history. It was not only a period of transition in which the tactical focus of naval warfare began to shift from boarding to heavy ordnance fire; it was also a time when shipbuilding placed heavy emphasis on high castles and size, achieving a previously unrivalled capacity for carrying infantry forces. This is perhaps most clearly reflected by the archaeological remains of the *Mary Rose*. Her heavy ordnance and placement of gun ports have been discussed above in relation to advancements within naval artillery and the newly given significance to long-distance battling; however, it is equally important to note that she was also equipped with high castles and carried large numbers of infantry forces, even after her rebuilding in 1536. Despite a general decrease in soldiers since her launch in 1511, she did, nonetheless, probably carry a crew of some 500 men into the Battle of the Solent (1545), most of whom drowned underneath the anti-boarding netting when she sank (Marsden 2003:10; Hildred 2011: 4ff.; Warming 2014). In addition to the Mary Rose, it should be mentioned that the 16th century was also witness to what can probably be regarded as the largest naval battle in European history, if understood in terms of a ship to men ratio, namely the Battle of Lepanto (1571). The galleys in this battle carried up to 400 men and the c. 400 galleys fighting at Lepanto may therefore have carried in total some 160,000 men, according to some estimates (e.g. Parker 1988:89).

Undoubtedly, the combination of large crews with soldiers in crammed formations and the increasingly effective use of ordnance fire entailed great losses of lives, even though certain measures were taken to protect the soldiers, such as special shipborne shields etc. The consequences of this unhappy marriage in the zenith of naval hand-to-hand combat could hardly have gone unnoticed. It is presumably what led the naval tactician Fernando Oliveira to remark about the general harmfulness artillery to humanity and his need to justify the use of such weapons in his naval treatise of 1555 (Oliveira 2008 [1555]: 41–42). Writing in a period which was witness to the ever more destructive and impersonal approach to waging war (Warming 2014), Oliveira was probably not alone in his sentiments. The violence, now generated in a detached and distant way, was something new, having interesting psychological repercussions that are known to result in the violence becoming more extreme (Shalit 1988:77). It can be supposed that such violence induced a certain amount of fear, particularly in the many soldiers who were aboard some of these ships (for notions of fear at sea, see Hammar, this volume). What were their thoughts upon embarking from the port, knowing that they would encounter enemy fleets who were capable of injuring and killing many of them before they even had the chance to play a part in the battle? Given the large number of infantry forces, the repercussions of this method of waging war certainly must have impacted those involved, their families and the society as a whole. Naval warfare during this period should therefore be seen as stimulus for ideological change and as a contributing factor in the scepticism about the rightness of war that emerged in the 16th century (Tallett & Trim 2010:6; Warming 2014).

While the period described above may rightfully be understood as the zenith of naval hand-to-hand combat, it should be noted that the practice was never completely abandoned (e.g. Gilkerson 1991). Boarding and anti-boarding operations remained important considerations in later fleets even after tactical focus had shifted towards heavy ordnance fire. It often played an important part in the final phases of naval battles, although not necessarily to the same extent as in the past. Moreover, for fleets lacking or inexperienced in effective shipboard ordnance use, boarding remained the primary method by which to conclude a battle at sea. Boarding actions could also have been undertaken as a counter-measure if the enemy vessel possessed superior firepower or when it was desirable to capture the enemy vessel instead of destroying it. The ship was not only a prize in and of itself, but may also have carried valuable persons or materials, such as food, treasure, weaponry or information that could have aided naval intelligence. Thus, while boarding tactics lost some of its importance to navies after the advent of successful heavy ordnance fire, it remained a widely applied practice in Europe, both amongst naval fleets as well as amongst privateers and pirates. Boarding is still employed and practiced by modern day institutions – including special military task forces – as well as pirates, the latter of which have even resulted in the revival of specialized anti-boarding tactics in our modern day, such as electric fences and anti-boarding netting.

Conclusion

Far from being a frivolous or heedless affair, naval hand-to-hand combat was conducted with considerable deliberation and played a crucial role in determining the outcome of naval battles in the past. Heavily influenced by both culture and environmental constraints, the practice of naval hand-to-hand combat assumed several different forms across Europe in different historical periods, making use of the prevailing military wisdom of the day and the technology available to them. Like on land, seaborne combat involved both defensive and offensive tactics. The extent to which these were carried out and emphasized varied from fleet to fleet and ship to ship. Sometimes, an offensive naval hand-to-hand combat force was the main concern of a fleet or ship and operated alongside boarding technologies designed to facilitate such actions; at other times, infantry forces merely constituted support for anti-boarding technologies, these being intended for sinking vessels or otherwise deterring enemy boarding actions. As mentioned, the technological advancements treated in the course of these pages are not all-encompassing nor are they treated at a level of detail that would allow a full comprehension of the actual naval hand-to-hand practices which were erected around these developments. They do, nonetheless, illustrate the extent to which efforts were invested into the development of boarding and anti-boarding technologies across the centuries, reflecting also a past awareness of the underlying principles that seem to govern the proceedings and various stages of naval warfare. The several different facets of this study, each of which have varying connections with the subject and which have the potential to address it from several historical and archaeological viewpoints, are likewise not intended to constitute any definite work on naval hand-to-hand combat. Instead, this chapter has served to clarify the significance of the role of hand-to-hand combat and bring out a few new aspects and topics for further consideration. As such, it should be understood as an introduction to a topic deserving of a fuller exploration. It is to be hoped that more specialized studies in the future will be able to shed greater light on these aspects of naval warfare in their regional and temporal varieties.

References

Source material and translations

Anonymous. *The King's Mirror (Speculum Regale – Konungs Skuggsjá)*. Translation by Larson, L. M. Scandinavian Monographs Volume III. New York: The American-Scandinavian Foundation. 1917.

Aristophanes. *The Knights*. Transl. by Murray, G. G. A., London: George Allen & Unwin. 1956. Available at: https://gutenberg.ca/ebooks/murrayaristophanesknights/murrayaristophanes-knights-00-h.html [Accessed 27.02.2018]

Constantine VII Porphyrogenitus. *De administrando imperio*. ed. & translation by G. Moravcsik & R. J. H. Jenkins. Washington: Dumbarton Oaks. 1967.

Constantine VII Porphyrogenitus. *De Cerimoniis Aulae Byzantinae libri duo*. ed. I. Reiskii. Bonnae. 1829.

de Contreras. *Das Leben des Capitán Alonso de Contreras von ihm Selbst erzählt*. Translation by Steiger, A. Zürich: Manesse Bibliothek der Weltliteratur. 1961.

Figueyredo, D. G., 2009 [1651]. *Memorial of the Practice of the Montante*. Translation by Myers, H. and Hick, S. The Oakeshott Institute. Available at: http://hroarr.com/manuals/iberian/Figueiredo-Diogo-Gomes-de-Montante-Translation-Myers-and-Hick-1651.pdf [retrieved 12.04.2018].

Godinho, L., 2015 [1599]. *Arte de Esgrima*. ed. Valle Ortiz, M. & Rivera, T. Santiago de Compostela: AGEA Editora.

Lucan. *Lucan: The Civil War Books I–X (Pharsalia)*. Transl. by Duff, J. D., Loeb Classical Library 220. Cambridge, MA: Harvard University Press. 1928.

Oliveira, F., 2008 [1555]. *Arte da Guerra do Mar: Estratégia e Guerra Naval No Tempo Dos Descobrimentos*. Lisbon: Edicoes 70.

de Palacio, D. G., 1986 [1587]. *Nautical Instruction*. Transl. by Bankston, J. Bisbee, Arizona: Terrenate Associates.

Polybius. *The Histories, Volume I: Books 1–2*. Translation by W. R. Paton. Revised by F. W. Walbank, Christian Habicht. Loeb Classical Library 128. Cambridge, MA: Harvard University Press. 2010.

Skylitzes, J., *Codex Skylitzes Matritensis*. Available at: https://www.wdl.org/en/item/10625/ [Accessed 03.10.2018].

Sturluson, S., *Heimskringla: A History of the Norse Kings*. Transl. by Samuel Laing. London: Norroena Society. 1907.

Thucydides. *Histories of the Pelopennesian War*. Volume 1. Translation by Jowett, B. Oxford: Clarendon Press. 1881. Available at: http://www.perseus.tufts.edu/hopper/text?doc=Perseus%3Atext%3A1999.04.0105%3Abook%3D7%3Achapter%3D41 [Accessed 12.03.2018].

Vegetius. *Vegetius: Epitome of Military Science*. Translation by Milner, N. P. 2nd revised edition. Translated Texts for Historians Volume 16. Liverpool: Liverpool University Press. 1996.

Weinrich, C., XXXVII. Chronico Gedanensi. In Claudius Annerstedt (ed.), *Scriptores Rerum Svecicarum. Medii aevi. Tome (part) III*. Uppsala 1871 and 1876.

Secondary sources

Bill, J., 2002. Castles at Sea: The Warship of the High Middle Ages. In Nørgård Jørgensen, A., Pind, J., Jørgensen, L. & Clausen, B. (eds.), *Maritime warfare in northern Europe: technology, organisation, logistics, and administration 500 BC–1500 AD: papers from an international research seminar at the Danish National Museum, Copenhagen, 3–5 May, 2000*: 47–56. Copenhagen: National Museum of Denmark

Bill, J., 2003. Scandinavian Warships and Naval Power in the Thirteenth and Fourteenth Centuries. In Hattendorf, J. & Unger, R. (eds.), *War at Sea in the Middle Ages and the Renaissance*: 35–51. Woodbridge: Boydell press

Barfod, J., 1990. *Flådens Fødsel*. Marinehistorisk Selskabs skrift nr. 22. København: Gyldendal.

Bauer Landauer, I., 1921. *La marina española en el siglo XVI: don Francisco de Benavides, cuatralvo de las galeras de España*. Madrid.

Bryce, T., 2007. *Hittite Warrior*. Oxford: Osprey Publishing Ltd.

Casson, L., 1991. *The Ancient Mariners: Seafarers and Sea Fighters of the Mediterranean in Ancient Times*. 2nd ed. Princeton: Princeton University Press.

Carman, J., 2009. Beyond the Western Way of War: Ancient Battlefields in Comparative Perspective. Ch. 4 in Carman, J. & Harding, A. (eds.), *Ancient Warfare: Archaeological Perspectives*: 39–56. Stroud, Gloucestershire: History Press Limited.

Cornelius, I., 1987. The Battle of the Nile – Circa 1190 B. C. *Military History Journal*, 7(4). Available at: http://samilitaryhistory.org/vol074ic.html [Accessed: 13.01.2018].

Crumlin-Pedersen, O., 2002. Description and analysis of the ships as found. Ch. 5 in Crumlin-Pedersen, O. & Olsen, O. (eds.), *The Skuldelev Ships I: Typography, Archaeology, History, Conservation and Display*: 96–304. Ships and Boats of the North vol. 4.1. Roskilde: The Viking Ship Museum.

DeVries, K., 1997. Catapults are Not Atomic Bombs: Towards a Redefinition of Effectiveness in Pre-Modern Military Technology. *War in History* 4: 75–91.

DeVries, K., 1998. The Effectiveness of Fifteenth-Century Shipboard Artillery. *The Mariner's Mirror* 84: 389–99.

Einarsson, L., 2008. Ett skeppsvrak i Ronneby skärgård. Kalmar Läns Museum. Available at:http://www.lansstyrelsen.se/blekinge/SiteCollectionDocuments/Sv/samhallsplanering-och-kulturmiljo/arkeologi-och-fornlamningar/Ettskeppsvrak.pdf [Accessed 15.2. 2018].

Ekman, C., 1946. Några data om Erik XIV:s sjökrigskonst. *Tidskrift i Sjöväsande 2*. Stockholm: Kungliga Örlogsmannasällskapet.

Eriksson, N., 2016. *Gribshunden* (1495): vraket efter ett medeltida kravellskepp. Marin-arkeologisk tidskrift 1: 4–10.

Erman, A., & Ranke, H., 1923. *Aegypten und aegyptisches Leben im Altertum*. Tübingen, H. Lauppschen Buchhandlung.

Fawcett, N., 1994. The Introduction of the Ram as a Weapons in Ancient Sea Warfare. *Akroterion* XXXIX: 83–95. Available at: http://akroterion.journals.ac.za/pub/article/viewFile/524/590 [Accessed 10.02.2018].

Friel, I., 1995. *The Good Ship: ships, shipbuilding and technology in England 1200–1520*. London: British Museum Press.

Friel, I., 2003. The English and War at Sea, c. 1200–c. 1500. In Hattendorf, J. & Unger, R. (eds.), *War at Sea in the Middle Ages and the Renaissance*: 69–79. Woodbridge: Boydell press.

Gilkerson, W., 1991. *Boarders Away – with Steel*. Lincoln, Rhode Island: Andrew Mowbray, INC.

Höglund, P., 2012. *Mars 1564: The History and Archaeology of a Legendary Swedish Warship*. *Skyllis, Zeitschrift für Unterwasserarchäeologie 12 (2)*: 142–147

Grotowski, P., 2010. *Arms and Armour of the Warrior Saints: Tradition and Innovation in Byzantine Iconography (843–1261)*. Leiden & Boston: Brill.

Guilmartin, J. F. Jr., 2011. The military revolution in warfare at sea during the early modern era: technological origins, operational outcomes and strategic consequences. *Journal for Maritime Research* 13(2): 129–137.

Gurney, O. R., 1952. *The Hittites*. London: Penguin Books.

Hildred, A., (ed.). 2011. *Weapons of Warre: The Armaments of the Mary Rose*. Portsmouth: The Mary Rose Trust Ltd.

Hjardar, K. & Vike, V., 2011. *Vikinger i krig*. Oslo: Spartacus.

Jesch, J., 2001. *Ships and Men in the Late Viking Age. The Vocabulary of Runic Inscriptions and Skaldic Verse*. Woodbridge.

Jesch, J., 2002. Sea-battles in skaldic poetry. In: Anne Nørgård Jørgensen, John Pind, Lars Jørgensen Birthe Clausen (eds.), *Maritime Warfare in Northern Europe. Technology, organization, logistics and administration 500 BC–1500 AD. Papers from an International Research Seminar at the Danish national museum, Copenhagen, 3–5 May 2000*: 57–64. Publications from the National Museum. Studies in archaeology & History, Vol. 6. Copenhagen.

Kirsch, P., 1990. *The Galleon: The Great Ships of the Armada Era*. London: Conway Maritime Press Ltd.

Konstam, R. A., 1988. 16th century Naval Tactics and Gunnery. *International Journal of Nautical Archaeology and Underwater Exploration* 17: 17–23.

López, I., & Lopez, I. N. 2012. *The Spanish Tercios 1536–1704*. Oxford: Osprey Publishing.

Luttwak, E., 2009. The Grand Strategy of the Byzantine Empire. Cambridge, Massachusetts, and London, England: The Belknap Press of Harvard University Press.

Mark, S., 2008. The Earliest Naval Ram. *International Journal of Nautical Archaeology* 37 (2): 253–272.

Marsden, E. W., 1969. *Greek and Roman Artillery: Historical Development*. Oxford: Clarendon Press.

Marsden, E. W., 1971. *Greek and Roman Artillery: Technical Treatises*. Oxford: Clarendon Press.

Marsden, P., 2003. *Sealed by Time: The Loss and Recovery of the Mary Rose*. Portsmouth: The Mary Rose Trust Ltd.

Mazza, E., 2016. 2,000-Year-Old Antikythera Shipwreck Famous for 'Ancient Computer' Yields New Treasures. *Huffington post*. Available at: https://www.huffingtonpost.com/entry/antikytherashipwreck_us_5768b582e4b015db1bca7547?ir=Science§ion=us_science [Accessed: 15.02.2018].

McGrail, S., 2001. *Boats of the World*. Oxford: Oxford University Press.

Melville, N., 2018. *The Two-Handed Sword: History, Design and Use*. Barnsley: Pen & Sword Military.

Mortensen, M., 1999. *Dansk artillery indtil 1600*. København: Tøjhusmuseet.

Mortensen, M., 2002. Early Danish naval artillery c. 1500–1523: The beginning of a new era. In Anne Nørgård Jørgensen, John Pind, Lars Jørgensen & Birthe Clausen (eds.), *Maritime warfare in northern Europe: technology, organisation, logistics, and administration 500 BC–1500 AD: papers from an international research seminar at the Danish National Museum, Copenhagen, 3–5 May, 2000*: 83–104. Copenhagen: National Museum of Denmark.

Murray, W., 2012. *The Age of Titans: The Rise and Fall of the Great Hellenistic Navies*. New York: Oxford University Press.

Nelson, H., 1943. The Naval Battle Pictured at Medinet Habu. *Journal of Near Eastern Studies*, II (1). Chicago: University of Chicago Press.

Parker, G., 1988. *The Military Revolution: Military innovation and the rise of the West, 1500–1800*. Cambridge: Cambridge University Press.

Pitassi, M., 2011. *Roman Warships*. Woodbridge: Boydell Press.

Probst, N., 1992. Nordisk søtaktik i 1500- og 1600-tallet - og Slaget i Køge Bugt den 1. juli 1677. *Marinehistorisk Tidsskrift* 25 (4): 3–23.

Ravn, M., 2016. *Viking-Age War Fleets: Shipbuilding, resource management and maritime warfare in 11th-century Denmark*. Maritime Culture of the North vol. 4. Roskilde: The Viking Ship Museum.

Rodgers, W. L., 1967. *Naval Warfare Under Oars: 4th to 16th centuries*. Annapolis, Maryland: Naval Institute Press.

Runuyan, T. J., 2003. Naval Power and maritime Technology During the Hundred Years War. In Hattendorf, J. & Unger, R. (eds.), *War at Sea in the Middle Ages and the Renaissance*: 53–67. Woodbridge: Boydell press.

Rönnby, J. (red.), 2012. *Skeppet* Mars *(1564). Marinarkeologisk fältrapport etapp I 2011*. Södertörn arkeologiska rapporter och studier. Södertörns högskola.

Rönnby, J. (red.), 2013. *Skeppet* Mars *(1564). Marinarkeologisk fältrapport etapp II 2012*. Södertörn arkeologiska rapporter och studier. Södertörns högskola.

Rönnby, J. (ed.), 2015. *Gribshunden* (1495): Skeppsvrak vid Stora Ekön, Ronneby, Blekinge. Marinarkologiska undersökningar 2013–2015. Blekinge museum rapport 21. Blekinge museum/Södertörns högskola.

Shalit, B. 1988. *The Psychology of Conflict and Combat*. New York: Praeger.

Sicking, L., 2010. Naval warfare in Europe, c. 1330–c. 1680. In Tallett, F. & Trim, D. (eds.), *European Warfare, 1350–1750*: 236–263. Cambridge: Cambridge University Press.

Sjöblom, I., 2015. Idenfiering och historiskt sammanhang. In Rönnby, J. (ed.), *Gribshunden (1495): Skeppsvrak vid Stora Ekön, Ronneby, Blekinge*: 3149. Blekinge Museum/Södertörns högskola.

Sjöblom, I., 2016. Svenska sjöfficerare under 1500-talet. Malmö: Universus Academic Press.

Spont, A., 1897. *Letters and Papers Relating to the War with France 1512–1514*. Publications of the Navy Records Society 10. London: Navy Records Society.

Staniforth, M., Kimura, J., Lien, L., & Sasaki, R. 2014. Naval Battlefield Archaeology of the Lost Kublai Khan Fleets. International Journal of Nautical Archaeology 43 (1): 76–86.

Stanton, C. 2015. *Medieval Maritime Warfare*. Barnsley: Pen & Sword Maritime.

Tallet, F., & Trim, D. J. B., 2010. *European Warfare, 1350–1750*. Cambridge: Cambridge University Press.

Usai, D. & Salvatori, S., 2007. The Oldest Representation of a Nile Boat. *Antiquity* 81(314) (Antiquity Gallery). Available at: http://www.antiquity.ac.uk/projgall/usai314/ [Accessed 18.02.2018].

Wallinga, H. T., 1956. *The Boarding Bridge of the Romans*. Gronningen: Wolters.

Warming, R., 2014. *Towards an Archaeology of Boarding: Naval Hand-to-hand Combat Tactics of Northwestern Europe in 16th Century*. MA dissertation. University of Southampton.

Warming, R., 2015. *Gribshunden*: Significance and Preliminary Investigations. Combat Archaeology. Available at: http://combatarchaeology.org/gribshunden-significance-and-preliminary-investigations/ [Accessed 15.2.2018].

Warming, R., 2017. Traces of Color Discovered on the Figurehead of *Gribshunden* (1495). Society for *Combat Archaeology*. Available at: http://combatarchaeology.org/traces-of-color-on-the-figurehead-of-gribshunden/ [Accessed 12/02/2018].

Understanding the Gundeck Experience

FRED HOCKER

Traditional studies of naval warfare in the age of broadside ordnance tend to concentrate on tactical and technical issues, such as the origins of coordinated line tactics, the development of more effective types of cannon, and different rates of fire achieved and their effects. Alternatively, the subjects are specific actions and their heroes. Nelson at Trafalgar or Cochrane's single-ship exploits have captured the imagination of historians as well as the public, to be turned into popular novels and films as well as learned articles. Where the experience of those directly engaged in naval battles is concerned, most writers have tended to fall back on lurid first-person accounts and imaginative fantasy. The life of a sailor on the gundeck is usually portrayed in highly anti-romantic terms, leaning heavily on the poor quality of the food, the harsh punishments, and the horrific effects of disease, shot and shell. Battle is a blood-soaked chaos compounded of fear, adrenaline, courage, knavery, primitive rage and noble sacrifice.

In studying conflict from any perspective, there are certain things that will always remain unknowable to someone who has not experienced combat first-hand. It is the paradox which plagues the scholar, the living history demonstrator and the recreational re-enactor. Until you have been shot at with live ammunition, with death a present and real possibility, it is not possible to comprehend the experience of war. No matter how carefully you recreate the clothing, food, and living conditions of a past army or navy, either as an academic study or as a living history experience, no one is trying to kill you, and you can hang up the funny clothes at the end of the weekend, wash off the smoke and accumulated dirt, and go home with no damage beyond a bad hangover.

This paper seeks a more scientific approach to understanding the gundeck experience, looking at the archaeological evidence for what happened in battle, in the broader context of the tactical and technical envelope defined by ships, weather, ordnance and the social structures of naval crews. Through such an approach we may be able to define some of the aspects of life and death on the gundeck more clearly, even if we cannot know it in a visceral way.

In 2013–2014, the Vasa Museum tested the performance of the main armament of a Swedish warship from 1628 by constructing and firing an accurate copy of a 24-pounder bronze *halv-kartog* (demi-cannon) under carefully controlled and measured conditions. In addition to assessing traditional ballistic properties, such as range and accuracy, as well as the effect of shot on hull structure, the project sought to measure some aspects of the experience of gun crews engaged in battle, both those firing heavy artillery and those on the receiving end. At the ergonomic level, we hoped to gain some idea of the working environment, such as the energy needed to move, aim and service a gun and carriage weighing over 1600 kg, the amount of smoke and noise generated inside the gundeck, and the physical risk from recoiling guns. Most modern histories presume that the noise is deafening, that smoke creates a choking environment in which the crew can barely see their own guns, much less the target, and that the work of handling big guns is exhausting. Some of these factors are alluded to in contemporary accounts, but somehow gun crews managed to overcome these issues to fire broadsides for hours or even days in extended engagements. How can this be?

We also wanted to evaluate what happens inside the target. Traditional accounts and medical records emphasize the predominance of splinter injuries over direct hits from ammunition, as shot passing through the wooden structure of the hull creates clouds of splinters expanding outward from the point of impact. This has been questioned in recent years, not least on the television program *Mythbusters*, in which popular beliefs, aphorisms, urban legends and movie tropes are put to scientific, experimental tests. In episode 71 (first broadcast on 17th January 2007), hosts Adam Savage and Jaymie Heineman built a replica section of a side of a ship, mounted pig carcasses behind it as human analogues, and fired several rounds from an American Civil War era 6-pounder field gun at it, before assessing penetration damage to the pigs. They saw little real damage to the "test subjects", with only small splinters produced and few of those penetrating deeply into the carcasses; they concluded that the danger of splinters was exaggerated, and that it was the shot that posed the real danger. They declared the myth "busted." This may help to explain why some naval battles, despite hundreds of rounds fired and observed to hit the target, resulted in relatively few casualties (see, for example, Fox 2009:94). It does not explain higher casualty rates in other battles of similar duration.

Our suspicion was that the structure of the ship being struck has a much more important and complex relationship to the result than either contemporary tests or modern experiments have presumed. In the 18th and 19th centuries, guns were tested against packed baulks of timber to assess penetrating power and measured in terms of the number of inches of oak a shot of given weight could pass through with a given powder charge (see, for example, Lafay 1850 or Douglas 1860; see also the discussion in Kahanov et al., 2012: 1995–1998). There is nothing wrong with this experimental premise. In an age when accuracy was questionable and volume of fire more relevant to the outcome of a battle, the results were a useful indicator of average performance. They are of less use to us in understanding what happens inside the target ship. Modern experiments with replica or original cannon usually substitute a simple wooden wall, with planks fastened to upright posts, for the complicated structure of a real ship (Hildred 2011: 123–129; Kahanov et al. 2012), and so the results may not be indicative of reality except at the grossest level of simplification.

In our tests, we fired the replica cannon at a detailed, accurate recreation of a section of *Vasa*'s side, built from similar materials and replicating even the small details of interior joinery. This has a much higher density of timber, with more layers than most previous test articles, and more variation in density due to the presence of the interior deck structure omitted in most other tests. The results proved to be counter-intuitive in some regards, but enlightening in general, and provide a much better picture of the actual risks experienced by gundeck crews.

Test parameters

The replicated gun is a type of lightweight siege gun originally developed for the Swedish army around 1620 (Figure 25). It has a shorter barrel and thinner walls than earlier guns of this size, reducing the overall weight by about half. The bore is 146 mm in diameter and 2650 mm long (approximately 17 calibre), firing a solid iron ball varying from 135–142mm in diameter, weighing 9.18–10.57kg. The mean diameter, 139mm, gives a weight of 9.96kg, almost exactly 24 Swedish *skålpund* (pounds). Gunners tables suggest that these types of guns, similar in performance to English drakes of the same period, produced a muzzle velocity in the high subsonic to transonic region (300–350 m/sec). After several proof rounds, we developed two working charges, of 2200g and 2650g, which gave average muzzle velocities of 300 and 360 m/sec, respectively. We also tested charges of 1100g, to simulate impact velocities at longer range without having to move the target so far away that it would be difficult to hit. Range and accuracy results are reported elsewhere (Hocker 2017).

The test article was a copy of a section of the side of *Vasa*, from around the waterline to just above the middle deck, 4.5 metres long, 3.5 metres high and incorporating three deck beams and one gun port (Figure 26). This replicated all parts of the hull structure found in the gundecks. The structure was built in relatively fresh oak, which would represent how *Vasa* first entered service. Crack propagation and splinter behaviour could be expected to change as the hull aged and the wood seasoned and decayed, or as it became wet (Fernández-González 2006: 17.65–17.66), but these variations were not addressed in this test.

The gun and test article were set up on a fully instrumented modern proving range at Bofors Test Center in Karlskoga, in western Sweden. The target was placed 30 metres from the gun, to minimize the chance of missing, and differing ranges were simulated by varying the powder charge. The gun was restrained by conventional breeching, attached to two 1-tonne steel slabs lying on the ground, and typical gun tackles, consisting of a single block mounted on the carriage and a double block mounted on the restraining slab, were attached to each side. The replica side was mounted by burying the foot of the structure in the ground and supporting it with struts (Figure 29). It was essentially unmovable, but numerous tests of smaller and larger weapons have shown that a projectile travelling at such speeds imparts almost no kinetic energy to the target due to inertial differences; bullets do not knock victims down, and cannonballs do not force ships backwards. Our main concern was that the target might fall under its own weight.

Instrumentation included pressure gauges inside the gun to assess breech pressure over time, sound pressure gauges in front of the muzzle and behind the breech to measure noise levels, a Doppler radar to measure velocity of the shot, and a multiple camera high-speed video aimed at both the gun and the target, to measure recoil speed and splinter speed. Penetration and distribution of splinters was not measured with pig carcasses; although they are a good human analogue for many types of tests, they are too variable to provide usable statistical data. Instead, the Defense Research Institute of Sweden (FOI) provided the types of test panels used in modern splinter analysis. These are calibrated panels of sandwich construction, with thin aluminium sheets on the outside, which have similar resistance to penetration as human flesh. They make it possible to measure splinter spread, impact speed and effectiveness consistently. A second panel, of ballistic soap covered with woollen cloth, was intended to test how effective the clothing of the time was as protection against splinters.

A total of 54 test rounds were fired, including three rounds to proof the gun and several rounds for training and demonstration purposes. Twenty-five rounds were fired to test basic ballistic performance, eight rounds were fired to test evaluate workload and rate of fire, and twelve rounds were fired at the ship side to assess effect against ship structure. Other rounds were fired to test evaluate workload the effect of chain shot on sails, and the dispersion of projectiles in case shot.

Ergonomics

Workload

The tests were carried out with a gun crew of eight adult men: a gunner (in command of the gun), a loader, two rammers, a powder monkey, a ball carrier, two haulers. Two rammers were required because the range required the use of a "safety" rammer, which took two men. A rammer of the original type would only have required one man. Many of the jobs can be shared, since the tasks covered occur at different moments in the loading/firing sequence. The haulers can also carry ammunition or ram when required. The only people who must have dedicated, specific roles are the gunner, the loader and the powder monkey, the last because he (or she, as is attested in some historical accounts) must leave the gun between rounds to fetch individual powder charges from the magazine. Powder monkeys are also not members of a single gun crew but may serve several guns at once.

Why then were gun crews typically made up of six to eight men? To a certain degree, there is some allowance for attrition in battle. A gun crew of eight can still serve the gun effectively if two, three or even four men are lost, although rate of fire will decline. Up to a point, adding men and separating tasks also increases rate of fire, but it increases the crowding in the restricted space around the gun and requires carefully choreographed and practiced movements. All members of the gun crew must fit into the space allotted to their gun with enough clearance to allow the gun to recoil, which effectively establishes a maximum gun crew of eight in the space allotted on *Vasa*.

In practice, this gun can be most efficiently served by a gunner, a loader and a dedicated rammer/sponger, assisted by four men who move the gun into or out of battery and assist in aiming it, as well as passing ammunition to the loader. Two movers would work, but they would need to change sides for certain tasks, which introduces too much complication in the choreography.

The gun and carriage weigh approximately 1600 kg. Two men can move the mounted gun over a flat, level surface with difficulty, either by pushing or by hauling on the tackles, but it is not a practical workload for an extended period. Cars of similar weight can be pushed by two people, but the higher friction in the wood-to-wood bearing surfaces of the trucks and axles makes the gun much harder to move and to steer. The greater mechanical efficiency of the tackles, which multiply the effort of human muscle power by a factor of three, is offset by using different muscle groups. Hauling largely uses the muscles of the arms and back, if the hauler is standing on the deck without something to brace his feet against, while pushing uses the much more powerful muscles of the legs. However, once the gun starts moving, it can be managed by two men; a third man with a handspike (a large lever) can get the gun started. In practice, hauling the gun into battery is assisted by gravity, since the crown of the deck means that the gun rolls downhill towards the side of the ship. If one takes advantage of the roll of the ship to help start the gun, two men might be all that is needed in some circumstances. If the gun must be hauled inboard to service it, then it must be hauled uphill, which would certainly require at least four men.

Historical accounts suggest that two men per tackle were common, which increased efficiency and speed. It also meant that one did not have to rely on the roll of the ship, and that the gun could be hauled in as readily as out.

Working environment

It is normally assumed that the muzzle blast of a heavy cannon is deafening, and that after only a few rounds the men in the gundeck would find it hard to hear the commands being given. Long-term hearing damage is also assumed in many accounts, and such damage is a common affliction among the men serving modern artillery pieces. Our tests suggest that this risk may not be as great as assumed, and that the situation is more complex than it may appear.

Sound pressure metres placed in front of the muzzle recorded levels six times higher than at the metre behind the breech, where the gun crew would stand. This is in open air, but on board a ship the difference would be even more dramatic, since the gun crew are screened from the muzzle of their own gun by the side of the ship; the muzzle blast occurs outside, and even the gun port is largely screened by the gun and its carriage. So sound levels inside the ship are probably not nearly as deafening or damaging as is usually assumed. This is not to say that they are insignificant. It is still a very big bang behind the gun, and the concussion of the muzzle blast is felt throughout the body. The noise of gas escaping from the touchhole is probably also significant, especially as this is higher in pitch, and thus more damaging to hearing.

A small amount of smoke is expelled from the touchhole, in a jet, as the gunpowder ignites (Figure 30). This would dissipate inside the ship but might be expected to accumulate in a longer engagement. The muzzle blast includes an immense cloud of dense, white smoke which is initially completely opaque, and would obscure the target, but it dissipates quickly. In our tests, the view of the gun was completely obscured after ignition, but the smoke cleared sufficiently within about 20 seconds to see the gun and its surroundings. Wind speeds were relatively low (less than 5 m/sec) for most of the tests. This suggests that in any weather which allowed two ships to approach each other, smoke would clear before the loading process was complete, so that it was probably not an issue in a single ship action. In a fleet action with many ships firing, the view to leeward would be gradually obscured, and ships towards the leeward end of an engagement might be gradually blinded as a battle developed. This could have the effect of slowing the rate of fire, as gunners waited for a better view of the target.

Recoil

During the proofing stage of the trials, the gun was fired without any breeching or other restraint, in order to evaluate recoil speed and distance. With the "service" charge of 2.65 kg of powder, the gun recoils approximately 7.5 metre on a level surface. With breeching, recoil was limited to just 1.5 metre, enough to bring the muzzle inboard so that the gun could be cleaned and loaded.

Analysis of the high-speed video provides more detail about the recoil behaviour. The gun and carriage accelerate from rest to a maximum speed of 3.4 m/sec (12.24 km/hour) in 0.15 seconds and are brought up short by the breeching within 0.5 seconds. The gun does not decelerate appreciably before the breeching arrests it. Human reaction time, from receipt of stimulus to action, usually expressed as simple reaction time (SRT), varies considerably, but is generally considered to have a lower limit for most people of about 0.2 seconds (Woods et al. 2015). This does not include the time needed for a person to clear the gun once he or she starts to move. It would thus be difficult for a member of a gun crew to step out of the way of a recoiling gun. The gun crew need to be clear before the gun is fired. One of the individuals found on *Vasa*, ("Johan") suffered a crushing injury to his right foot, resulting in the loss of his big toe; this could have been caused by a cannon running over his foot.

Wounding

The results of shot impact varied, with two factors predominating: impact velocity and the location of the strike. One factor has a clear relationship: a ball travelling at higher speed produces smaller splinters travelling at higher speed than a ball travelling at lower speed, a phenomenon noted in the era of broadside gunnery (Gibbon 1863) and confirmed by modern experiment (Kahanov et al. 2012). In fact, the initial velocity of small splinters is slightly higher than the exit speed of the shot; some splinters were measured at transonic velocities. This is because the splinters are not created directly by the shot, but by the pressure wave moving ahead of it through the timber, and the ball slows down as it passes through the timber. In general, thicker timber slows the shot more than thinner timber, but the relationship is not direct. The number of layers in the structure and air gaps create small differences (see Hocker 2017). We did not notice an especially large difference in the size of splinters relative to shot velocity, but slower shot did produce marginally larger splinters.

The location of the strike, and thus the amount of structure through which the shot passes, had more of an effect on the size and distribution of the splinters. A round hitting the thinnest part of the hull (in this case, no more than 0.45 m of oak) creates a parabolic cloud of small splinters, with most of the mass concentrated on the line of flight of the ball and leaves an exit hole on the inside not much larger than the ball (Figure 31). Most of these splinters weigh less than 10 grams. These splinters have a large surface area for their mass and are thus slowed rapidly by air resistance (drag); few of them travelled more than 5 metres from the point of impact. A round striking in thicker structure allows the shock wave to expand outward, spalling off much bigger splinters on the inner surface, in some cases completely shattering knees and standards supporting the deck beams (Figure 30). These splinters can be over a metre long and weigh in excess of 10 kg. Their initial velocity tends to be lower than the shot, but they can still travel at velocities over 200 m/sec, and they may fly farther. Their flight path is less regular, and they spread out over a wider area than smaller splinters from thinner structure.

The penetration of small splinters is poor. Few of them caused penetrating wounds in test panels (Figure 34), although most would have resulted in bruising, and to be hit in the eye would still be crippling. More of a surprise was the effectiveness of wool cloth in stopping small splinters, even those travelling at the speed of sound (Figure 34). A person could be standing less than 0.5 m from such a strike and emerge essentially uninjured if not hit by the cannonball itself. This is like the result achieved by *Mythbusters* and observed in some other tests which did not use accurate replicas of ship structure.

Large splinters are a completely different story. Jagged chunks of oak weighing a kilogram or more cause deep, penetrating wounds and blunt force trauma which can be devastating, if not lethal. Such splinters not only penetrated the test panels deeply in most cases but demolished the test frames and buckled the panels.

What this suggests is that wounds due to cannon fire, even from what would be considered heavy artillery (18-pounders and up), are extremely random in their distribution. While shot velocity determines splinter velocity, splinter size determines how dangerous the splinters are. The paradox is thus that the best defence against heavy cannon is a lightly built ship. Shot will punch clean holes and pass completely through the ship, leaving a trail of small, fast, and largely harmless splinters. In this case, the ball itself poses the greater risk, but occupies so little volume that it would be an unlucky sailor who was struck by one.

The tests also showed that no ship built in the 17th century had thick enough structure to stop a 24-pound cannonball, even one travelling at relatively low velocity. Against lighter guns, thicker structure could provide a useful defence. It was also not possible for an attacking ship to target those areas which would cause the most devastating damage, as they were not readily visible from the outside of the enemy ship, especially at any range, and the accuracy of smoothbore cannon was too poor to hit them reliably. Gunnery thus focused on volume of fire over accuracy, since enough rounds fired at a ship would eventually create enough big splinters to make a difference. A smaller, lightly built ship with practiced gun crews thus stood a chance against a bigger ship in the right circumstances.

Conclusions

Some of the results obtained in the tests confirmed the suspicions of earlier theorists, who could not measure some parameters, such as the velocity of shot or the volume of sound. Other suspicions proved to be less well-founded. Shot placement appears to have a greater effect on the generation of splinters than velocity, at least in a target with highly variable thickness, as was typical in 17th-century ships. The heavy timbers bracing the beams are the source of the most dangerous splinters, while the unreinforced areas between beams, while appearing to offer less protection also offer less risk of large, dangerous splinters. The interior of the gundeck is a loud, dirty place, but not to the degree that it presents a serious hindrance to serving the guns. The crew are effectively shielded from the worst of the noise and most of the smoke generated by artillery, and if there was enough wind to allow a ship to manoeuvre, there was enough wind to clear the smoke in front of the target in about the time it took to load.

For a man or woman serving on the gundeck of a wooden warship in the 17th century, combat was no doubt a terrifying, exhilarating, noisy, smoky, bloody experience fraught with risk. Yet gun crews managed to function in this environment, serving their guns and following the commands of their gunners and officers. The tests of the *Vasa* 24-pounder carried out in 2014 help to explain why this was so, as well as why casualty rates could vary so widely. It also allows us to quantify and study analytically some of the aspects of naval warfare in the age of the broadside, even if we cannot ever understand what it was like to be there.

Acknowledgements

This project was carried out under the leadership of the Friends Association of the Vasa Museum, with major financial support from The Marianne and Marcus Wallenberg Foundation, the Barbra Osher Pro Suecia Foundation, The Fulbright Foundation, Lantz Metall AB, and the National Maritime Museums of Sweden.

Figure 28: A 24-pounder cannon and carriage, as fitted to Vasa in 1628 (photo: Vasa Museum)

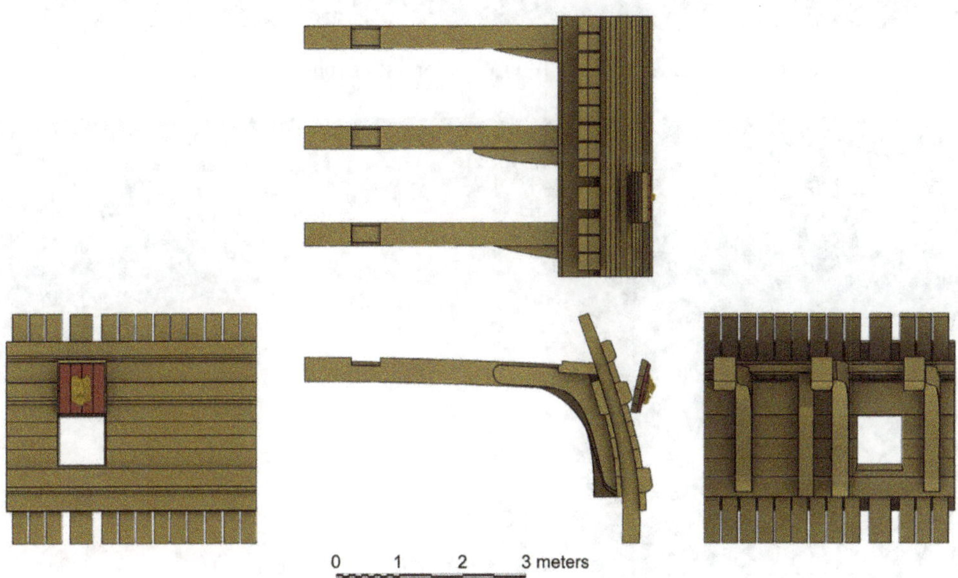

Figure 29: The reconstructed section of ship side used to test penetration and splinter damage (drawing by Fred Hocker)

Figure 30: Ship side target mounted at Bofors Test Center for testing (photo by Sofia Hedenstierna)

Figure 31: Smoke and flame generated at the touch hole by a service charge, approximately 8 m/sec after ignition (photo: Bofors Test Center)

Figure 32: Splinters generated by a strike in the thinnest part of the hull structure; the impact velocity was 350 m/sec, splinters are traveling at an initial velocity of 345 m/sec (photo: Bofors Test Center)

Figure 33: Splinters generated by a strike in an area of heavy reinforcement; the impact velocity was 340 m/sec, splinters are travelling at an initial velocity of up to 180 m/sec (photo: Bofors Test Center)

Figure 34: Test panel showing splinter strikes within 50 cm of the path of the ball, after penetration in the thinnest part of the hull structure (the same round as Figure 32) (photo by Richard Belles)

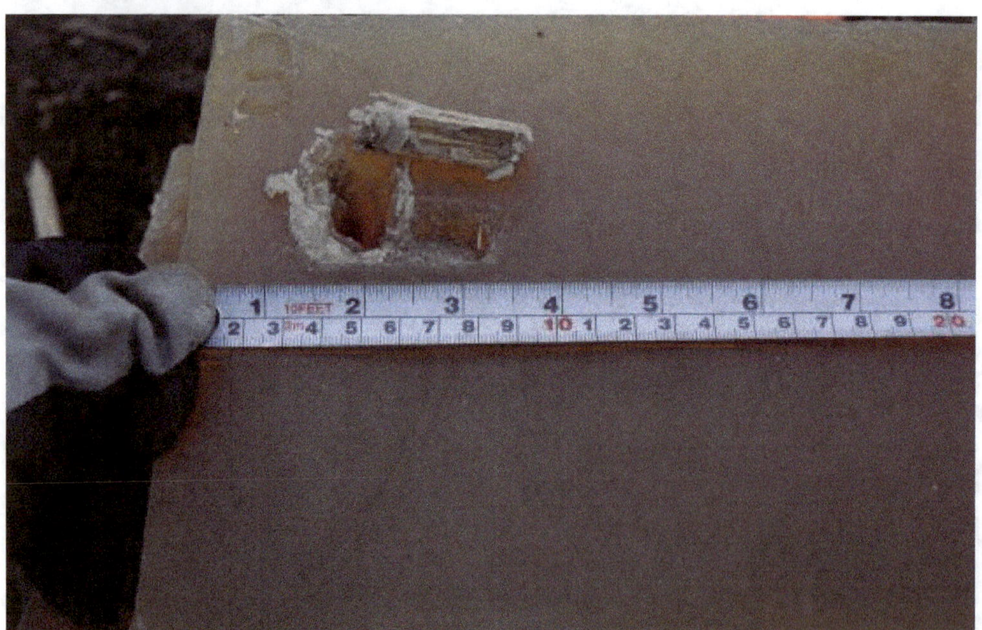

Figure 35: The only splinter which penetrated the woollen cloth over the ballistic soap; the resulting wound would not have reached any vital organs (photo by Sofia Hedenstierna and Richard Belles)

References

Douglas, H., 1860. *A Treatise on Naval Gunnery*, 5th ed. London.

Fox, F., 2009. *The Four Days' Battle of 1666: The Greatest Sea Fight in the Age of Sail.* Barnsley. (Originally published 1996 as A Distant Storm).

Fernández-González, F., 2006. *Ship structures under sail and under gunfire.* In: Technology of the Ships of Trafalgar, 3–5 November 2005. Escuela Técnica Superior de Ingenieros Navales, Universidad Politécnica de Madrid, pp. 17.1–17.146.

Gibbon, J., 1863. The Artillerist's Manual, Compiled from Various Sources, and Adapted to the Service of the United States. New York and London.

Hildred, A., 2011. *Brass guns, in Weapons of Warre: The Armaments of the Mary Rose, Alexzandra Hildred* (ed.), pp. 17–129. Archaeology of the Mary Rose 3. Portsmouth.

Hocker, F., 2017. *Ships, shot and splinters: the effect of 17th-century naval ordnance on ship structure.* In: J. Litwin (ed.), Baltic and beyond: Change and continuity in shipbuilding Gdańsk 2015. Proceedings of the 14th International Symposium on Boat and Ship Archaeology, pp. 221–228. Gdansk.

Kahanov, Y., J. B. Tresman, Y. Me-Bar, D. Cvikel and A. Hillman, 2012. Akko 1 Shipwreck: the effect of cannon fire on the wooden hull. *Journal of Archaeological Science*, 39: 1993–2002.

Lafay, J. J., 1850. Aide-Mémoire d'Artillerie Navale. Paris.

Woods, D. L, J. M. Wyma, E. W. Yund, T. J. Herron and B. Reed, 2015. Factors affecting the latency of Simple Reaction Time. *Frontiers in Human Neuroscience* 9: 131. Published online 2015 Mar 26. doi: 10.3389/fnhum.2015.00131

Lost at Sea
– Complementary Digital Method for Analysing Skeletal Remains in Situ

MATILDA FREDRIKSSON & SABINE STEN

It may be difficult to fully comprehend what it really was like aboard a warship in the 15th and 16th century. Seeing a museum ship like the *Vasa* today, we may first be struck with amazement over its size. However, imagine living aboard such a ship together with several hundred people, one soon realises that it would be quite crowded and far from a pleasant stay. Add to this an ongoing war, and an attempted evacuation during the capsizing of a ship in the middle of a battle and the picture darkens further.

Marine archaeology and osteology may be used to shed light on the lives and health conditions of the crew aboard the sunken ships. The classic approach, at excavations, is to collect the human skeletal remains from the wreck or the sea bed and to analyse them in an osteological laboratory. New technological advances and documentation techniques may, however, allow a new form of marine osteoarchaeology to take form without collecting the skeletal remains from the sea bed. The aim is not to replace classic osteology, but to create an alternative method that may be applied at sites where a non-invasive approach has been chosen, or at sites that are hard to reach and excavate.

The aim of this article is to underline the type of information that is generally possible to retrieve from human skeletal remains found at marine archaeological, and other hard- to- reach, sites through a physical analysis, and ways of using that information to better understand the lives of those men, women, and even children lost at sea. The aim of this article is also to underline the possibilities of performing non-invasive in-situ osteological analysis of skeletal remains at marine archaeological sites by using digital documentation. The method is still in its cradle, and much work is yet to be done.

The classic osteological approach

The classic osteological approach is, as previously stated, to retrieve the skeletal remains from the marine archaeological site in order to analyse them in an osteological laboratory. Retrieving skeletal remains from a site is, however, a far more complicated task than it may appear at first glance. Firstly, there are several legal issues to be handled. Shipwrecks that sank before 1850 in Swedish waters are protected by the cultural heritage act, and special permits are needed in order to perform an archaeological excavation and/or retrieval of artefacts or skeletal remains from the site (KulturMiljölagen SFS 1998:950 RAA 1990. Lag 2013:548; Iregren 2004; www.lansstyrelsen.se). Secondly, there are many factors affecting the possibility of retrieving the skeletal remains from the site, the depth, the position and state of the individual (will the skeletal remains be solid and strong enough to endure handling). Thirdly, there are several ethical issues of retrieving skeletal remains from archaeological sites and the handling of them post excavation (ICOM 2011; White et al. 2012:357; Jennbert 2015:296–298). ICOM (2011) set of rules state that human skeletal remains should only be collected from archaeological sites if they can be kept in safe conditions, and in a respectful way. The ethical discussion concerning reburial/redeposit or storage need to be had before applying for the permits to disrupt a site. The most likely scenario is that the skeletal remains, if retrieved, is considered vital for future research, and that they need to be kept in the name of science in a storage room in a museum, university or other institution, to keep them available for research in the future. It is also important to note that many people see the sea as a last resting place, something that in modern cases, where retrieval of the deceased is not possible, occasionally leads to the decision to protect wreck sites through prohibiting diving and to declare burial/grave peace in the area. This was the chosen procedure in the case with the *M/S Estonia*, a passenger ship that sank in the Baltic Sea in 1994 (Estoniasamlingen.se).

Once the decision and the permission to retrieve skeletal remains from a marine archaeological site are final, precautions need to be taken concerning retrieval method, possible conservation, future storage or reburial of the skeletal remains. The skeletal remains may also be sent for conservation before the osteological analysis is performed.

The classic approach to osteology has been a vital source of information, just as the three following examples, the warships *Vasa*, *Kronan*, and the *Mary Rose*, will illustrate, but perhaps new osteological documentation and analysis methods may be used either in addition or as an alternative method in the future.

The *Vasa*, 1628

The warship *Vasa* sank during her maiden voyage in the Stockholm archipelago August 10th 1628 (During 1996:189; During 1997:135; Kvaal & During 1999:170; Villner 2012:30; the Vasa museum 1), and it is estimated that about 85 to 150 people were aboard the ship at this time. This estimation is based on the amount of personal wooden spoons aboard the ship, and the addition of family members and other guests who had been invited to join the crew for part of the journey. The visitors were to be put ashore in Vaxholm before the ship completed its first journey to the naval base in Älvsnabben, in the Stockholm archipelago (Villner 2012:30) where approximately 300 to 600 soldiers were to board (Kvaal & During 1999:172; the Vasa museum 2). The *Vasa* only had wind in her sails for about 15 minutes before she capsized and took in water through her open gun ports. Most of the people aboard managed to save themselves, but approximately 30 individuals died in the accident, most of who are thought to have been trapped aboard (the Vasa museum 2).

The salvage of the *Vasa* ship was initiated in 1959 and completed in 1960 (The Vasa Museum 1), and a total of 15 individuals were stated to have been lifted from the wreck and the sea bed in the initial phases (During 1996:190–191). Today that number has been estimated to 17 (the Vasa Museum 1). The first osteological analyses were performed by Nils-Gustaf Gejvall who was put in charge of the evaluation of the skeletal remains at the Wasa board's conservation unit in Beckholmen, Stockholm, in 1962 after a formal inquiry to the Swedish National Heritage Board in January the same year (ATA, Vitterhetsakademien, ank. 31.1.1962, Dnr. 001152). Gejvall performed the first osteological analyses in 1963 and continued the analyses on the individuals found outside the wreck in 1967 (During 1996:190–191; Kvaal & During 1999:172), but the results were never published (Kvaal & During 1999:172; Iregren 2003:123). The human skeletal remains that were salvaged from within the ship were, after the analyses, placed in a temporary grave in the sacred grounds at the Galärvarvet cemetery on Djurgården, Stockholm, 10th August, 1963. The skeletal remains had been packed in a very specific manner in order to allow them to be lifted and reanalysed at a later stage (During 1996:190–191; During 1997:139; Kvaal & During 1999:172). The grave was reopened in 1988 when the osteologist Ebba During had been given the task to perform new osteological analyses of the skeletal remains. Unfortunately, the skeletal remains had been partially waterlogged, and the damp conditions in the temporary grave had resulted in heavy mould growth and the breakdown of bone tissue (During 1996:194; Kvaal & During; During 1997:135; 1999:172–173).

The new osteological analyses performed by During showed that many of the individuals had several healed bone fractures (During 1994:67-68, The Vasa Museum 1). Only a few pathological changes were noted, and the three most common changes were enamel hypoplasia, pathological changes of the cervical vertebrae (During 1994:68; During 1997:150), and eburnation (During 1994:73). The enamel hypoplasia can be seen as parallel horizontal lines in the enamel and is connected to malnutrition or illness in childhood affecting the enamel formation process (During 1994:68; During 1997:150). The pathological changes in the cervical vertebrae appear in several different forms among the individuals, including signs of Schmorl's nodes, compressed triangular shaped vertebrae, ossification of the *ligamenta flava*, osteoarthritis, and osteophytes. The underlying reasons for the occurrence of the pathological changes in the cervical vertebrae differ greatly, but to a large extent include inflammation, injuries, and physical strain. Eburnation due to cartilage damage, the polishing of the bone through bone to bone contact, were noted in the hip joint (*acetabulum*) on the coxae and the femoral head in one individual, and on the knee caps in another. During also noted a severe deformation of the metatarsals on one individual (likely a crushed foot), and osteochondritis dissecans (a compression injury between two joints where a small piece of bone or cartilage is sprung loose or formed during the healing process) in both elbows on one individual (During 1994:73; During 1997:150). She also noted some skeletal variations where one individual had spina bifida occulta (During 1994:75; During 1997:150), unfused superior vertebral arches (Free medical dictionary), and sutura metopica persistens, where the frontal cranial suture remains unfused through adulthood (During 1994:75; During 1997:150).

During noted that two women (During 1994:45; During 1997:144; the Vasa Museum 1) and a child were among the deceased (During 1994:50; During 1997:144; the Vasa Museum 1), something that did not come as a big surprise since the ship had not yet been boarded by the approximately 300 to 600 soldiers awaiting her at the naval base in Älvsnabben, and still carried the invited guests during her descent (the Vasa Museum 1; 2).

During estimated that the average stature for the deceased adult individuals were at about 167 cm (160–179 cm) and, therefore, much shorter than we are today (During 1994:51–53; During 1997:44; the Vasa museum 1). The average stature estimated in 2005, was 179.4 cm for men, and 165.5 cm for women (sbc.se). During stated that the low average stature was likely due to malnutrition in childhood (During 1994:51–53; During 1997:44; the Vasa Museum 1). Malnutrition was common during this time, due to the period called the Little Ice Age that occurred in the 1620s, where the cold temperatures and long winters lead to bad harvests and famine (Fagan 2000; the Vasa Museum 1). During's age assessments imply that most individuals were between the ages of 20 and 40 years old, where the youngest was a child younger than eight, and the oldest was a man in his sixties (During 1994:50; During 1997:144; the Vasa Museum 1). Additional DNA studies show that one of the crew members originated from outside of Scandinavia, and that two of the men aboard were brothers (the Vasa Museum 1).

Unfortunately, some errors occurred during the analysis and documentation process, and new osteological and forensic archaeology studies were, therefore, conducted on the human skeletal remains in 2017 and 2018 (conversation with PhD Fred Hocker, January 2018). The previous studies of the human skeletal remains did not take the context into consideration, something that underlined the importance for a contextual analysis to be performed. The new forensic archaeology study, performed in 2017 by Alison Miller Simonds (2017), showed that the original context of the finding could not only be used to identify individuals and rearrange the bone element setup of previously studied individuals, but could together with psychological research be used in order to highlight some of the last moments aboard the ship. Miller Simonds (2017) stated that most individuals are likely to have attempted to escape the sinking ship, but not all. One of the men aboard appears to have been trying to help one of the women to safety. They are stated to have perhaps been related and that the woman was one of the invited guests for the maiden voyage. At least four of the men aboard the ship are stated to have been common sailors, something that Miller Simonds partly based on the fact that at least three of them appear to have attempted to evacuate according to safety routines. One of the individuals, perhaps an officer, is thought to have been either unconscious or paralysed by anxiety due to his position aboard the ship. It is also stated that some of the invited guests aboard the ship may have panicked and searched for shelter in the quarter galleries, instead of heading for an exit. Miller Simonds (2017) states that it is more likely that the individuals drowned rather than died from their injuries, the reason being that the only noted perimortem injury was a broken tibia (Miller Simonds 2017). The osteological analyses have, unfortunately, not been available at this point since the research is still ongoing. However, according to the site formation process and the ocular analysis of the skeletal remains, it has been stated that the reassembly of bone elements correspond to the results from the forensic archaeology study (conversation with PhD Fred Hocker, January 2018). This underlines the importance of reanalysing skeletal remains, especially since new technology and analysis methods are developed.

The *Kronan*, 1676

The warship *Kronan* sank in the battle of Skandia on June 1st, 1676 during a battle in the Baltic Sea, in the Swedish economic zone (Einarsson 2001:140; Villner 2012:31; Kjellström & Hamilton 2014:34). The warship *Kronan* capsized during the repositioning of the ship and exploded before sinking. Approximately 800 of the 850 crew members aboard *Kronan* were lost in the disaster. Approximately 200 of these men are stated to have drifted ashore on the eastern shore of the Swedish island Öland (Villner 2012:31; Kjellström & Hamilton 2014:34), implying that up to 600 individuals may have gone down with the ship. The event is stated to only have taken a couple of minutes (Villner 2012:38–39), something that is likely to explain why so many lives were lost. Approximately 650 kilos of human bones were excavated and retrieved from the wreck site in the late 1990s (Villner 2012:31).

The age assessment of the men aboard *Kronan* show that most of the individuals were around 20 to 35 years of age. There are, however, several younger individuals aboard, consisting of both teenagers and preteenagers between the ages of 9 to 11, and some older men between the ages of 40 to 60 (Villner 2012:33). The osteological analysis also resulted in several stature assessments, indicating that the average stature was 171 cm (156 to 182 cm), something that has been underlined to be more than average for Swedish soldiers even in the 1850s. This has been stated to imply that the individuals aboard may have been well fed through most of their lives (Villner 2012:33).

The first osteological analyses were performed by Ebba During in 1997 on the 500 kilos of human skeletal remains collected up until that point (Kjellström & Hamilton 2014:35). The MNI (Minimum Number of Individuals) estimation based on the human femurs (thigh bones) performed by During in 1997, was set to at least 260. The actual number of individuals at the entire site is, however, likely to be higher than this since another 150 kilos of human skeletal remains were collected in the late 1990s (Kjellström & Hamilton 2014:35). The noted injuries among the crew include shallow cuts, deep cuts, smaller incisions, and cut off pieces of bones. During stated that the vast amount of traces of shallow cuts were connected to sharp force trauma shortly before death (Villner 2012:31; Kjellström & Hamilton 2014), this based on injuries noted on approximately 27 individuals (Villner 2012:38–39).

Ebba During suggested, together with Jan Lindberg, forensic investigator at the Forensic medical institute in Stockholm, that the cuts noted on the skeletal remains from *Kronan* were connected to a situation where the crew panicked and that officers swung their swords around in a desperate attempt to flee the ship. The theory of how these injuries occurred was highly questioned and alternative theories have been presented (Iregren 2003:132). New research implies that the injuries were inflicted post-mortem during salvation attempts of cannons aboard *Kronan*. The salvation crew had, according to this theory, used sharp blades in order to clear debris and similar objects, in order to clear a path through the sunken ship. This argument is based on the fact that the cuts are placed in areas, such as between the tibia and the fibula that would not be exposed to superficial cuts incurred through panicked strikes against your comrades (Kjellström & Hamilton 2014). A behaviour that may also be debunked through the study performed on the human skeletal remains from the *Vasa* ship by Miller Simonds (2017). Considering the conditions aboard the ship, it is, however, highly likely that these injuries may be connected either to falling objects, or to the flying debris and splinters connected to the explosion that resulted in the wrecking of the ship. The explosion theory is highly likely since some individuals who appear to have been positioned behind cannons lacked these superficial cuts on the lower part of their bodies (conversation with PhD Fred Hocker, January 2018). The theory of the injuries being connected to flying debris and splinters have been strengthened by the canon experiments performed by researchers connected to the Vasa Museum and the Friends of the Vasa Museum foundation at the Bofors Test Center, in Karlskoga, in 2014 (Hocker 2017:193–194 and Hocker this publication).

The experiment was conducted through firing cannonballs with a 24-pounder cannon on a partial replica of the hull of the *Vasa* ship to create a better understanding of the ballistics, effect, and ergonomics, connected to the use of cannons in naval battles (Hocker 2017:195). Even though the main objective of the experiment did not focus on injuries inflicted on human bodies by flying debris, it did result in a greater understanding of the formation and force of the splinters. Since the researchers could draw further conclusions concerning impact energy, it also allowed them to draw conclusions regarding the pointed ends of splinters penetrating flesh, breaking bones, or inflicting blunt force trauma. They stated that any individual directly hit by a cannonball would most likely be inflicted with fatal injuries.

They also stated that an individual within the six-metre range of a cannon ball entry, through the knee of the hull, is likely to be hit by large and heavy splinters. These splinters may cause not only severe, but even fatal injuries, including both sharp and blunt trauma (Hocker 2017:198). Flying splinters and debris would also be a factor during an explosion aboard a ship, and this research underlines that standing within the pressure zone of the explosion may put you at huge risk of being fatally injured. This could also, therefore, explain the presence of shallow cuts among *Kronan*'s crew.

The *Mary Rose*, 1545

The warship *Mary Rose* sank in the salty strait of the Solent, in the Atlantic sea on 19th July 1545 (Stirland 2013:66–67). The *Mary Rose* was one of Henry VIII's flagships and it led the English fleet out of the Portsmouth harbour, together with the flagship *Henry Grace a Dieu*, to meet the French fleet in the Solent in England. The winds had been unfavourable the day before, but as the winds changed, they decided to head out to fight. As the *Mary Rose* was trying to turn and position herself, a ghastly wind caught her sails and pushed her starboard side down. She started to take in water through her opened gun ports and shortly began to sink. Approximately 415 men were aboard at the time, and the sinking occurred so fast that only about 30 men managed to get out (Stirland 2013:3-4). Many of them are thought to have been trapped aboard the ship or under the anti-boarding netting that covered the exposed decks (Stirland 2013:66). The English did not only lose the *Mary Rose*, they also suffered a great defeat in the battle against the French (Stirland 2013:3–4).

The *Mary Rose* was rediscovered in 1971 (Bell et al. 2009:167) and was put under the Historic Wreck act in 1973, in order to protect the site. The Mary Rose committee, formed in 1967, realised the importance of the wreck and concluded that the wreck should be fully excavated and recovered for conservation and permanent display (Stirland 2013:9) The first excavation, in 1981, was of the bow of the ship, and both the different floor levels, personal possessions, and archaeological artefacts could be noted (Stirland 2013:9). The ship was eventually salvaged on 11th October, 1982 (Bell et al. 2009:167; Stirland 2013:9). All human skeletal remains were lifted immediately from the site and were put into rinsing baths for desalination before being sent for osteological analyses (Stirland 2013:9).

It has been estimated that about 179 of the 380 individuals that went down with the ship have been retrieved. Many of them only consist of a smaller number of bone elements, whereas 92 individuals have been estimated to make up relatively intact skeletons. The large number of individuals aboard may be used as a guideline for the living conditions, both in the area and aboard a warship (Villner 2012:30).

The osteological analysis implied that most individuals were men in the age span 18 to 30. Other age groups were, however, also represented through both older and younger individuals, ranging from the age of 10 to 40+ (Villner 2012:32; Stirland 2013:81). The stature assessment resulted in an average of 171 cm, just like on *Kronan* (156 to 182 cm) but ranged between 159 and 180 cm (Villner 2012:33; Stirland 2013:82).

One skeletal variation noted among many of the individuals aboard the *Mary Rose* is the unfused acromiale of the scapula. The unfused scapula may be an indicator that a certain type of activity pattern has occurred through childhood into adulthood. The movement pattern that has been regarded as the most likely explanation is the motion and force needed to draw a longbow. The individuals with this skeletal variation have, therefore, been assumed to be the archers that were aboard the ship on their way to battle (Stirland 2013:129).

The osteological analysis also showed that many of the individuals aboard the *Mary Rose* had suffered from malnutrition. Some appeared to have lacked specific nutrients, whereas others appeared to have undergone complete starvation. The skeletal changes could be seen both in the form of rickets, osteomalacia, and scurvy. All these changes are highly connected to vitamin deficiency. In the case of rickets, it may be noted in the bent long bones, and it is caused by severe vitamin D deficiency in early childhood. In the case of osteomalacia, it may be noted in the sternum, ribs, pelvis and the spine. This is commonly also connected to the lack of protein and fat in combination of lack of vitamin D, which results in the demineralisation of the skeleton weakening the bone tissue, allowing it to be compressed when put under a loadbearing stress. Scurvy, on the other hand, occurs during prolonged vitamin C deficiency. This highly affects the immune system of the individuals, exposing them to infections and inflammations, and limiting their odds of being able to fight them. Scurvy mainly affects the body's connective tissue and may result in severe bleeding, and haemorrhaging (Stirland 2013:90–91; Villner 2012:34). In the case of childhood scurvy it may be possible to note ossified haematomas, new bone formation around the shaft of the bones where the bleeding occurred. It may also be possible to see traces of it on the cranium (ex. eye sockets, cribra orbitalia) through an increased and visible porosity (Stirland 2013:94–95). Other notes of malnutrition in childhood could be noted on the teeth on some individuals. This through the presence of enamel hypoplasia, such as aboard the *Vasa* ship, where disruption of the enamel formation occurred due to either long periods of illness or prolonged malnutrition in childhood (Stirland 2013:98).

Considering that the men aboard the *Mary Rose* consisted mainly of soldiers, there have been very few noted fractures: some broken ankles, one strained ankle, a twist and pull fracture of both the tibia and a fibula in one individual (shearing), at least one confirmed fractured nasal bone, some broken sternums, a heel (*calcaneus*) injury, fractured spine injuries, ulna injuries, and a few broken ribs. Notes have also been made of osteoarthritis, eburnation, and a hip injury that could be noted both on the femoral head and in the acetabulum (Villner 2012:34; Stirland 2013:101–106). There are, however, very few injuries that may be clearly connected to battle. Stirland (2013) states that at least 14 head injuries could be noted and that some have been penetrating, whereas others have been gracing or shallow. Most of these injuries are likely to have been inflicted in battle and by several different weapons. One of the individuals is described to have survived being shot with an arrow through his helmet, despite his luck in surviving that attack, he did not survive the day. It is believed that he, just as so many of his comrades, drowned during the sinking of the ship (Villner 2012:34; Stirland 2013:107).

New digital research concerning the human skeletal remains from the *Mary Rose* site is currently being conducted, by the Mary Rose Museum, Oxford University, and Swansea University, through the Virtual Tudors project (The virtual Tudors project).

How can we develop new methods and create new opportunities within marine osteoarchaeology?

With the costs of retrieving and conserving a fully intact wreck from the sea, it is rather unlikely that 'a new Vasa Museum' is likely to emerge any time soon. It is, therefore, unlikely to perform a full excavation and retrieval of a wreck, all its artefacts, and the crew aboard. We can still learn a lot more from the individuals retrieved from the wrecks *Mary Rose*, *Kronan*, and *Vasa*, but there are more human fates to be discovered, and more mysteries to be unravelled. If we are to look further and closer at the wrecks and their crews resting at the bottom of the sea, we will need to find new ways to work with the marine archaeological cultural heritage.

With new advanced documentation equipment and techniques, it may be of interest to explore the possibilities of applying them in a marine archaeological context. Documentation techniques, such as photogrammetry, where an object is documented in situ from all angles and then rendered into a 3D image, are no longer just used for documentation on land sites such as Çatalhöyük, 7500–5700 BC, (Berggren et al. 2015), Turkey, and Sandby borg, 400 AD, (Gunnarsson et al. 2016), Sweden, but also in the maritime archaeology to document shipwrecks, underwater sites, and artefacts on the seabed (Eriksson et al. 2015; Eriksson & Rönnby 2017; SMTM sketchfab). The documentation has in most cases been collected for illustrative purposes, and not as a method for data collection.

The project group 'Skeppet *Mars* 1564', in charge of the marine archaeological research at the naval ship *Mars*, has during the last seven years used digital documentation techniques in order to document and analyse the wreck and the surrounding sea bed (Eriksson et al. 2012; Rönnby et al. 2013; Eriksson et al. 2015; Eriksson & Rönnby 2017). The general idea has been to use non-invasive methods in order to retrieve as much information as possible from the site without disturbing the sediments, artefacts, and the wreck itself. The idea of digital marine osteoarchaeology was born through this approach, and the documentation of the *Mars* site was used in order to test the possibility of using this documentation instead of the physical skeletal remains as a basis for osteological analysis (Fredriksson 2015). Only one human femur (Figure 38) has been located at the site so far, therefore, animal bones found at the site has also been included. Such as bones from cattle (Figures 36, 37 & 38) and pigs (Figures 41, 42 & 43). The results clearly showed that it was possible to retrieve information concerning species, bone element, bone element side, age, trauma, and they also gave an indication of the taphonomic conditions at the site. Further comparative studies were made based on skeletal remains in three different formats: physical skeletal remains (from the Viking Age harbour Birka, Sweden); two-dimensional documentation of skeletal remains (from the naval ships *Mars* and *Gribshunden*, Sweden); and three-dimensional reconstructions of skeletal remains (from Sandby borg, Sweden, and Çatalhöyük, Turkey) (Fredriksson 2017).

The method of using photogrammetry as a source material for digital osteological analysis was tested on documentation from the land based archaeological sites of Çatalhöyük, Turkey, and Sandby borg, Sweden. The analysis results show that the photogrammetry was limited at the available rendering of the 3D reconstructions. The limitation was due to the low-resolution rendering creating smoothening of edges, but still allowed the osteologist to retrieve information concerning species, age, trauma, bone element side, and the taphonomic conditions at the sites. It is also important to underline that the 3D images allowed the osteologist to rotate, zoom in, and adjust the visual angle of the skeletal remains, something that created many opportunities for data collection. Both the two-dimensional documentation and the three-dimensional reconstructions of skeletal remains allowed the osteologist to retrieve information such as species, bone element, age, sex, trauma, and taphonomy. This shows great promise for further development of the method, and it may perhaps also be applied within a forensic context. The method may be applied in a forensic context when an unknown bone element has been discovered, this in order to access if the bone element is human or not, before calling in a full team of forensic divers (Fredriksson 2017:77–79).

The use of the method to identify skeletal remains on the sea bed through digital techniques/photogrammetry is still in its cradle. Both a bachelor thesis and a master thesis have been written at Uppsala University Campus Gotland, focusing on development and application of method for analysing skeletal remains in situ on the seabed (Fredriksson 2015; Fredriksson 2017).

The ethical discussion concerning the retrieval of human skeletal remains from both land sites and marine archaeological sites often occurs (Iregren 2004:265). The question is how we, as osteologists, may handle a situation where we need to perform an osteological analysis of human skeletal remains in a context where the retrieval of the skeleton from the sea bed is out of the question. How can we identify skeletal remains on the sea bed without retrieving the bones? Is it possible to use image material in order to perform a proper and satisfying analysis? These questions are also relevant within forensic science.

There is a big difference between analysing skeletal remains through image material and holding and touching the physical bone element. An analysis of skeletal remains on the sea bed through digital documentation may not be compared to the practical 'hands on' work in an osteological laboratory. Scientific methods such as isotopic analysis, to study the individual's diet, origin etc., are also limited.

In order to, in the future, be able to retrieve as much information as possible about the deceased individuals and their lives, the digital technique and methods may be developed and applied where it is difficult or even impossible to retrieve skeletal remains. The digital methods are not here to replace the physical osteology, but to create new opportunities to study what may otherwise remain hidden down on the seabed.

Acknowledgements

We would like to thank the following people for aiding us in our work: Professor Johan Rönnby at Södertörn University, PhD Alex Hildred and collections curator Simon Ware at the Mary Rose Museum, first curator Leena Drenzel at the Swedish History Museum, Professor Ian Hodder and PhD Scott Haddow at Stanford University, PhD Fred Hocker, Nina Eklöf, and PhD Fredrik Svanberg at the Swedish National Maritime and Transport Museums, PhD Fredrik Gunnarsson at Kalmar county museum, and all the researchers and divers who participated and contributed in the *Mars* project.

Figure 36: A bovine proximal radius (see arrow) documented that the site of the naval ship *Mars*. The results of the osteological analysis of the digital documentation indicates that the individual was older than 12–18 months at the time of death (photo by Daniel Tapia)

Figure 37: A bovine sacrum (see arrow) documented at the site of the naval ship *Mars*. The results of the osteological analysis of the digital documentation indicates that the bone showed signs of possible traces from butchering (photo by Kirill Egorov)

Figure 38: A human femur from the right side of the body documented at the site of the naval ship *Mars*. The results of the osteological analysis of the digital documentation indicates that the femur (see arrow) showed signs of possible sharp force trauma against the knee (the distal part of the femur). The analysis also indicates that the individual was at least 22 years of age at the time of death. ROV-film documentation

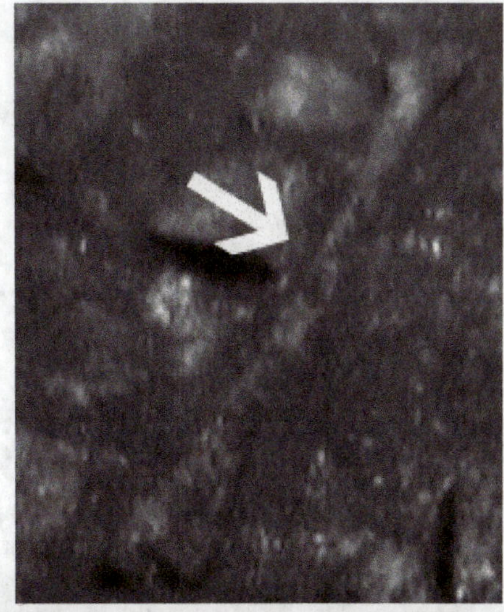

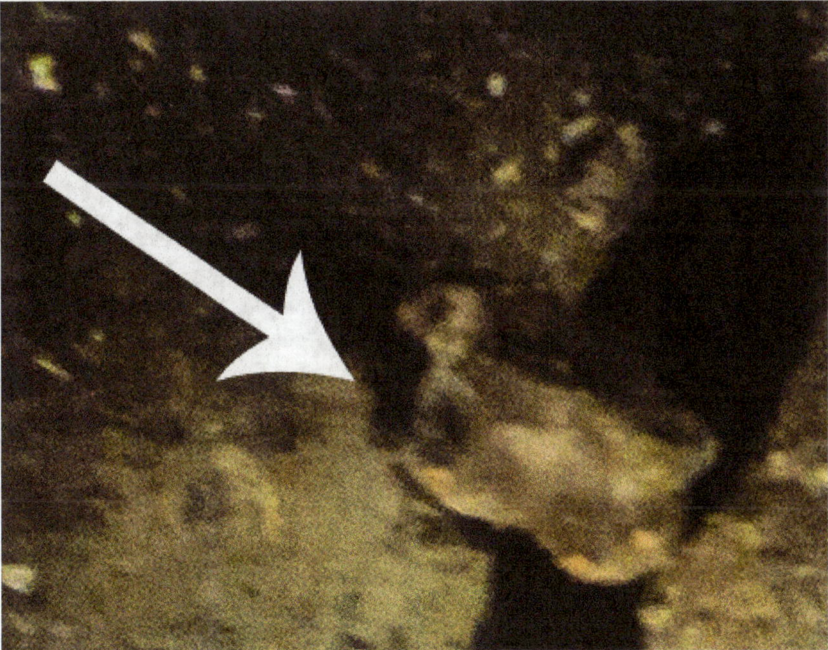

Figure 39: A bovine ankle bone (*talus*, see arrow) documented at the site of the naval ship *Mars*. The results of the osteological analysis of the digital documentation indicates possible signs of trauma connected to the butchering process. Anatomically the bone is placed in the hind legs (photo by Kirill Egorov)

Figure 40: A pig femur (see arrow) from the right side of the body documented at the site of the naval ship *Mars*. The results of the osteological analysis of the digital documentation indicates that the bone had either absorbed foreign substances from the marine sediments, and or, been exposed to fire. The proximal part is missing (photo by Tomaz Stachura)

Figure 41: A pig tibia, distal part, from the right side of the body (see arrow) was documented at the site of the naval ship *Mars*. The results of the osteological analysis of the digital documentation indicates that the individual was at least two years of age at the time of death (photo by Tomaz Stachura)

Figure 42: A hipbone (*coxae*, see arrow) from the right side the body of a pig was documented at the site of the naval ship *Mars* (photo by Tomaz Stachura)

References

ATA. Vitterhetsakademien. Ank. 31.1 1962. Dnr. 001152. Nils-Gustaf Gejvalls anställning i Vasa projektet.

Bell, L., S. Lee-Thorp, J. Elkerton, A., 2009. The sinking of the Mary Rose warship: a medieval mystery solved? Elsevier. Journal of Archaeological Science 36. pp. 166–173.

Berggren, Å. Dell 'Unto, N. Forte, M. Haddow, S. Hodder, I. Issavi, J. Lercari, N. Mazzucato, C. Mickel, A. Taylor, J. S., 2015. Revisiting reflexive archaeology at Çatalhöyük: integrating digital and 3D technologies at the trowel's edge. Antiquity, 89: 433–448.

During, E., 1994. *De dog på Vasa*: skelettfynden och vad de berättar. Vasastudier 16. Stockholm: Vasamuseet.

During, E. 1996., Historien om en osteologisk analys. In: Björklund, A. (red.), 1996. *Mitt i strömmen*: en vänbok tillägnad Lars-Åke Kvarning. Stockholm: Statens sjöhistoriska museer. pp. 189–208.

During, E., 1997. The skeletal remains from the Swedish man-of-war Vasa: a survey. HOMO 48 (2). pp 135–160.

Einarsson, L., 2001. *Kronan*. Kalmar: Kalmar länsmuseum.

Eriksson, N., 2015. Skeppet *Mars* (1564). Fältrapport etapp III 2013. Södertörn arkeologiska rapporter och studier.

Eriksson, N., Höglund, P., Lundgren, I., Lundgren, R., Rönnby, J. (red.), Sjöblom, I., Skog, F., 2012. Skeppet *Mars* (1564). Fältrapport etapp I 2011: Inledande skeppsdokumentation, identifiering av kanon, observerade föremål och avgränsning av vrakplatsen. Södertörn arkeologiska rapporter och studier.

Eriksson, N., Rönnby, J., 2017. *Mars (1564): the initial archaeological investigations of a great 16th-century Swedish warship*. In: The International Journal of Nautical Archaeology. 46.1. 2017:92–107.

Fagan, B. M., 2000, *The Little Ice Age: how climate made history, 1300–1850*, Basic Books, New York, NY, 2000.

Fredriksson, M., 2015. The skeletal remains of the naval ship *Mars*: An osteological pre-study for analysing digitally documented skeletal remains in a marine context. Bachelor's thesis. Uppsala University Campus Gotland. Sweden. https://www.academia.edu/12829552/The_skeletal_remains_of_the_naval_ship_Mars_An_osteological_pre-study_for_analysing_digitally_documented_skeletal_remains_in_a_marine_context.

Fredriksson, M., 2017. Digital marine osteoarchaeology: The problematization of bodies and bones in water. Master's thesis. Uppsala University Campus Gotland. Sweden. *https://www.academia.edu/33576769/Digital_marine_osteoarchaeology_the_problematization_of_bodies_and_bones_in_water*.

Gunnarsson, F., Viktor, H., Nilsson, N., Hallberg, P., Larsson, F., 2016. Det digitala Sandby borg: Årsrapport 2015. Kalmar länsmuseum 2016.

Hocker, F., 2017. Ships, shot and splinters: the effect of 17th-century naval ordnance on ship structure. In: Litwin, J. 2017. Baltic and Beyond: Proceedings of the fourteenth international symposium on boat and ship archaeology. Gdansk 21–25 sept 2015. Change and continuity in shipbuilding. Session: Experimental Nautical Archaeology. ISBSA 14. National Maritime Museum Gdansk. Pp. 193–200.

ICOMs etiska regler. 2 ed. 2011. Stockholm: ICOM. Available at: *http://icomsweden.se/wp-content/uploads/2010/12/etiska-regler_webb-1.pdf*

Iregren, E., 2003. Människor i vraken: en etisk diskussion om marinarkeologi, utställningar och sportdykare. In: *Åländsk odling*. 2003 (1962), pp. 123–139.

Iregren, E., 2004. Human in Wrecks. An ethic discussion on marine archaeology, exhibitions and scuba diving. In: Swedish Archaeologists on Ethics. Ed. Karlsson, H. Bricoleur Press. pp. 265–286.

Jennbert, K., 2015. Kunskapskulturer och etik i arkeologisk utbildning och forskning. In: Iregren, E., Jennbert, K., Etiska perspektiv inom arkeologi. Studenter och lärare i Lund reflekterar över ämnesetiska frågor. Report series. Institute of Archaeology. Lund University. pp. 293–306.

Kjellström, A., Hamilton, M. D., 2014. The taphonomy of maritime warfare: a forensic reinterpretation of sharp force trauma from the 1676 wreck of the Royal Swedish Warship Kronan. In: Martin, D. L., Andersson, C. P., 2014. *Bioarchaeological and forensic perspectives on violence*: How violent death is interpreted from skeletal remains. Cambridge University Press. United Kingdom. pp. 34–50.

Kulturminneslagen SFS 1998:950. RAA 1990. Lag (2013:548). Kulturminneslagen. Skeppsvrak. Underrättelser från riksantikvarieämbetet och Statens historiska museer 1990:1. Stockholm. Available at: *https://www.riksdagen.se/sv/dokument-lagar/doku ment/svensk-forfattningssamling/kulturmiljolag-1988950_sfs-1988-950*

Kvaal, S. I. & During, E. A., 1999. A dental study comparing age assessments of the human remains from the Swedish warship Vasa. In: International Journal of Osteoarchaeology. Vol. 9. Issue 3 May/June. 1999. pp.170–181.

Miller Simonds, A. N., 2017. Who are you? An archaeological examination of the human remains associated with Vasa. Master's thesis. Department of History. East Carolina University.

Stirland, A. J., 2000. *The men of the Mary Rose*: Raising the dead. The History Press. United Kingdom.

Rönnby, J., (red.). Eriksson, N., Holmlund, J., Jonsson, K., Lundgren, I., Lundgren, R., Sjöblom, I., Skog, F., 2013. *Skeppet Mars (1564) Marinarkeologisk fältrapport etapp II 2012*. Södertörn arkeologiska rapporter och studier.

Villner, K. 2012. *Under däck: Mary Rose - Vasa - Kronan*. Stockholm: Medström.

White, T. D., Black, M. T., Folkens, P. A., 2012. Ethics in Osteology. In: White, T. D., Black, M. T., Folkens, P. A., 2012. *Human osteology*. 3rd ed. Amsterdam: Academic Press. pp. 357–378.

Internet sources

Arkeologi och fornlämningar. http://www.lansstyrelsen.se/Stockholm/Sv/samhalls-planering-och-kulturmiljo/arkeologi-och-fornlamningar/guidelagstiftning/ Pages/default.aspx.

Estonia samlingen: http://www.estoniasamlingen.se/content.aspx?idx=2&sub=4&ex=n [2018-01-15].

The Vasa Museum 1. The skeletons: https://www.vasamuseet.se/forskning-samling/ skeletten [2018-02-16].

The Vasa Museum 2. The Accident: https://www.vasamuseet.se/vasas-historia/olyckan [2018-02-16].

Free medical dictionary. Spina bifida occulta: http://medical-dictionary.thefreedic tionary.com/spina+bifida+occulta [2018-02-20].

The virtual Tudors project: http://www.virtualtudors.org/ [2017-12-21]

The Swedish National Maritime Museums (SMTM) sketchfab page: https://sketchfab.com/maritima [2018-02-20]

Statistiska centralbyrån (SCB). Press release 2005-11-07 concerning average weight and stature in Sweden. https://www.scb.se/statistik/LE/LE0101/1980I05/Pressmeddelande%20%20Vikt%20och%20l%C3%A4ngd.pdf [2019-04-15]

Oral sources

Conversation with PhD Fred Hocker, Director of Research at the Vasa Museum, January 2018.

The Consequences of New Warships
– From Medieval to Modern and our Dialectical Relationship with Things

JONATHAN ADAMS & JOHAN RÖNNBY

The general question in this paper concerns human relationships with our things and the ways in which material culture is entangled in societal change.

At the beginning of the Modern period, the design, construction, rig and armament of certain large ships undergo major modifications in connection to a new strategic thinking regarding the role of navies, as well as collective and individual conduct during battle. The building of these new powerful ships was a complex activity demanding considerable material resources and new technologies. This maritime transformation was part of a dynamic period of social upheaval in Europe in which fundamental changes in politics, economics, religion and the arts accelerated the creation of a modern world from the roots of medievalism. The new warships of the 15th and 16th centuries are therefore regarded by us as an unusually good subject to study if one wants to address questions related to material culture, agency and causality in history.

The maritime archaeological and historical cases presented here, therefore all concern early modern state formation, and although they focus on the Baltic Sea area during the period 1480–1570, their relevance is far wider. The new ships, with their guns and large crews, without doubt played a part in the transition to a modern new world that was global and exploitative. Revealing this process then allows new ways to address the much-debated question regarding how material culture is implicated in societal change. We argue then that things can surely have important consequences, but the role and impact of material culture must be understood in relation to specific historically-determined human agency.

Medieval to modern

In the change from the Medieval to the early modern period, some historical events are seen as breakpoints. Such is the case with the fall of the Eastern Roman (Byzantine) Empire in 1453 through the conquest by the Ottomans. Another such event is the Christian recapture of Moorish Spain in 1492 or

Columbus's so-called discovery of America by means of three small carvel ships that same year.

More importantly though, for tracing and defining the transformational processes that create the Modern period are a series of interrelated political, economic, social, religious and cultural changes happening in Europe around the turn of the 15th century. During this time, much of what has been associated with modernity, like globalism, rationality and individualism, slowly begins to become visible. Perhaps the most obvious sign of changing conditions across much of Europe at the end of the Middle Ages concerns power. Historians usually refer to this as the "state formation process". Within the framework of new states, all-powerful monarchs could now more systematically take control of their different countries. This included new systems for power distribution, resource utilization, technological development, taxation and implementation of policy including the use of violence. This last aspect meant setting up new standing armies and navies (e.g. Andersson 1987, Glete 1993, 2000, 2002).

A significant aspect of this change is also one of scale. Power in 14th century Europe was often exercised in geographically segregated and politically more autonomous regions. Through processes of dynastic alliance, smaller polities merged and rationalised military and economic control over much larger areas. Voyages of discovery and conquest further expanded the known world and offered new resources to Europe's new rulers through exploitation and colonialism (see, for example, Wallenstein 1980, 2011).

In this changing world, shipbuilding was an activity that became steadily more important for the maritime and globally ambitious early-modern "princes" during this time (Adams 2013:148, Glete 2000). The young states' abilities to gather resources and know-how opened the way for the building of ships on a bigger scale, to do so more systematically and to manage the whole process with new centrally organised administration. Technically the 1400s are recognised as a transitional period in Northern Europe when it came to ship design and construction. This involved the supplanting of the long-established Nordic clinker method of construction, in which hull planks overlapped and were fastened through the overlap, by a technique that came to be known as 'carvel', a term believed to be derived from the Portuguese ship type 'caravella'.

In carvel construction, the planks were laid flush and fastened to the frame elements and not to each other. Put simply, the technique was developed in the Mediterranean and was adopted in the north. Earlier forms, however, show that a plank-on-frame approach to boat and ship building, albeit achieved through different construction sequences, had been present in Northern Europe for centuries. However, it is the Mediterranean carvel-built ships: caravels and the larger carracks, that were variously seen, captured, bought and then copied or commissioned that were a primary stimulus for the enthusiastic adoption seen in every Northern European maritime nation (for a detailed discussion of the two methods and this transition see Adams 2013).

The rig also changed as larger ships began to be fitted with several masts carrying what came to be known as the 'ship rig' with square-sails on a fore and main mast and a lateen sail on the after mizzen mast. For warships, guns started to be mounted aboard in ever-increasing numbers and sizes during the 15th century along with the structural adaptations such as gun ports necessary to do so (for early modern weapons and warfare see, for example, Hall 1997, Hildred & Rule 1984, Tallet & Trim 2010, Hildred 2011). Keith Muckelroy (1978:3) has argued that ships in general were the most complex and advanced technology created by societies until the industrial revolution, and these great new early modern warships are surely a good example of this.

These new large three or four-masted carvel ships enabled voyaging over greater distances and for greater duration. They carried heavy loads, could carry hundreds of soldiers and were equipped with deadly black powder guns. It is clear, however, from archaeological material that these new, large, carvel-built ships were not just a snap invention in response to a sudden demand from the rulers of the new states. The interrelated technological adaptations that enabled their development had their roots far back in an earlier period. The "invention" of the new ship was more of a process where the ships in general became larger, sturdier and better armed by the end of the Middle Ages. The great warships of the 16th century, known as carracks, came from somewhere (see Unger 1994, Bill 2002:47–56, Adams 2013: chapter 4).

A question then in relation to this is what role ships and seaborne weapons technology played in the general process of transition from medieval to modern time? It is rather obvious that we humans create artefacts, machines and technologies to fulfil different needs and aspirations. But once the "things" exist, as part of the totality of material culture, they will also impact on us and our behaviour. What does it mean for the societal development when some individuals or sectors of society have access to a new powerful tool and ideological instrument? How does that change the agendas of those in control or those attempting to gain control?

As a general question, this concerns how one should understand and describe the relationship between humans and things. So, before we return to the early modern period, we will try to clarify our own perspective and theoretical assumptions regarding this connection.

A materialist perspective?

The relationship between humans and things is of course a central theoretical issue in the discipline of archaeology. A basic starting point for archaeological research, all the way back to the late 19th century, has been that material culture and physical objects can be seen as products and results of different cultural and societal conditions. It has also often been said in various ways that it is not the things themselves that the archaeologist really studies, it is the people behind them (Mortimer Wheeler 1954:v; Johnson 2010, Olsen 2012:7). However, over the years and in different disciplinary contexts, i.e. within archaeology and beyond, the ways to understand and formulate this relationship has varied widely. Things have been seen and explained as the products of nations, race, function, adaptation to nature and evolution, and even as the cultural equivalent of the genetic phenotype (see also Adams & Rönnby 2013:50).

A new research trend within the humanities, known as the "material turn", started to be clearly visible during the mid-1990s. This perspective meant arguing for the importance of material culture and the role of things in relation to humans and society. The discussion is to be found in archaeology (see for example Whitmore 2008:546–562, 2014:1–44, Olsen et al. 2012) but also in several other disciplines (see Knappet & Malafouris 2008, Harvey 2009, Karlholm 2017).

If one just wants to underline the importance of things, there is of course nothing to object to as an archaeologist. The relationship between material culture and humans is, as expressed above, fundamental for the discipline (compare Malmer 1984). The claim for a need for "returning materials to archaeological theory" (Alberti et al. 2013) therefore seems to be strange and unnecessary, but should probably primarily be seen as a counter reaction to the earlier post-structuralist/post-processual focus on meaning and interpretation at the expense of studies actually linked to the archaeological material remains.

Theoretically, this "turn back to things" often have been called *New Materialism*, a name that implies that this is something new in comparison to older forms of materialism, such as positivistic, empirical or historical materialist perspectives. To simplify a little, three things are usually held to be central to the new materialism: a reappraisal of science, a focus on the agency of things and a sort of "flat" symmetrical ontology (see Choat 2017:3).

In terms of the discipline of archaeology specifically, a strong approval of science is maybe something that partially goes against the postmodern, post-processual grain but is otherwise nothing new. A strong link to natural scientific methods and theories has been constant in the field of archaeology since the 19th century and, not least in connection with the processual archaeology of the 1970s and 1980s (see discussion in Johnson 2010:12–50).

Seeing things and material phenomena as agents in themselves and advocating a so-called symmetrical relationship between us and our things can at first sight appear as an attractive and useful perspective for an archaeologist (for a maritime archaeological advocate see Dolwick 2009). To highlight a certain type of ship, as Nordic Viking ships, Hanseatic cogs or Dutch fluyts, or even the physical space aboard, as a historical agent may then provide a suitable and fertile interpretative framework (see Eriksson 2014). Our view, however, is that the question of the nature of the agency of things and its relationship to us humans is a much more complex issue, a subject that also entrains ideological and political aspects which seem to have been neglected in most cases.

We regard "New Materialism" not just as a way to emphasise the significance of things but something which should be understood as part of a larger post-humanist concept. A feature of this concept is to challenge a fundamental premise of the Enlightenment: that the human is a unique subject. On the contrary, human beings are now said not to have a prime position or unique role regarding understanding and interpretation of the world. Nature, animals and things are just as much "starting points" and subjects as humans. The approach has inspired environmental and animal rights activists, as well as various groups of people who have rightly considered that earlier definitions of the human subject have been restricted and characterized by racism, gender and other forms of exclusion. Therefore, in the defence of oppressed groups, posthumanism appears to be something democratic and radical (Hornborg 2017: 106 note 2).

But the claim for self-acting things and the demotion of the human being as an active subject appears to us to be somewhat paradoxical and contradictory. The central concept of "reification", "alienation" and "commodity fetishism" are in fact in Marxist theory, examples of how the social structure and power conditions are masked and mystified by things being animated and attributed to a false meaning and role. This is a part of the capitalist system through which it exerts control and promotes inequality (cf. Hornborg 2017:96). The oppression and suppression of certain categories of people throughout history can instead from this perspective be seen as an example of the unjust reduction of certain humans' possibilities as active subjects (compare also the discussion about "objectification" in Nussbaum 1995).

The reduction of human importance can also be seen as an anti-intellectual and theological perspective, in which people's ability to critically understand the full scope of existence is denied. An interesting example to consider in this context is Bruno Latour's so-called Actor-Network Theory (ANT) (for an introduction often cited in archaeology see Latour 2005). We believe that this perspective should not just be seen as an innocent argument for things as "actants" and symmetry, or for the importance of assembling empirical data, but also as part of a larger mindset rejecting the Enlightenment's belief in reason and possibility of understanding. As Latour himself put it "we have never been modern" (Latour 1993).

If we agreed to this, we would have to accept both the impossibility of critical sociology or explaining our universe. And, probably indicating a hidden personal theological agenda by Bruno Latour, it would exclude the ability to question and scrutinize the logic of religion and the existence of God (Skirbeck 2017 see also discussion in Hornborg 2013, 2017, White 2013, Noys 2016, Choat 2017, McCarthy 2017).

A historical dialectic possibilism

However, the attention to how things and "assemblages of things" influence our history is undoubtedly an important perspective. The notion of how people and things are linked together in "hybrid" social entities is also an interesting and helpful point in the new materialist discussion. As a perspective however, this is hardly anything new in social science. Understanding the material world as social and as part of historical and economically related situations has always been an important subject, not at least for scholars inspired by Marxism (see, for example, Österberg 1977, 1989:81–125).

We also believe that there is no contradiction in acknowledging that things have an important role and yet emphasizing that human agency is of a different nature to that of a rock or a warship. In our opinion, it is not a simple "symmetrical" relationship. It is certainly so that humans and non-humans are jointly part of changing the world, but that does not mean that they do it in the same ways. Historically-determined power relations must be considered if one is to understand the motives, liaisons and the capacities of the different actors. In this context it has been suggested that studies of the state, due to the way it concentrates power, can shed special light on this process (McCarthy 2017:13) as shown in the case studies below.

Regarding the relationship between humans and our things we also consider the dialectical aspect important. As stated before by many archaeologists, material culture is meaningfully constituted (see Hodder 1982, 1986) and once in existence 'acts back' on society. We shape things out of need and aspiration, but once they exist, they change our individual and collective behaviour, i.e. the opportunities they provide for good or ill, and the constraints they impose. The relationship starts to change us and the society we live in. This "entanglement" with things and how this dialectical relationship works and has worked throughout history is a central question for all studies involving humans and material culture (see Hodder 2012, Hodder & Lucas 2017). Compare also the theory of affordances in the Gibsonian sense (see Gibson 1979:29).

Maybe then, objects and the material surroundings are a framework of constraints but also of possibilities. In this historically-determined physical reality, on this "platform" or "stage", people actually "make their own history". Within the discipline of geography, a similar and long-established perspective regarding the role of landscape is known as "possibilism" (Östman 1985). A possibilistic viewpoint combined with an idea of a dialectic relationship between humans and their surroundings is then very similar to the perspective used in historical materialism. What classic Marxist materialism argues in addition to this, however, is also a rather strict and rigid concept of class-struggle as an explanation of change in history. A perspective which could be explained by the structure of Karl Marx's and Friedrich Engels's contemporary late 19th century society.

So, our standpoint regarding "things" is that they surely have important consequences, but that the impact and role of material culture must be understood in relation to specific historically determined human agency. We will now try to demonstrate that in five different examples of archaeological contexts or interpretative "stories". They vary in scale and in scope but all reveal aspects of state building and "the new ship" of the 15th and 16th centuries.

Story 1: "In navi nostra GRIFFONE"

During the Middle Ages, the North German Hanseatic cities were the leading shipbuilders in the Baltic Sea region. The type of ship that is usually associated with them is the cog. A handful of shipwrecks of this type have been found in Northern Europe (see, for example, Adams & Rönnby 2002). Medieval seafaring on the Baltic, however, includes a few other types of ship, reflected very well by several of the 25 vessels revealed in the 1930s when the Medieval harbour in Kalmar was drained (Åkerlund 1951).

A tradition states that the first "modern" carvel ship in the Baltic Sea was built in Gdansk in 1465. This should have happened after a large Western European carvel ship *Peter of La Rochelle* had been left for a long time in the harbour of the German city for repair (Mozejka 2019).The shipbuilders in the town were then able to study the ship's construction in detail and soon started building similar ships. The story is of course a simplification. It may, however, contain an element of truth regarding the approximate time and manner concerning how the "know-how" about the new carvel construction was spread to the Baltic (Adams 2013: 93, Friel 1994:80, 1995).

The end of the Middle Ages is an exciting and turbulent period in Scandinavian history. The Kalmar Union, in which Denmark and Sweden were united, remained a reality until 1523. The kings based in Denmark, however, had for some time considerable trouble in controlling the Swedish part of the area. This region was, for periods at the end of the 1400s, ruled by Swedish noblemen, called "*riksföreståndare*".

In addition to estates and property, these powerful men also owned several larger and smaller ships. Sten Sture the Elder, for example, had his own small fleet which included at least one larger "kravel" (carvel). One source also states that Sten Sture the Younger, in the year 1519, ordered a large ship, named *Stora Svan* from Gdansk. For the wealthiest and powerful noblemen, investing in new large ships was a way to maintain their position and prestige. One example is the powerful Ivar Axelsson-Tott on Gotland who in 1485 had at least one large carvel-built vessel in his private fleet (Glete 1976:46, 1977:33). Even a Swedish bishop like Hans Brask (1448–1536) had his private small fleet. Perhaps one of the most renowned examples from this period is the fearless Danish Admiral Sören Norby. During the period 1524–1526 he had a small private fleet operating from Gotland, attacking Swedes, Danes and Germans alike (Larsson 1986).

However, the first known state-organized naval fleets in the Baltic area were linked to the Danish king Christian I (1426–1481). From 1487 there is an early record of 12 ships belonging to King Hans (also known as Johannes) (1455–1513). Judging by the names of these ships and the number of their crew, one can assume that many of these ships were relatively large carvels. The total number of vessels in the fleet at this time was 29, the others being owned by various noblemen and assembled by the king following the old Medieval system of the "ledung".

The second large ship mentioned in the list from 1487 is *Griffen,* in a later source also called *Gribshunden* (*"The Griffon Hound"*). This ship is also mentioned the year before when king Hans, on the 16th of May 1486, signs a document on board the ship, "in navi nostra GRIFFONE." The list mentions 30 seamen to which should probably be added around 100 soldiers to get the full size of the crew (Sjöblom 2015:38–39).

The late medieval Danish kings' coat of arms (the Oldenburg family) has a painting of a griffon in one of the fields. Maybe the name of the ship the "Griffen" actually refers to that? If so, it can be seen as an example of how the name of the names of the king's largest warships start to change from evoking religious figures and themes to those linked to royal power and its associated symbols (Rönnby 2019). The same trend can be seen in England at the same time where the religious names of the first half of the 15th century give way to dynastic names under Henry Tudor (Adams 2013: 96).

This ship figures again eight years later in written sources. King Hans was at this time on his way to Kalmar to negotiate with Sten Sture the Elder to try to restore the Union and secure the throne of Sweden. The power hungry and aggressive Swedish nobleman Sture had procrastinated for as long as possible but at last it was agreed that a meeting would take place in Kalmar. But in the summer of 1495, when his fleet was halfway from Copenhagen, anchored outside the town of Ronneby in today's southern Sweden, fire breaks out on board *Gribshunden.* The sources say that many noblemen, along with gold, silver and the king's "best fatabur" (meaning his "household") were lost when the great carvel went to the bottom. The king never met Sten Sture that summer, but two years later in 1497 Hans was finally crowned as king also over the Swedish half of the united Nordic kingdom.

It seems that the start of the ship-technology innovations of the late Middle Ages may have an important origin in capital-rich Mediterranean cities such as Genoa and Venice. They had resources as well as a need to create safe and efficient ships for both trade and war. As leading-medieval trading centres with long-distance contacts, the conditions for combining different building traditions were good. For ocean adaptation, shipbuilding on the Iberian Peninsula also seems to have had an especially important role.

A central area for the continued development, spread and construction of the new ships at the beginning of the early modern period also seems to have been the current coast of France, Belgium and the Netherlands. Flanders in particular was one of Northern Europe's major trading centres during the

Middle Ages, and there were several wealthy trading cities here such as Bruges, Ghent and Antwerp. They had already longstanding, close contacts with Mediterranean counterparts, so they had access to both know-how, and not least, financial resources for new shipbuilding. Dendrochronological studies of wood from the wreck of *Griffen/Gribshunden* show that the oak timbers for the building of the ship were cut in this area a little bit upstream of the river Mause valley in 1482/83 (Linderson 2012). The Danish Oldenburg kings had connections in Flanders and it is very likely that the *Griffen* was built somewhere here at the Atlantic coast, very possibly on direct orders of the king Hans or his father (Rönnby 2019).

The wreck of *Griffen* has been found and rests on the seabed in less than 10 metres of water (Rönnby 2015, Eriksson et al. 2019). The dendrochronological analysis of the timbers shows that she was built sometime after the winter of 1482/83. The provenance of the timber is northeast France which may indicate that King Hans bought part of his fleet abroad.

The hull has opened and fallen outwards, and various parts of the ship lie scattered on the bottom. From these remains, and through a systematic analysis of the place, one can study in detail an example of a ship constructed in the 1400s. *Griffen* was around 30 metres long, an unusually big ship for her time. She was also rigged with three masts. The floors running across the keel are made from large grown oak timbers and these, together with the other framing elements, are sandwiched between flush-laid inner and outer oak planking, forming a modern 'carvel' construction. The upper hull both fore and aft was built into 'bow- and stern castles' respectively and, as opposed to other parts of the hull, have been clinker-built or at least lapped (as was *Mary Rose* built in 1510).

Beamshelves and concreted bolts through the side of the hull indicate the level of the main deck where many small, wrought iron guns would have been located as well as in the castles. Systematic use of guns on board ships was a relatively new practice during this time. However, there are sources indicating that the first attempts by Danish kings to use guns on board ship goes back to 1380 (Rosborn 2018, see also Mortenson 2002).

Eleven wrought iron guns have been found on the wreck. They all seem to have been rather small, around 1,5 metres long with the diameter of the barrel around 0,1 metres. The barrels of this type of early gun were formed by a number of iron staves aligned longitudinally, around which a series of rings and collars were fitted. They had separate chambers constructed the same way but thicker to be able to resist the explosive force of the charge. The chamber fitted into the rear of the barrel and had to be wedged into place. The wooden sledges where the barrels were fitted are well preserved.

In 1493, Hans sent some of his ships to England under the command of Chancellor Johan Jepsen for a negotiation. Two ships are known by names from the trip, the *Griffen* and the *Swan* and Anders Bryggere is skipper on the *Griffen*. The armament on one of the ship is mentioned (unclear which of them). 68 guns are listed, but also 10 swords, moulds for casting and 200 lead shots (Barfod 1990: 81, 128, Sjöblom 2015: 39).

The historical account that the king had his household with him 1495 seems to be confirmed by the complex find material on the seabed. Underwater excavation midships has shown how beer, meat and fish were packed in marked barrels. One of the barrels contained a large amount of bones from sturgeon. Other household finds include a tin plate and a wooden beaker with the royal crown engraved in it.

Chain mail as well as parts of crossbows and several bolts give a good impression of the kind of medieval warfare technology which was still in use when *Griffen* sank. A "hand cannon" have also been found on board. This kind of small firearm was held by the soldiers with one arm and also had a simple firing mechanism. It is a very early example of this type of guns. Crossbows and small handheld firearms side by side on the ship clearly show the transition period between the Middle Ages and the modern period (Rönnby 2019).

The historical account that the king had his household with him seems to be confirmed by the complex finds of bones, clothing, barrels and kitchen equipment. Chain mail as well as parts of crossbows and bolts also give a good impression of the kind of medieval warfare technology which still was in use when *Gribshunden* sank. A long beam that served as a central support for the triangular forecastle had a large sculpture of a huge grinning "dragon" devouring a screaming man. This symbolic head was once projected from the bow of the ship in the manner of a figurehead. Contemporary illustrations indicate that this kind of "front figure" seems to have been rather common on big ships. Iconographic parallels connect it to the monstrous images and sculptures that can be seen in late medieval churches and cathedrals, but also on late medieval maps and in books. Paintings and illustrations depicting biblical sea monsters, dragons and fantasy animals such as griffons (Rönnby 2019).

It is easy to imagine how the horrifying image of the bow of the ship worked as a kind of tool for symbolic psychological warfare. In a combat situation, with the high forecastle looming over the waist of an opposing vessel, the enemy crew encountered not only gun shot, arrows and other projectiles but also a slavering monster in the action of swallowing a human being. The clear message that they were next in line must have been obvious to the sailors aboard an enemy ship.

Structurally the ship has much in common with what one can see in the well-known Catalan votive ship model from Mataro, in Spain. Dating from the middle of the 1400s, this model is often depicted when construction of late medieval ships is discussed. *Griffen* is furthermore contemporary with Christopher Columbus' famous ship *Santa Maria* from 1492 (but bigger!). An interesting circumstance in this context is that we know that there were contacts between Denmark and shipbuilding power-holders in the Iberian Peninsula during the mid-15th century. One of Henry the Navigator's captains on an expedition along the African west coast 1448 seems to have been Danish (Landström 1964:170). Some sources also indicate that Danish ships were sailing far to the west and maybe could have crossed the north Atlantic before Columbus' famous expedition (see Møller Jensen 2007, Ullidtz 2017).

Griffen/Gribshunden is the earliest and the best-preserved example so far discovered by this first generation of large northern European carvel-built ships (compare Adams & Rönnby 2013b, Arnold 1978, Cervin de Rubin 1967, Gerout 1989, Grenier 1988, 2007, Keith 1984, 1985, Redknap 1984, Rule 1982, Salisbury 1961). The recovered figurehead of the grinning monster and the other material finds also give us an unparalleled insight into the nature of everyday life on board, the practice of warfare and of the associated symbolism that surrounded one of the new princes who was changing Europe at this time. King Hans carvel-built griffon still partly belongs to the Middle Ages but was on her way to meet the early modern period when she burned and sank at Stora Ekön outside Ronneby.

Story 2: A new state and new fleet

King Hans reigned into the next century but there was to be no stability in Nordic relations. In 1513, Christian II ascended the throne as the struggle between Sweden and Denmark passed to a new generation. King Christian attempted to secure power through wholesale political assassination in an event known as the Stockholm Bloodbath. In short, this left very few of the Swedish nobility alive, but the purge was not complete. Gustav Eriksson Vasa was not present in Stockholm and consequently avoided death. He assumed the mantle of leadership and began a new phase of rebellion in 1521. In the beginning he was very successful but after the initial victories, he realized that he could never ultimately succeed without taking Stockholm and that was impossible without ships to cut the city off from the sea. Lübeck, which had its own interests in opposing the Danish king, was more than willing to help, and therefore allowed Gustav Vasa to buy the vessels he needed. So, in the summer of 1522 a dozen ships arrived from the German city to Stegeborg in the mouth of Slätbacken.

The arrival of this new squadron in Sweden has often been regarded as the birth of the Swedish navy in traditional national history writing. One can assume that most of the new vessels were old merchant ships of varying sizes. However, some of them appear to be modern carvel-built ships. Especially one which is significantly different from the others, namely the *Lybska Swan*. She must have been much larger than the others because she was valued at 7,600 Lübeckian marks, which was two and a half times more than any of the other vessels. Her displacement has been estimated to have been around 750 tons (Glete 1977:37, Glete 2010:349–350, 735). In size this makes her comparable to the Tudor king Henry VIII's warship *Mary Rose* (1510–1545).

Gustav Vasa immediately used his new fleet to blockade Stockholm, cutting the city off from the open sea during the winter of 1523, forcing the city to surrender the following Midsummer. It was in the great cabin on the *Swan* that the Danes signed the surrender documents under the oversight of the newly-crowned Swedish king in June that year. A certain confusion has arisen in historical literature about the fate of *Lybska Swan*, but it is mostly suggested that she was lost the following year in a storm. In order to save his ship and the precious equipment on board, the commander Staffan Sasse, beached the ship on the northern shore of Öland (see Daggfelt 1963).

A shipwreck that is very likely to be the remains of one of the new carvels in Gustav Vasa's new fleet lies between a depth of 30 and 55 metres below a small rocky island in the central Stockholm archipelago (Adams & Rönnby 1996, 2002, 2013b see also Cederlund 1994, 1995). The main mast measures 19 metres, indicating a keel length of around the same. The width can furthermore be estimated to be between 6.5 and 7 metres from the length of the beams. A probable depth of the hold would have been between 3–3.5 metres, according to an English formula used in the latter half of the 16th century (Salisbury 1966). These dimensions indicate a ship of approximately 150–200 tons (compare Ekman 1946: 216 and Glete 2010: 696 who estimates the ship to about 250 tons).

In connection with marine archaeological investigations, a number of chamber-loaded iron guns have been documented, still attached to their wooden sledges with heavy hemp ropes. The larger examples are approximately 3.5 metres in length and give a brutal and powerful impression: early modern power unmasked. Having come to power, Gustav Vasa began almost immediately to build his own ships in the mid-1520s. Holding a permanent and standing fleet now became a significant part of the new state's ambitions. Organizing and financing this would have consequences for the organisation of society at large and how the concept of Sweden as a territory changed.

To be able to build all these new ships, the king established shipyards along the Swedish east coast. Access to good oak trees seems to have been important for the location, but the young and rather insecure state also needed to negotiate the places for building with local landowners and nobility. Sweden, unlike England and other Atlantic states, did not have a long tradition of extensive marine activities. The Swedish medieval towns' seafaring had been limited. Knowledge of the sea and seafaring was based locally and often connected to fishery and archipelago activities.

Until the middle of the century, the shipyard in Stockholm was located at Strömmen, right below the castle and then moved to the current Blaiseholmen. The Master Shipwright who had the main responsibility in Stockholm during the first time was Hans Hake. Master Hake probably hailed from Gdansk which shows the need for the king to collect the necessary skills for building the new fleet from abroad. Jakob Henriksson and Holgerd Olsson were also working in Stockholm as important shipwrights. The latter, also known as Mäster Hollinge, played an import role regarding the early Vasa kings' building of new ships during the second part of the 16th century.

Several of the king's new ships are known by name, *New Holken*, *Kiljen* and *Lilla Kravelen*. The King's new flagship, however, became *Stora Kravelen*, which was completed around 1530. It has been interpreted from documents that she was about 50 metres long and that her main mast was 37 metres high (Ekman 1942). She was probably also relatively wide and has been estimated to have had a displacement of as much as 1800 tons (Glete 2010:683).

Stora Kravelen participated successfully in the battle of Bornholm in 1535 and the siege of Copenhagen in 1536 during international conflicts with Denmark, the so-called *Grevefejden* (1534–1536). From the German enemy, she received the nickname "The Great Cow", possibly an indication that her sailing qualities were not so excellent. Olaus Magnus writes in his description of the Nordic region that the king has a ship that can embark 1000 men, which probably refers to this ship (Ekman 1942a).

The *Grevefejden* were followed by a Swedish civil war, *Dackefejden* (1542–1543) and then the *Russian War* (1555–1557). Archipelago warfare along the Småland coast at this time, outside Viborg and along the river Neva, led Gustav Vasa to also build *galärer* (galleys) according to the Mediterranean concept, not unlike the experimental galleasses and row-barges of Henry VIII of the 1540s (Adams 2013: chapter 4).

During this time, *Stora Kravelen* was not used at all and in 1552 when she was 25 years old, the ship was taken out of service. It is possible that there are still the remains of this ship four metres below the square at the corner of Biblioteksgatan and Birger Jarlsgatan in Stockholm (Hjulhammar 2010). In 1555 a new great ship was built in Stockholm, called the *Elephant*. The building of the ship was initially led by Mäster Jacob Laiko, also known as Finnish Jacob, but was then taken over by Master Hollinger. The ship has been estimated to be the same size as *Vasa* of 1628, approximately 1200 tons (Glete 2010: 683).

After having taken part in a sea battle on 14th–15th August 1564 north of Öland, the *Elephant* sailed towards Kalmar for repairs. But in a hard north-easterly gale, the ship sailed onto a skerry outside Köpingsvik, today called Elefantengrundet. The mainmast cracked and had to be cut away. Heavy objects were thrown overboard which successfully lightened the ship enough to be freed from the rock. The *Elephant* then almost managed to reach her destination, the shipyard at Björkenäs. But here, the temporary seal that had been fitted after the grounding was removed too early. Water began to flow in, and the *Elephant* sank 150 metres from land. A comprehensive salvage operation began immediately afterwards to lift her. Stone cairns were built around the hull and divers were used, "men who could go under water". Despite all the effort in the spring of 1565, the salvage attempts were unsuccessful, and they were forced to leave her on the bottom (see Ekman 1942b, Rönnby & Adams 1994).

Parts of the *Elephant*'s hull were examined during the 1930s in a pioneering marine archaeological operation conducted by naval officer Carl Ekman. Still, much remains of the lower hull of Gustav Vasa's last "kravel" at a depth of six metres at Björkenäs. The frame timbers are heavy and the use of naturally grown pieces for knees and floors as well as the use of long scarf joints in the futtocks show the availability of good quality oak timber, the power and wealth of the crown to procure it and the presence of a work force with the ability to build in the new carvel fashion and on this scale. However, the construction has an idiosyncratic system of "fillets" or backing pieces set along the seams on the inside of the planks (also seen on the warship *Mars*). These are rebated into adjacent futtocks, presumably to retain the caulking medium (Adams 2013:89), indicative of local specialisation in the attempt to adopt and refine a new craft of fundamental importance.

Master Hollinger, who had been involved in building the *Elephant* in Stockholm, built *Sankt Erik* at Björkenäs shipyard in Kalmar in the late 1550s. The ship was, in principle, almost as large as the *Elephant*, possibly with slightly smoother lines because she is mentioned for her good sailing qualities. The ship was completed in 1559 and participated in Prince Erik's courtship expeditions to England attempting to marry Elisabeth I. It was a time of increasingly international dynastic alliances and maritime contacts. However, it seems the English Tudor queen was not so impressed by the Swedish Vasa prince or his resources, and Erik's attempts were fruitless (see Sjöblom 2003, 2009).

Story 3: The matchless warlord?

After *Sankt Erik*, the next mission for Master Hollinger at the shipyard in Kalmar was to build a flagship for Erik, now king Erik XIV. The new ship, which was called *Mars*, was built quickly during 1563. A new war, called the *Nordic Seven-Years' War*, with Denmark and Lubeck had just started, and *Mars* was needed in the fleet. The expanding new Swedish state challenged Denmark and the still powerful old trading Hanseatic town of Lubeck. Ostensibly, the war was caused by political insults; among other thing, the Danes continued to use the Swedish three crowns in their coat of arms. However, the real reason was sea power and thus the control of resources particularly in the Baltic, for example, the right to tax the important trade to towns such as Riga and the shipping of the Gulf of Finland.

The power-hungry king Erik's ambition for Sweden to be the leading Baltic sea power stood in direct competition with his prime rival, the Danish king Fredrik I. He was also increasing and modernizing his fleet (see Barfoot 1995). The Danish king's maritime ambition was also demonstrated in 1561 when he creates the first permanent lighthouses on Kullen, Anholt and Skagen. It was a new attitude to "maritime space" (see below).

In the summer of 1563, *Mars* sailed from Kalmar to Stockholm where she was equipped with guns and was made ready for war. At the beginning of May, the following year, a Swedish fleet of about 35 ships sailed south and met the enemy north of Öland in the central Baltic Sea. *Mars* was the largest ship in the fleet and the admiral on board was the experienced Jakob Bagge (see Sjöblom 2003: 55–61, Wolke & Hårdstedt 2009: 36–47).

The tactical concept during this time was based on partnering a large heavy ship with two smaller, more easily operated vessels. These should protect the bigger Swedish ships from being boarded. *Mars* was also equipped with long beams which could be run out of the gun ports and push an enemy ship away. The distance fighting tactics worked well the first day of the battle and *Mars* managed to sink the Lybeckian ship *Långe Barken* using her heavy artillery.

However, the following day *Mars'* manoeuvres were not so successful. In adverse winds, the ship was left alone long enough for two Lübeckian ships to close in on her. They managed to attach themselves with grapnels and got a large force aboard armed with boarding pikes and incendiary devices. The ship caught fire and in the heavy smoke, Admiral Bagge made the decision to strike the colours and surrender. About 100 Swedes were taken on board the enemy ships, while the burning *Mars* was boarded by between 300 and 400 men of the enemy contingent. But then the fire must have reached the powder magazine and the ship blew up and sank. Around 600–700 soldiers and seaman went down with her (compare Ekman 1939, Glete 2010, Ekman & Unger 1942, Eriksson & Rönnby 2017).

The 16th century was a transitional period in maritime warfare. At the beginning of the century, warships were used as platforms to bring the opposing forces together for hand to hand combat, albeit assisted by ordnance of various sorts. Shipboard guns were by then numerous but relatively small and mounted to fire over the gunwale, waist rail, from the fighting tops and particularly in the fore and after castles. The castles were ingenious in the way that they could be used both in boarding actions, especially where the projecting bow castle could be driven over the waist of the enemy vessel, but also enabled effective defence should the enemy board. The large numbers of guns were mostly intended for use in actions of this sort, being too small to destroy the enemy ships themselves. The largest of these early modern carracks can be seen as floating fortresses, but also more generally as the equivalent to castles on land regarding being important signs and symbols for those in power (Adams 2013:95–96). Their limitations were related to their size and height, creating windage, and to the relatively inefficient rig (compared to what was to come).

However, a progressive change was occurring throughout the century. Naval artillery became steadily more efficient and larger examples began to be placed on ships. Carrying larger guns gave the capability of severely damaging or sometimes sinking an enemy vessel without closing. However, the laws of physics meant that placing guns weighing two to three tons each on a ship in any numbers required rethinking hull design and construction. Placing them low enough in the hull to retain stability meant placing them within the hull. The answer was to fire them though lidded gun ports. To control such an action also required manoeuvrability, and this meant improving the rig, both in terms of the ease and speed with which sails could be adjusted and changed but also cutting sails flatter to work more efficiently, enabling ships to sail closer to the wind.

This was the start of a new form of naval warfare in which the initial phase of an action was stand-off gunnery, although boarding continued to be the way that many ships used in combat throughout the age of sail (see, for example, Kirsch 1990, Rodger 1996). The increased use of guns must also have changed the demands on the men on board during combat. Instead of a situation where "battle rage" in close combat was needed, it now became more important to stay at one's task and cooperate effectively, even in the excessive noise and smoke with splinters flying all around you.

All the seafaring nations of northern Europe developed their fleets along these lines, though at different rates related to specific needs and various cultural factors. Based on a protracted period of experiment, England developed a particularly successful form of galleon, the name given in some places at this time for ships of this general type. The English form was heavily constructed but with good sea-keeping qualities, an efficient rig and it was heavily armed for its size. They also had a lower profile compared to earlier generations of 'high-charged' carrack derivatives. Some scholars attribute the English victory over the generally bigger and more numerous ships of the Spanish Armada in 1588, at least in part, to these qualities although strategy and weather also played their part. What is certain is that these ships were significantly more capable for naval warfare, long-distance trade where security was paramount and for voyages of exploration and colonisation. They are rightly seen as an important breakpoint for the tactical change, although the actions of the Armada demonstrated that the change had already occurred, driven by the likes of Admiral Sir john Hawkins whose personal experience of actions against Spain in the 1460s had convinced him that the days of the 'great ship' of the Henrican period were over. Interestingly, the events outside of Öland in 1564 and especially the success of *Mars* on the first day of battle show that this was also an ongoing process in the Baltic Sea. The outcome of the second day, however, shows that the older way of conducting a battle at sea used by the Danes and the Lübeckians still worked well.

The sinking of this newly built leviathan of the Swedish fleet was a triumph for the allied forces and they were quick to use this for propaganda purposes. Pamphlets describing the victory over the large Swedish ship were soon in print. Already in these sources, the great size of *Mars* is mentioned, and in the diary from the Lübeckian admiral, she is called *Mars Makalös* ("Matchless"). Since then, the size of *Mars* has often been mentioned in different sources.

The Lübeckian chronicler, Die Herren von Hövel, says that the ship was 10 feet longer than the church of St Peter in Lübeck (Eriksson 2019). This has been used by later researchers to argue that *Mars* must have been at least 52 metres long (Ekman 1939: 5, Anderson 1939: 296–299). It is uncertain whether this refers to the distance between the stem and stern post, which later became the common way to define the length of a ship, or if it also includes the beakhead, the counter and the rudder. *Mars* was, however, found in 2012 on the sea floor and from new archaeological information and the position of the main mast, it has been suggested that von Hövels comparison to the church relates to the total length of the ship. Between the posts *Mars* would therefore have been around 45 metres (Eriksson 2019).

An additional confusion in determining how "matchless" *Mars* really was, is the disparity in sources regarding the number of guns carried. In an almost contemporary chronicle, written by Erik Johansson Tegel (1563–1636), it says that the large ship *Mars* carried 125 bronze guns 'and other firearms'. But according to the Danish admiral, Herulf Trolle, in the battle of 1564, *Mars* had 169 bronze guns and four of iron, a total number of 173. Later still, as many as 200 are mentioned by various authors (Eriksson 2019).

The exact number of guns on board however, was found in a document by professor Jan Glete. On this occasion it seems to have been 107. The list of guns is as follows:

> Two hela kartoger (40-pdrs), two tre kvarts kartoger (30-pdrs), two not-slangor (long 20-pdrs), seven halva kartoger (20-pdrs), 10 fältslangor (10-pdrs), four tre kvarts slangor (7-pdrs, 20 halva slangor (3-pdrs), six dubbla falkonetter (2-pdrs) and 50 falkonetter (½-pdrs) of bronze and four stone guns, two of 8, one of 7, and one of 5 tum (Ten of the 50 falkonetter were used aboard *Mars* ship boat) (Glete 2010:634, note 49).

This is impressive fire power for a ship from this period. But many of the guns were evidently rather small and the power of *Mars* can of course not match the 60 guns (48 24-pounders) on *Vasa* (1628) let alone the heavy guns on *Kronan* or on *Svärdet* from 1676. In an action against one of these later warships, the matchless *Mars* would not have had a chance.

Regarding displacement, Jan Glete, using a combination of different sources, suggested that the tonnage of *Mars*, could have been in the order of 1800 tonnes (Glete 2010:358, 679–683). This is rather heavy considering the length mentioned above and the kind of armament which was on board, and professor Glete's calculations have recently been questioned (Eriksson in press). However, even though it is likely that the size of *Mars* has been over-estimated by many there are some circumstances regarding her construction that show she was an extraordinarily large and heavy ship for her period. The first is the presence of two gundecks. The *Elephant* built, 1554, sailing in the same fleet and with a very similar construction and probably just a couple of metres shorter then *Mars*, had just one-gun deck (see Ekman 1942c, Rönnby & Adams 1994: 42-54, Adams 2013). But above the modern carvel hull configured for two gun decks, *Mars* still had high fore and aft castles, similar to the carracks of the first half of the century. The result was an extraordinarily high ship which may have been an attempt to combine the old tactic of closing and boarding, with the new battle tactics of stand-off gunnery.

A ship built in this way, with so much weight above the water line, needs to be rather wide and it also needs to be well ballasted. There are in fact written sources saying that heavy iron was used for this. Divers have also found a surprisingly large number of lead ingots. They are usually interpreted as raw material to melt down for casting shot, but such heavy ingots would also function very well as ballast. Stone ballast may have been judged insufficiently heavy on its own for a ship like *Mars*.

So, in the sense of a hybrid between earlier carrack derivatives and the new galleons to come, maybe king Erik's ambitious Swedish Flagship *Mars* from 1564 truly was a matchless ship?

Story 4: Maritime Space

The landscape is the environmental and cultural space where technology and things such as ships were needed, developed and used. The trajectory of change in shipbuilding can be seen together with a similarly fundamental change in the scale of state, both in terms of geography and power. The Medieval political map of Europe looked much like a patchwork quilt of rela-tively small, volatile administrations. Henry VIII's first wife was Catherine of Aragon, not Catherine of Spain. English forces rampaging through France in the Hundred Years' War could do so not just because of longstanding territorial claims but also because of the lack of a unified opposition. Then during the 16th century, through processes of conquest, political and dynastic alliance, the plethora of Lordships and Dukedoms predominant in 14th and 15th century Europe steadily resolved into the larger power blocks that anticipated today's nation states. These much-enlarged emergent states soon started to compete on an international stage and that meant by sea as well as on land.

A greater scale brought with it a fundamental reality: the larger geographic regions all had coastlines, and this meant that competition between them, i.e. competition that looked outwards rather than inwards would of necessity be maritime. It was a change in the ways maritime space was experienced and understood. This too involved scale: everything from fishing, to global exploration, warfare, trade and colonial enterprise. This is manifested in the ways geographic space was conceptualised, used and represented.

There are also indications that this conception of maritime space was also applied differently in different places. An interesting contrast here is the situation of the Baltic surrounded by competing emergent states, including Sweden, whereas England was part of an island group. In the 'new country' of the early Vasas they tried to encircle a sea through military expansion as well as naval development. On the island of Tudor England, it worked the other way round. Security and prosperity were linked to an outward looking aspiration for maritime control. Indeed, it may be that this historically-based outward-facing maritime stance was a factor in England's rise from a secondary medieval power to one of post-medieval, global dominance achieved and maintained through sea power.

Perhaps one of the most revealing illustrations of the changing percep-tions of the maritime world in Europe are the *mappae mundi* and *portolan* charts, since they provide a time line from the thirteenth to the 16th century during which knowledge of the world was expanded principally by the sea. The *mappae*, though appearing to be crude maps, are ways of representing cultural, historical and religious relationships of the world in the contexts of contemporary, Christian and Classical centres of importance (Harvey 2006). In contrast the *portolans* represent geographic space and practical interests in navigation. In both forms we see the progressive additions of newly discovered lands until the mid-15th century, where it is the *portolan* and its descendent charts that indicate the ascendancy of Renaissance, humanist thinking and the political and economic importance of distance and direction between the old and new worlds.

In almost every theatre of maritime activity whether commerce, industry or naval endeavours, voyage distance and duration were increasing. Such voyaging necessitated increased specialism in crews and thus heightened the sense of identity and of being different from those ashore. It also both demanded and promoted an increasingly professional class of vocational seafarers linked to a growing community in the rapidly expanding dockyards as well as the necessary administrative structures. Beyond the port towns, those interfaces between the familiar and the exotic unknown, New Worlds revealed by transatlantic voyaging, circumnavigation and first contact, conferred the sort of esoteric knowledge discussed by Helms (1988), not just for commanders and masters but for every member of the crew.

All this is also linked to the new ships' possibilities and during the period necessitated new changes in vessel configuration, not necessarily size (though ships in general became larger) but in the space organized as work areas, cargo stowage and accommodation. For voyages of a few days and less, especially in the undecked vessels of the High Medieval period, accommodation was not differentiated with significant internal structure. But as voyage length got longer, extending to weeks or months in the case of transatlantic fishing and whaling, capacity and accommodation became factors reflected in the sea-keeping design and construction of the hull as well as with the partitioning by which internal space was organized.

Maritime space was being understood in new ways and space aboard ship was being reconfigured in response. There is a parallel here between the organisation of space on board ship with similar changes in medieval houses identified by Johnson (1993). Over the course of the period under discussion, both in the house and on board ships, space is increasingly sub-divided partly for function and role but also to address notions of identity, status and privacy: cabins for a navigator, a barber-surgeon or a carpenter aboard the *Mary Rose*; parlours and bedrooms in the medieval house.

Specialization in the practice of seafaring brought with it an increasing specialization of the material culture aboard, everything from clothing, adornment, style and decoration, which together with idiosyncratic vocabulary, all heightened a sense of belonging to a maritime community, the two being mutually reinforcing. At the beginning of the period, things carried aboard that were exclusively maritime were relatively few, navigation instruments for example. Even at the time the *Mary Rose* sank, many of the objects used aboard for the sailing of the ship or carried by the crew as personal possessions, including their clothes, were the same as they would have used ashore. Of those objects specific to tasks on board, many were made by or for the person concerned. Gun Captains on the *Mary Rose* for example may have made their own linstocks, the swagger stick-like holder for the slow match used to touch off the gun. Individually carved and decorated with appropriate symbolism, for example a dragon's head, they were both functional and a badge of office specific to the owner.

But by the end of this period we are on the way to a maritime world in which much more of what is worn, carried and used aboard is not only specifically maritime in design, function and nomenclature but, particularly in naval vessels, institutional rather than individual.

Story 5: The hold of Neptune

Some interesting manifestations of the relationship between spatial organization and professional specialization in the early modern context can be drawn from the Swedish warship *Neptunus* (*Neptune*) built in 1566 in Västervik (Rönnby & Sjöblom). *Neptunus* was built directly after the sinking of *Mars* and was the royal fleet's largest warship. The king's order was to build a slightly longer ship than *Mars* but with a more curved hull compared to the old flag ship. Maybe an adjustment to gundecks and an attempt to gain better sailing performance and capacity? (Rönnby & Sjöblom 2016).

The space below deck must have been rather crowded with guns and equipment for warfare praxis. However, a big ship like this was also a complex society with a crew of up to 1000 people, which in fact was larger than most Swedish cities at that time. Everyone had to eat, sleep and fulfil their tasks, which required similarly complex logistics and organization.

From the investigations of the warship *Mars*, we know that the *Neptunus* "byssa" (the galley), was probably located far down the ship in front of the main mast, probably set into the "trossdäck" (orlop deck) in the manner seen on *Vasa* (1628). Here, in this relatively small space built up with bricks, one could contain fires sufficient for preparing food in many different ways for the various groups of people aboard. The smoke found its way up through gratings in the decks above. In connection to the galley there was also a large wood store and several tonnes of meat and fish packed in barrels (regarding food on board, compare Spens 1942, Söderlind 2004, Dobbs 2009).

All these aspects of the ship's operation and daily life had to be placed under various occupational and professional specialists for the ship to run smoothly. However, the responsibilities of some of these tasks might not seem to us particularly logical. An example of this has been found in written documents by the historian Ingvar Sjöblom and concerns the activities of a person aboard the *Neptunus* called "eldkarlen" ("The fireman"). His place seems to have been deep down in the ship around the kitchen area. We know of his various duties from an inventory list from 1570. As "fireman" he was obviously in charge of the safe management of the galley fires and prevention of accidental fire in general, but he also had several other areas of responsibility that at first sight seem rather incongruous. First, the list takes up things about cooking that one might assume to be under the charge of a head cook: two iron frying pans, two copper cauldrons, six gridirons and one large grill skewer. The list then mentions something called the "fångbult" ("the jail") and 15 manacles. Life on board was strictly regulated and there were severe punishments for what today would seem minor transgressions. An illustrative example is the navy regulations from 1571 concerning food which stated that those who spilt their beer or wasted bread "shamelessly" could be sentenced to be dragged under the keel three times or be put in the "fångbult" for three days.

However, as well as also being the jailer, the inventory shows that the fireman's area of responsibility was still more extensive. It mentions various tools including crowbars, augers and hammers, etc., as well as rolls of lead sheeting, buckets, and animal skins. This was equipment to extinguish fires, repair holes in the hull and to fix the ship's pump.

One can from this see the "fireman" as a sort of under officer whose responsibility on board clearly encompassed cooking, imprisonment, leak repair and maintenance of the all-important pumps located down in *Neptunus'* hold. In other words, his responsibilities were determined by the organisation of space within the ship rather than by what might have been more logical combinations of responsibility. This space in the hold was apparently the fireman's domain and he was responsible for everything in this part of the ship. The large new ships, like the new contemporary early state they served, needed to be organized and systematized (see Sjöblom 2016). In this way, the careful but still rather haphazard organization of professional responsibility for the "eldkarlen" deep down in the ship's hull corresponds with wider processes of social development during the 16th century.

Discussion

Depending on the perspective, one can highlight different causes and driving forces for the change from Medieval to Modern. One way is to argue is that the concepts underlying Renaissance thinking meant, new approaches regarding art, literature, architecture and science, but also resulted in new ideas about the organization of society. The Reformation also undermined the ideologically and economically powerful Catholic Church which had had a conservative influence on the earlier Medieval society. From this viewpoint, it is a new ideological concept that explains the change.

Another, well-argued way to explain the driving forces behind innovation is to see it as a new form of economic exploitation. The Medieval feudal system with is material preconditions was breaking down and a new system built around a monetary economy and the commodification of labour was taking place (Platt 1996). A classic study arguing for such a perspective is Perry Andersson's "The development of the absolute state" (1987). This way of describing the reason for the change has an advantage because it integrates explanation of all aspects of the transformation, i.e., the economic, ideological and social together. An expansion of this perspective is also the so called "World System Theory" describing the way in which the new capitalistic economy became global during the 16th century specifically, shaping both core and periphery, long distance trade with commodities and accumulation of wealth in Europe (Wallerstein 1980, 2011).

In the case of State formation, many historians have also pointed to the role of war in this change, the transformation process sometimes being referred to as the 'Military Revolution' (Glete 2000:9-16, Rogers 1995). In the European power struggle, vital components were the new standing armies and then in response to an increasingly maritime world, standing navies. This of course required a new systematic organization of both resources and people.

Different general theories and perspectives such as the ones above are of course both illustrative and important. However, general theories should not be confused with reality, for they necessarily lack details and cannot cover all the various aspects that together drove the change from the Medieval to the Modern state. We therefore believe that overall explanation should be complemented with investigations of different fields and material. Doing this gives us a chance to better understand how the process of societal change really works (see also Adams 2013).

A possible way to do that within the discipline of archaeology is to examine material culture and the historical human agents' dialectical interaction with these things. There are of course several interesting examples of material culture from the early modern period which then can be discussed. A classic case is the new physical medium for printing – the printing press. It enabled the spread of new ideas and plays an important part in both processes of Renaissance and Reformation. Other important physical materials were of course gold and silver from America but also commodities like sugar or spices such as nutmeg. The demand and the enormous efforts made to procure exotic products and commodities like these had a surprisingly great impact on European society (Milton 2001, Nordin 2010:47–70).

As is evident by now, the authors of this paper obviously also believe that the development and existence of new ships and tools for naval warfare is another field which is of great importance for our understanding of the early modern period. The physical ships enable new discoveries and they play a crucial role in the late Medieval game of power. They are big expensive investments, requiring specialist building knowledge, theoretical calculations and an advanced organization to be created in order to manage and use them effectively. These circumstances diminished the number of possible national competitors to the new state builders and accelerated the state formation process. But the need for ships, guns and fleets was also driven by other states and rulers with similar ambitions. This created an ongoing need to construct better, stronger and more powerful ships before the enemy did. Moreover, the changing conditions on board the new ships and the need to handle the crews and the equipment demanded new ways of organisation and ideological motivations.

This *societal material entanglement* with the new warships is clearly visible in the Baltic examples discussed above. During the 15th century, the king's ships and fleets were challenged by various noblemen, warlords and bishops still powerful and wealthy enough to have their own carvel-built warships and even small fleets. Building larger ships, both as power symbols and as superior war machines, became important for kings such as Christian I, Hans and Christian II to match their ambition for a strong Nordic kingdom. When the Swedish nobleman Gustav Vasa started his uprising in the 1520s, he had to borrow resources from Lubeck to be able get the necessary ships to match the Danish kings. During the second half of the 16th and early 17th century, the intensive efforts of the new Vasa dynasty to build a powerful modern fleet has far-reaching effects on the entire society in terms of resource exploration and organization.

The *New ship* was in many respects, a materialization of the new early modern period. They are part of a new societal structure and the European princes' need for overseas trade, demonstration of power and not least, warfare. The increased naval professional segregation and the specialized material culture this led to also went hand in hand with a growing importance of maritime affairs to society at large.

The consequences that the developments within the maritime sphere had for the society, and the human dialectical entanglement with the new carvel warships, is therefore an important part of the change from Medieval to Modern.

Figure 43: Ship with a dog-like monster on the bow from a description of a pilgrimage to Jerusalem by Conrad Grünenberg in 1486. https://www.flickr.com/photos/bibliodyssey/3993238058/sizes/o/

Figure 44: The figurehead of *Gribshunden* (1496) being salvaged in 2015. The monstrous figure would have been positioned beneath forecastle of the ship (photo by Ingemar Lundgren)

Figure 45: Guns visible at wreck site *Mars* 1564 (photo by Ingemar Lundgren, Ocean Discovery)

Figure 46: French ship with a prominent "monster" on the bow. From a translation of the Eneiden by Octavien de Saint-Gelais in 1500. The wood that the *Griffens/Gribshund* is built from comes from the north side of the Ardennes and it is possible that the ship was also built on the coast nearby. L'Énéide, traduction d'«OCTOVIAN DE SAINT GELAIS », précédée d'une Épître à Louis XII. https://gallica.bnf.fr/ark:/12148/ btv1b8470048t/f13.image.r=fr%20861

Figure 47: The Arrival of the Pilgrims in Cologne 1490 by Vittoria Carpaccio. At the same time as the new carvel ships made the world larger the use of the central perspective in paintings also gave the pictures an almost global perspective

References

Adams, J., 2013. *A Maritime Archaeology of Ships. Innovation and social change in medieval and early modern Europe.* Oxford: Oxbow Books.

Adams, J. & Rönnby, J., 1996. *Furstens fartyg: marinarkeologiska undersökningar av en renässanskravell.* Stockholm: Sjöhistoriska museet.

Adams, J. & Rönnby, J., 2002. Kuggmaren 1: the first cog find in the Stockholm archipelago, Sweden. The International Journal of Nautical Archeaology. 31.2.

Adams, J. & Rönnby, J. (ed.), 2013a. *Interpreting shipwrecks: maritime archaeological approaches.* Southampton: Highfield.

Adams, J. & Rönnby, J., 2013b. One of His Majesty's 'BesteKraffwells': the wreck of an early carvel-built ship at Franska stenarna, Sweden, In: *The International Journal of Nautical Archaeology*, Vol. 42.1, Sid. 103–117.

Alberti, B., Jones, A. & Pollard, J. (ed.), 2013. *Archaeology after interpretation: returning materials to archaeological theory.* Walnut Creek, Ca: Left Coast Press Inc.

Anderson, P., 1987. *Den absoluta statens utveckling.* 3. uppl. Lund: A/Z förlag.

Anderson, R. C., 1939. The *Mars* and the *Adler. Mariner's Mirror*, 25:3 (1939), 296–9 doi: 10.1080/00253359.1939.10657346

Arnold, J. B. III & Weddle, R., 1978. The Nautical Archaeology of Padre Island, the Spanish Shipwrecks of 1514. New York.

Barfod, J. H., 1990. Flådens fødsel – Den danske flådes historie – 1533. Marinehistorisk Selbskabs Skrift nr 22. København: Marinehistorisk Selskab.

Barfod, J. H., 1995. Christian 3.s flåde – Den danske flådes historie 1533–1588. Marinehistorisk Selbskabs Skrift nr 25. København: Marinehistorisk Selskab.

Bill, J., 2002. Castles at sea – The warship of the High Middle Ages. In: Nørgård Jørgensen, Anne (ed.) *Maritime warfare in northern Europe: technology, organisation, logistics and administration 500 BC–1500 AD: papers from an international research seminar at the Danish National Museum, Copenhagen, 3–5 May 2000.* Copenhagen: National Museum.

Brown, A., 1988. *The Renaissance.* London: Longman.

Braudel, F., 1981. *Civilization and Capitalism 15th–18th Century, Vol. 1 The Structures of Everyday Life.* Berkley, Los Angeles: University of California Press.

Burwash, D., 1969. *English Merchant Shipping: 1460–1540.* Newton Abbot: David & Charles.

Choat, S., 2017. Science, Agency and Ontology: A Historical-Materialist Response to New Materialism. *Political Studies.* Vol 66, Issue 4, pp. 1027–1042. https://doi.org/10.1177/0032321717731926

Cederlund, C. O., 1994. The Royal Ships and Divine Kingdom. *Current Swedish Archaeology* 2: 47–85.

Cederlund, C. O., 1995. Svanen Som Blev en Anka. Vrakidentifiering och marknadsföring av nationella myter. *Tvärnsitt*, 1. Swedish Science Press. Uppsala.

Cervin de, Rubin, G. B., 1967. The Catalan Ship, in Jobé, J. (ed.), *The Great Age of Sail*: 19–33. Cambridge.

Cohen, G. A., 1978. *Karl Marx's theory of history: a defence.* Princeton, N. J.: Princeton U.P.

Daggfeldt, B., 1963. Lybska Svan. *Tidskrift I Sjöväsendet* 1963: 3–27.

Dolwick, J. S. The "Social" and Beyond: Introducing Actor-Network Theory. In: *Journal of Maritime Archaeology* 4(1): 21–49. DOI: 10.1007/s11457-009-9044-3

Dobbs, C., 2009. The Galley. In P. Marsden (ed.), *Mary Rose: Your Noblest Shippe. Anatomy of a Tudor Warship*: 124–135. Portsmouth: Mary Rose Trust.

Einarsson, L., 2008. In navi nostra Griffone- Griffen i djupet. I: *Gränsland. Blekingeboken Årg 86. Karlskrona: Blekinge hembygdsförbunds förlag.*

Ekman, C., 1939. The Swedish Ship Mars or Makalös, *The Mariner's Mirror*, 25.1, pp. 5–10.

Ekman, C., 1942a. Stora Kraveln. Lybeck, O. (red.). *Svenska flottans historia: örlogsflottan i ord och bild från dess grundläggning under Gustav Vasa fram till våra dagar. Bd 1, [1521–1679].* Malmö: Allhem.

Ekman, C., 1942b. Svenska Flottans sjötåg fram till Kalmarkriget. Lybeck, O. (red.) *Svenska flottans historia: örlogsflottan i ord och bild från dess grundläggning under Gustav Vasa fram till våra dagar. Bd 1, [1521–1679].* Malmö: Allhem.

Ekman, C., 1942c. Stora kraveln Elefanten. Lybeck, O. (red.) *Svenska flottans historia: örlogs-flottan i ord och bild från dess grundläggning under Gustav Vasa fram till våra dagar. Bd 1, [1521–1679].* Malmö: Allhem.

Ekman, C., 1946. Skeppstyperna under Gustav Vasas och Erik XIV:s tid. *Sjöhistorisk årsbok.*

Ekman, C. and Unger, G., 1942. Svenska flottans sjötåg fram till Kalmarkriget. Lybeck, O. (red.) *Svenska flottans historia: örlogsflottan i ord och bild från dess grundläggning under Gustav Vasa fram till våra dagar. Bd 1, [1521-1679].* Malmö: Allhem.

Ericson Wolke, L. & Hårdstedt, M., 2009. *Svenska sjöslag.* Stockholm: Medström.

Eriksson, N., 2014. Urbanism under sail: an archaeology of fluit ships in early modern everyday life. Diss. Huddinge: Södertörns högskola. Internet: http://urn.kb.se/resolve?urn=urn:nbn:se:sh:diva-24415.

Eriksson, N., 2015. Skeppet Mars (1564). Fältrapport etapp III 2013. *Södertörn arkeologiska rapporter och studier.* Södertörns högskola.

Eriksson, N., 2019. How Large Was *Mars*? An investigation of the dimensions of a legendary Swedish warship, 1563–1564 The Mariner's Mirror. Vol. 105 (2019), Issue 3.

Eriksson, N. & Rönnby, J., 2017. *Mars* (1564): the initial archaeological investigations of a great 16th-century Swedish warship. In: *The International Journal of Nautical Archaeology.* 46.1. 2017: 92–107.

Eriksson, N., Irskog, S., Persson, T., Rönnby, J., Sandekjer & M., Sjöblom, I., 2019. *Gribshunden*: medeltidens modernaste skepp., *Blekingeboken.* 2019 (97). Karlskrona.

Friel, I., 1994. The Carrack: The Advent of the Full Rigged Ship. 1994, in: Unger, R., (ed.). *Cogs, Caravels and Galleons. p 77 - 90.* London: Conway Maritime Press.

Friel, I., 1995. *The Good Ship: Ships, Shipbuilding and Technology in England* 1200–1520. London.

Gerout, M., Reith, E., & J. M. Gassend, 1989. Le Navire Génois de Villefranche un naufrage de 1516? *Archaeonautica*, 9. CNRS. Paris.

Gibson, J. J., 1979. *The Ecological Approach to Visual Perception.* Boston: Houghton Mifflin.

Glete, J., 1976. Svenska örlogsfartyg 1521–1560. Flottans uppbyggnad under ett tekniskt brytningsskede. *Forum Navale. Skrifter utgivna av Sjöhistoriska Samfunde,* Nr 30.

Glete, J., 1977. Svenska örlogsfartyg 1521–1560. Flottans uppbyggnad under ett tekniskt brytningsskede. *Forum Navale. Skrifter utgivna av Sjöhistoriska Samfundet* Nr 31.

Glete, J., 1993. *Navies and nations: warships, navies and state building in Europe and America, 1500–1860.* Stockholm: Almqvist & Wiksell International.

Glete, J., 2000. *Warfare at sea: 1500–1650: maritime conflicts and the transformation of Europe.* London: Routledge.

Glete, J., 2002. *War and the state in early modern Europe: Spain, the Dutch Republic and Sweden as fiscal-military states, 1500–1600.* London: Routledge.

Glete, J., 2010. *Swedish naval administration, 1521–1721: resource flows and organizational capabilities.* Leiden: Brill.

Grenier, R., Bernier, M-A. & Stevens, W. (eds), 2007. The Underwater Archaeology of Red Bay. Basque Ship-building and Whaling in the 16th Century. Ottawa: Parks Canada.

Hall, B. S., 1997. *Weapons and warfare in Renaissance Europe: gunpowder, technology and tactics*. Baltimore: Johns Hopkins Univ. Press.

Harvey, K. (ed.), 2009. *History and material culture: a student's guide to approaching alternative sources*. London: Routledge.

Helms, M. W., 1988. *Ulysses' sail: an ethnographic odyssey of power, knowledge, and geographical distance*. Princeton, NJ: Princeton University Press.

Hjulhammar, M., 2010. *Stockholm från sjösidan: marinarkeologiska fynd och miljöer*. Diss. Stockholm : Stockholms universitet.

Hildred, A. & Rule, M., 1984. Armaments from the Mary Rose. *Antique Arms and Militaria*. May 1984: 17–24.

Hildred, A. (ed), 2011. *Weapons of warre: the armaments of the Mary Rose. [P. 3/4]*. Portsmouth, England: Mary Rose Trust.

Hodder, I., 1982. *Symbols in action: ethnoarchaeological studies of material culture*. Cambridge: Cambridge U.P.

Hodder, I., 1986. *Reading the past: current approaches to interpretation in archaeology*. Cambridge: Cambridge Univ. Press.

Hodder, I., 2012. *Entangled: an archaeology of the relationships between humans and things*. Malden, MA: Wiley-Blackwell.

Hodder, I. & Lucas, G., 2017. The symmetries and asymmetries of human – thing relations. In: *Archaeological dialogues*. Vol. 24 No. 2. Cambridge: Cambridge University Press.

Hornborg, A., 2013. Technology as Fetish: Marx, Latour, and the Cultural Foundations of Capitalism. *Theory, Culture & Society*. 0(0) 1–22. DOI: 10.1177/0263276413488960 tcs.sagepub.com.

Hornborg, A., 2017. Artifacts have consequences, not agency: Toward a critical theory of global environmental history. *European Journal of Social Theory*, vol. 20, no. 1, pp. 95-110. DOI: 10.1177/1368431016640536.

Johnson, M., 1993. *Housing Culture: Traditional Architecture in an English Landscape*. London: University College London Press.

Johnson, M., 2010. *Archaeological theory: an introduction*. 2. ed. Chichester: Wiley-Blackwell.

Karlholm, D., 2017. När konsten blev subject. I: Burman, A. & Lennerhed, L. (ed). *Samtider. Perspektiv på 2000-talets idehistoria*. Göteborg: Daidalos.

Keith, D. H. et al. 1984. The Molasses Reef Wreck, Turks and Caicos Islands, B.W.I.: A preliminary Report. IJNA, 13,1: 45–63.

Keith, D. H. & Simmons, J. J., 1985. Analysis of hull remains, ballast, and artefact distribution of a sixteenth century shipwreck, Molasses Reef, British West Indies. *Journal of Field Archaeology*, 12: 411–424.

Kirsch, P., 1990. *The Galleon. The Great Ship of the Armada Era*. London: Conway. Maritime Press.

Knappett, C. & Malafouris, L. (ed.), 2008. *Material agency: towards a non-anthropocentric approach*. New York: Springer

Landström, B., 1964. *Vägen till Indien. Upptäcksresor till lands och sjöss från expeditionen till Punt 1493 f. Kr till upptäckten av Godahoppsudden 1488 e. Kr*. Forum.

Larsson, L. 1986. *Sören Norrby och östersjöpolitiken 1523-1525*. Lund: Biblitoteca Historica Lundensis.

Latour, B. 2005. *Reassembling the social: an introduction to actor-network-theory*. Oxford: University Press

Latour, B. 1993. *We have never been modern.* Cambridge, Mass: Harvard Univ. Press

Levey, M. 1967. *Early Renaissance.* Harmondsworth: Penguin.

Linderson, H. 2012. Dendrokronologisk analys av Ekö-vraket, Saxemara i Blekinge skärgård. *Nationella Laboratoriet för Vedanatomi och Dendrokronologi Rapport 2012:1.* Lund

Marsden, P. (ed) 2009. *Mary Rose: your noblest shippe: anatomy of a Tudor warship.* Portsmouth, England: Mary Rose Trust

Marx, K. 1985. Kapitalet. Första boken, supplement. Lund: Arkiv-Zenit.

McCarthy, D. R. 2017. *Objects in Motion: Marx, Latour, and the Historical Processes of Powerful Things.* University of Melbourne. https://ecpr.eu/Filestore/PaperProposal/ 13aad5c9-04f8-4906-be81-b1bbb3cdf0ad.pdf

Malmer, M. 1984. Arkeologisk positivism. Fornvännen 79. Stockholm

McCarthy, D. R. 2017. Objects in Motion: Marx, Latour, and the Historical Processes of Powerful Things. Draft. *https://ecpr.eu/Filestore/PaperProposal/13aad5c9-04f8-4906-be81-b1bbb3cdf0ad.pd*

Milton, G. 2001. *Muskotkriget: kampen om de ostindiska kryddöarna.* Lund: Historisk media

Mozejka, B. 2019. Peter von Danzig. The Story of a Great Carvel 1462-1475. The Northern World, Volume: 86. Leiden: Br

Mortenson, M. H. 2002. Early Danish naval artillery c. 1500-1523. The beginning of a new era. In: Nørgård Jørgensen, Anne (red.) *Maritime warfare in northern Europe: technology, organisation, logistics and administration 500 BC-1500 AD: papers from an international research seminar at the Danish National Museum, Copenhagen, 3-5 May 2000.* Copenhagen: National Museum

Muckelroy, K. 1978. *Maritime archaeology.* Cambridge: Cambridge U.P.

Mortimer W, Sir R. E. 1954. *Archaeology from the Earth.* Oxford: Clarendon Press.

Møller Jensen, J. 2007. *Denmark and the crusades, 1400–1650.* Leiden: Brill

Noys B. 2016. Matter Against Materialism: Bruno Latour and the Turn to Objects. In: Middeke M., Reinfandt C. (eds) *Theory Matters.* Palgrave Macmillan, London. DOI https://doi.org/10.1057/978-1-137-47428-5_6

Nordin, J. M. 2010. Det emblemiska silvret. Sverige i den atlantiska världen vid 1600-talets mitt. I: Lihammer, A. & Nordin, J. M. (red.) *Modernitetens materialitet: arkeologiska perspektiv på det moderna samhällets framväxt.* Stockholm: Statens historiska museum

Nussbaum, M. 1995. "Objectification". Philosophy & Public Affairs. 24 (4): 249–291. doi:10.1111/j.1088-4963.1995.tb00032

Olsen, B. 2006. Ting-mennesker-samfunn. Introduksjon till en symmetrisk arkeologi. *Arkeologisk Forum* nr 14.

Olsen, B. 2012. *Archaeology: the discipline of things.* Berkeley: University of California Press

Platt, C. 1996. King Death. *The Black Death and its aftermath in late-medieval England.* London: University College London Press.

Redknap, M. 1984. The Cattewater Wreck: the investigation of an armed vessel of the sixteenth century. Greenwich: National Maritime Museum. Archaeological Series No. 8. *British Archaeological Reports: British series No. 131*

Roberts, M. 1968. *The Early Vasas.* A History of Sweden, 1523-1611. Cambridge: Cambridge University Press.

Rodger, N. A. M. 1996. The Development of Broadside Gunnery 1450–1650. *Mariner's Mirror,* 82, 301–24. doi: 10.1080/00253359.1996.10656604

Rogers, C. J. (ed.) 1995. *The military revolution debate: readings on the military transformation of early modern Europe.* Boulder: Westview Pres

Rosborn, S. 2018. *Att använda krut*. Foteviken museum. https://www.fotevikens museum.se/pdf/Eldvapen.pdf 2018-10-16

Rule, M. 1982. *The Mary Rose*. London: Conway Maritime Press

Rönnby, J. (ed.). 2012. *Skeppet Mars (1564). Marinarkeologisk fältrapport etapp I 2011*. Södertörn arkeologiska rapporter och studier. Södertörns högskola.

Rönnby, J.(ed). 2013. *Skeppet Mars (1564) Marinarkeologisk fältrapport etapp II 2012*. Södertörn arkeologiska rapporter och studier. Södertörn högskola.

Rönnby, J. (ed.). 2015. Gribshunden (1495): Skeppsvrak vid Stora Ekön, Ronneby, Blekinge. Marinarkologiska undersökningar 2013–2015. Blekinge museum rapport 21. Blekinge museum/Södertörns högskola

Rönnby, J. 2019. Furstar, nya skepp och början på det moderna. *Gribshunden, Griffen, Gripen, Gränslös nr 10, 2019*. Centrum för Öresundsstudier. https://journals.lub.lu.se/grl/issue/view/2934/526

Rönnby, J. & Adams, J. 1994. *Östersjöns Sjunkna Skepp*. Stockholm: Tiden.

Rönnby, J. & Sjöblom, I. 2016. Havsguden från Västervik – om skeppet Neptunus och vasakungarnas nya stora kravlar. Red Palm, Veronica. *Västerviks historia II*. Västervik: Västerviks Museum.

Salisbury, W. 1961. The Woolwich Ship. *Mariners mirror*. 47: 81-90.

Salisbury, W. 1966. Early Tonnage Measurement in England. *Mariners mirror*. 52.1: 41 - 51.

Shanks, M. 2007. Symmetrical archaeology. *World Archaeology*, 39:4. 589-596, DOI: 10.1080/00438240701679676.

Skirbeck, G. 2015. Bruno Latour´s antropology of the moderns. A reply to Maniglier. *Radical philosophy*. 189 (jan/feb 2015). https://www.radicalphilosophyarchive.com/commentary/bruno-latours-anthropology-of-the-moderns

Spens, E. 1942. Livet ombord och i land under äldre vasatid. Lybeck, O. (red.) *Svenska flottans historia: örlogsflottan i ord och bild från dess grundläggning under Gustav Vasa fram till våra dagar. Bd 1, [1521-1679]*. Malmö: Allhem

Sjöblom, I. 2003. Makalös motgång. *Svenska slagfält*. Ericson, L., Hårdstedt, M., Iko, P., Sjöblom, I. & Åselius, G. Stockholm: Wahlström & Widstrand/Publisher Produktion, 2003

Sjöblom, I. 2015. Identifiering och historiska sammanhang. In: Rönnby, J. (ed.). Gribshunden (1495): Skeppsvrak vid Stora Ekön, Ronneby, Blekinge. Marinarkologiska undersökningar 2013–2015. *Blekinge museum rapport 21*. Blekinge museum/Södertörns högskola

Sjöblom, I. 2016. *Svenska sjöofficerare under 1500-talet*. Diss. Stockholm : Stockholms universitet.

Söderlind, U. 2004. *Matvrak – kosthållning och måltidsordning ombord svenska örlogsfartyg under 1600-talet*. Licenctiatavhandling. Stockholm University.

Tallett, F. & Trim, D. J. B. (red.) 2010. *European warfare, 1350-1750* . Cambridge: Cambridge University Press

Ullidtz, P. 2017. Medici, Columbus og kong Hans. Renaessance, Oppdagelserejser, Unionskonge. Köpenhamn: Books on Demand GmbH.

Unger, R. (ed.). 1994. *Cogs, Caravels and Galleons*. London: Conway Maritime Press.

Wallerstein, I., M. 1980. *The modern world-system 2 Mercantilism and the consolidation of the European world-economy, 1600-1750*. New York: Academic Press.

Wallerstein, I., M. 2011 [1974]). *The modern world-system. 1, Capitalist agriculture and the origins of the European world-economy in the sixteenth century*. Berkeley, Calif.: University of California Press

White, H. 2013. Materiality, Form, and Context: Marx contra Latour. In: *Victorian Studies* 55(4):667-682. DOI: 10.2979/victorianstudies.55.4.667

Wigforss, E. 1970. *Materialistisk historieuppfattning. Industriell demokrati.* [Ny utg.] Stockholm: Tiden

Witmore, C., L. 2007. Symmetrical archaeology: excerpts of a Manifesto. *World Archaeology,* 39:4, 546-562, DOI: 10.1080/00438240701679411

Witmore, C., L. 2014. Archaeology and the New Materialisms. *Journal of Contemporary Archaeology,* Vol 1, No 2 (2014). DOI: 10.1558/jca.v1i2.16661

Zettersten, Axel. 1890. Svenska Flottans Historia I, 1522 - 1634. Stockholm.

Åkerlund, H. 1951. *Fartygsfynden i den forna hamnen i Kalmar.* Uppsala: Almqvist & Wiksells.

Østerberg, D. 1977. *Makt och materiell: samhällsteoretiska essäer.* Göteborg: Korpen.

Østerberg, D. 1989. *Tolkande sociologi.* Göteborg: Korpen.

Östman, P. 1985. *Geografi som vetenskap. En introduktion.* Stockholm: Liber Förlag.

Life and Death on *Mars* (1564)

INGVAR SJÖBLOM

A floating society

The admiral ship *Mars* was the largest warship in the strong Swedish fleet, consisting of 37 ships, during the battle of Öland in 1564 (Sjöblom 2003; Sjöblom 2016:66–67, 332). The ship was considered to be the same size in population as many contemporary towns in Sweden and can therefore be regarded as an independent floating society. But it was obviously a very special "town", with its crew of just men and specific professions and equipment requested for war at sea. However, despite the special character analysis of its crew and the conditions aboard, new light can be shed on the 16th century society, which it served.

The aims of the text are therefore to investigate different questions related to the crew on this great warship. What different kinds of occupations occurred on *Mars*? The crew size differs in previous research, so how large was the crew really? How were different positions divided on the warship? Where did the crew originate from and to which social strata did they belong?

Case studies on single Swedish warships during the 16th century, is a theme rarely investigated. There are some early exceptions. Navy captain Carl Ekman was interested in the naval operations during the Nordic Seven Years' War and wrote about the number of crew personnel on *Mars* and other ships in the fleet as *Elefanten* (Ekman 1942; Ekman 1946:73–76). Similarly, the pioneer, Axel Zettersten, made early important studies of this subject (see Glete 2000b). Zettersten wrote his masterpiece about the Swedish navy in the 1890s (Zettersten 1890, 1903). Today, the naval records are more complete than a hundred years ago due to the marine collections having been brought together in the archive. Despite this, his discussions still have their value as a catalogue over the roles of the mariners in the Swedish Navy (Zettersten 1890:33–185). The latest exception of case studies is our study on the building and manning of the large warship *Neptunus*, which replaced *Mars* after it sank, (Rönnby & Sjöblom 2016).

General discussions on manning the Swedish navy during the 16th century are to be found in new research by Jan Glete and Ingvar Sjöblom (Glete 2000a:40–59; Glete 2010:583–593; Sjöblom 2016:86–113). For the earlier period, Martin Neuding Skoog has studied military institutions in late medieval Sweden (Neuding Skoog 2018). His thesis focuses on the total war organizations function and recruitment strategies. For the later period, there are two important investigations regarding the role of the crew in the Swedish navy during the 17th century. The first is AnnaSara Hammar's study about the social order among the warship crew during 1670–1716 (Hammar 2014). Patrik Höglund is preparing a thesis on the conditions on board ships in the Swedish Navy during the 17th century. (Höglund 2020 in prep).

General studies for belligerent Danish and Lübeckian navies during the Nordic Seven Years' War, have been made by Herbert Kloth and Jørgen Barfod. (Kloth 1923; Kloth 1925; Barfod 1995) Research on European naval seamen can be found in Royen, Bruijn and Lucassen (1997). Another related exception of 16th century warship society is Ann Stirland's research on the men on Henry VIII's warship *Mary Rose* (sank 1545). Her interesting study is mainly based on the results from the osteological research (Stirland 2012:47–74). Of the 415 crew members on the Mary Rose (some sources mention an additional 300 men aboard the day she sank), the bone remains consist of about 40 per cent of the total crew (Stirland 2012:53). Maybe a future marine archaeological investigation of the *Mars* wreck site will reveal osteological remains to compare to the results from the *Mary Rose* (see Fredriksson & Steen this volume).

The number of men and crew positions

In the Swedish navy, there were in general, naval officers (admirals and captains), mariners (*sjöfolk* or *skeppsfolk*) and soldiers (*knektar*). Sometimes, the naval officers were included among the mariners. More often the wider term seamen (*båtsmän*) was used instead of mariner. Seamen included, not only common seamen, but also petty officers, staff personnel (secretaries, surgeons, chaplains, cooks, craftsmen etc.) and gunners. (Sjöblom 2016:88–89, 468–483; Glete 2010:585). The soldiers were generally administrated in the army organization (army records), even though they were sometimes included in the naval administration (Sjöblom 2016:99–101; Glete 2010:586; Ekman 1946).

Only two weeks before the large Swedish fleet left Stockholm in May 1564, aiming to defeat the united Danish–Lübeckian navy, the salary in money (coins) was paid to the personnel. The salary payroll list in the Shipyard accounts is the best source to reveal information about the crew and the categories of personnel on *Mars*. There were also other forms of payment such as clothing, food and enfeoffment (Sjöblom 2016:39, 60).

The two noblemen Nils Ryning and Hans Kyle's record of the spring salary payroll shows that it was paid at Stockholm castle on 16th April, 1564 (Skgh 1564:I vol. 10:1). The crew covered male society members, from aristocracy to craftsmen, and soldiers and seamen. Not surprisingly, the top trio of naval officers came from the highest level within the Swedish society. The admiral Jakob Bagge originated from Denmark (Norway). He moved to Sweden along with his father and made a long career as bailiff, army captain and colonel. His vice-admiral (*underamiral*) was the aristocrat and knight Arvid Turesson of the house Trolle. Surprisingly, Trolle was ranked beneath Bagge even though he came from a higher society level. He also had Danish links. Arvid Trolle was a cousin of the admiral of the opposing Danish fleet, admiral Herluf Trolle. The Captain Christoffer Andersson (*Grip*) had a background in the Royal court (Sjöblom 2016:66–67, 327, 330).

The spring salary payroll list over the *Mars* crew divided the crew into mariners, gunners and hired seamen. The number of personnel was 315 mariners and 32 gunners. The list contains 347 persons on *Mars*, divided into annually employed workers and hired personnel. The number of soldiers is not known but estimated by Carl Ekman.

In the payment list, the names and salaries were written down and the reveals different roles on board the warship.

Table 1: *Mars* crew according to the payroll list for the spring salary 16th April, 1564.

Officers	Admiral	1	3
	Vice admiral	1	
	Captain	1	
Petty officers	Master	1	14
	Vice-Master	3	
	Quartermaster	10	
Navigation	Pilot	10	10
Food supply	Supply secretary (*Proviantmästare*)	1	5
	Cook	3	
	Supplier (*Skaffare*)	1	

Craftsmen	Carpenter	9	12
	Turner	1	
	Sail maker	1	
	Hooper	1	
Administration	Office secretary	1	2
	Ship secretary	1	
Spiritual care	Chaplain	1	1
Medical care	Surgeon (*Bardskär*)	2	2
Signalist	Drummer	1	1
Artillery	Gunner	32	32
Seaman (annual employed)		33	265
Seaman (hire)		232	
Soldier		325*	325*
Total		672	672

Source: RA, Skeppsgårdshandlingar 1564:I, vol 10.1. *Estimation (Ekman 1946:76)

The table is based on the Shipyard accounts, excluding the number of soldiers, which has been estimated by Carl Ekman (Ekman 1946:76). His assumption is based on the provision accounts being compared to the consumed food on other warships in the fleet. The provision account includes 27 vessels. *Elefanten* (The Elephant), second in command after *Mars*, was included, but only with an inventory list. This means that there are no sources of how many crew members on board consumed supplies or how long they were at sea. It is possible to conduct further research and compare the sources in order to find out the names of the soldiers. I have compared this data over consumed supplies with other larger Swedish warships. The result is as follows:

Table 2: Crew and number of weeks at sea in supplying accounts.

Warships	Crew	Weeks
Sankt Erik	530	28
Herkules	460	26
Svenska Hektor	404	26
Engelen	179	24
Sankt Christoffer	182	26

Source: RA, Skeppsgårdshandlingar 1564:I, vol. 10.1.

The table shows the total number of crew members, soldiers included. One can try to calculate the number of soldiers (as Ekman did), by comparing the total amount of men from the supply accounts with the spring salary list for mariners. The list of supply accounts is over a period of between 24 to 28 weeks or roughly six months duty. During wartime, the number of soldiers on board the warship was generally as large as the number of mariners (Sjöblom 2016:98–100). However, during the total time at sea, the crew varied and differed. At the start, the mariners manned ship (during April/ mid of May) before the soldiers embarked the ship. They also embarked, sometimes for duty on land before the mariners left the ship. The soldiers were only present when the ship was needed for war and fighting.

For instance, the warship *Sankt Erik* which has been estimated to 1100 tons of displacement (Glete 2010: 683) was reported to have had 530 persons aboard. In the spring salary, the number of mariners on *Sankt Erik* was 211, which means that there should have been 319 soldiers. But according to Ekman, *Sankt Erik* had just 225 soldiers during the battle of Öland on 30th to 31st May (Ekman 1946). This example shows the difficulties in calculating exactly the crew, even during wartime.

It is possible that *Mars* had the capacity for 350 to 375 soldiers even though the warship most likely had 325 soldiers on board during the battle (Table 1). The army captain responsible for the soldiers on board *Mars* is at present unknown. One troop/file of soldiers (rote, 38 persons) are known by their name (See appendix, table of the infantry). Among them were the petty officer, provost (*prefekt*) Markus Olsson and file master Michill Joensson (Skeppsgårdshandlingar 1564:I Vol. 10:4. Claes Jöranssons löneregister över skeppsknektarna., 33v-34r.). Of the 672 crew members 384 persons (almost 60 per cent) are known by their name (see below).

Naval officers, staff personnel and their responsibilities

During the 16th century, the naval officer had great responsibility. He led the warship in combat, maintained lines of communication, carried out trade of war, was responsible for transporting supplies, patrolling and customs duty. He was also responsible for recruitment, the payroll, administration, discipline and legal issues. However, he did not have to navigate or set sail. For these duties, it was the petty officers (masters and pilots) who were responsible (Sjöblom 2016:622). Sometimes the responsibility for setting sail and navigation were a part of the naval officers' responsibility, but this later became integrated into their duties during the 17th century.

The petty officers consisted of masters, pilots and quartermasters. The Master on *Mars*, Mats Persson (Skulte) was well known in the Swedish society. He was also the Mayor in Stockholm. There were also three vice-masters (*underskeppare*), two seasonally employed and one for hire. On *Mars* there were nine quartermasters. One of the quartermasters also had his valet (*tjänare*) present. Even if valets were rarely noticed on *Mars*, there is evidence that the naval officers had valets on board the warship (Sjöblom 2016:422–423). The seamen were divided in quarters (*kvarter*) and each quarter into files (*rotar*). During the Nordic Seven Years' War, sometimes the quartermaster was known as the ¼ master in the naval administration (Sjöblom 2016:276). He was responsible for one quarter of the seamen, commonly a hundred persons. A larger warship had four quarters and a smaller two quarters (Spens 1945:138). All ten pilots were hired for duty on *Mars*. They also came from different parts of Sweden and were possible experts on different parts of the Swedish coastline. Four came from Stockholm, five from Älvsborg and one from Korpa in Finland.

Another prominent group of specialists were the secretaries and the most important being supply secretary Peter Poyss. He had the largest salary of all the crew in the spring salary payroll. The office secretary received half of the supply secretary's salary. One remark is that neither the naval officers nor the master received salaries according to the spring salary payroll. Either they were paid at some other point or in some other way. At least admiral Jakob Bagge and vice admiral Arvid Trolle received enfeoffment which probably yielded a good profit to cover the amount of overall salary. Peter Poyss received 200-mark silver coins (*penningar*). It is comparable to a half year's salary for the best paid captain in the fleet.

Next in line regarding level of salary, was the office secretary Bertil Eriksson. He received 100-mark silver coins in salary. It is interesting to discover the presence of office secretaries in the navy. Even the warship *Elefanten* had an office secretary in the crew. It was Johannes Hendreiÿ who also received 100-mark silver coins for his spring salary. *Mars* ship secretary, Anders Tidemansson, was hired and received 20-mark silver coins for his spring salary. This was almost double the payment compared to the seamen.

Mars crew also had two surgeons (*bardskär*). The master surgeon, Hans Berg, received 50-mark silver coins and the surgeon, Hans Wybelt, received 20-mark silver coins in his spring salary. *Mars* also had a chaplain, Mr. Erik Larsson, responsible for the spiritual care. He also received 20-mark silver coins. The drummer, Anders Ingelsson, was responsible for forwarding drum signals to the crew. Three cooks and one supplier were responsible for the food supplies on the ship. They were possibly located in the cooks' galley or at the orlop deck in order to supply the crew with food.

Gunners

The artillery on *Mars* is briefly described in this text and will be further investigated in forthcoming research (see Sjöblom 2012; Sjöblom 2013; Sjöblom 2014; Sjöblom 2016:84–85). The gun master and the 31 gunners were of course responsible for the artillery on *Mars*. The number of gunners is, in relation to the number of guns on the battery decks, one gunner assigned to two guns. The gun crew consisted of soldiers. Each gunner is a squad leader responsible for a gun crew working with and servicing two guns (Sjöblom 2016:109, Mothensen 1999:337f).

The naval artillery was used for fighting at a distance. Cannon balls were preferable for long distance fighting, and special ammunition (i.e. grenades etc) were used when the distance narrowed. When fighting in close combat, the soldiers used the same fighting technique as for land warfare (Sjöblom 2016:82-85). Furthermore, the largest guns on *Mars* were the full cannons (five tons of weight) which probably required a larger gun crew than the half culverines. (Sjöblom 2016:84 footnote 42). The gun master Esbjörn Staffansson is notorious. The second day of battle, on 31st May 1564, beat to quarters (battle stations) was ordered, the gun master was drunk and "slept deeply". When he woke up, he fired a half cannon, despite there not being any enemies in sight. When he realized what he had done, he committed suicide by lying down on the barrel of a newly-fired gun (Ekman 1942:512). Twenty-nine of the gunners received between six to 16-mark silver coins in the spring salary payroll (ten marks in medium salary). The gun master Esbjörn Staffansson was best paid among the gunners and earned 34-mark silver coins. Calmar Nils seems to be second in command according to the accounts, because he received 28-mark silver coins. Next in line in the payroll was Jakob Skotte. Due to his name, he originated from Scotland and received 20-mark silver coins.

Craftsmen

Of the nine carpenters, five were annually employed and four were hired seasonally. The turner and sailmaker were both annually employed. There were also people with surnames related to their craftsmen duties. This may indicate that some seamen and gunners had a previous occupation or knowledge as craftsman. Evidence of the latter is demonstrated in their names Nils Skaffare (supplier), Lasse Fiskare (fisherman), Sven Skräddare (tailor), Joen Bagare (baker), Erik Sågare (sawyer), Erik Svarvare (hooper) and Sven and Jöns Grytgjutare (pot molder) from Linköping. All these persons were notified as gunner or seaman in the spring salary payroll list. Among the hired seamen, we also find Erik Larsson with the mysterious title "flÿcke". His purpose and role have not yet been figured out. Altogether, there were some people with surnames related to their craftsmen duties, but others were employed as seamen or gunners.

Foreign extraction

One surprising fact is that some of the crew members originated from enemy countries. Why did some personnel fight in the Swedish Navy on *Mars* against their native countries? We can only imagine the reason. One hypothesis is that it was not so problematical during the 15th and 16th centuries to serve for another country. At least the eleven hired German and six hired Danish seamen indicate this possibility (RA, Skgh 1564 vol 10: f.41r). This was also noticed in previous research by Carl Ekman. His interpretation is that these German and Danish seamen were prisoners forced into Swedish duty (Ekman 1946:74). However, this cannot be true because they were paid salaries for their duties as hired seamen on *Mars*. (See appendix) They were paid an average salary level of ten-mark coins of silver.

The name also indicates which country the crew members came from. For instance, some of the gunners originated from Germany, France and Scotland. A gunner was highly trained, and it is understandable that skill and experience was sometimes necessary to be found abroad. Among the gunners were Jacob Huit von Hamburg, Hans von Hamburg, Nicolaus von Fransos (France) and Jacob Skotte (Scotland). In some cases, a nick-name was used as surname to indicate a person's native country. This was obvious for those persons with the surnames "Jute" (Jutland/Denmark) or "Bagge" ("norrbagge" Norway, Denmark) (Sjöblom 2016:66f, Neuding Skoog 2018:84–87).

Three of the six hired seamen from Denmark had "Bagge" as a surname. As mentioned before, the admiral Jakob Bagge emigrated from Norway, which the surname indicates. This was not the case for the seaman Joen Bagge from Öregrund and the pilot (*styrman*) Tord Bagge from Älvsborg. Even though their surname was Bagge, they were not related to the admiral Jakob Bagge. There were also other examples of native Swedish persons with "Bagge" as a surname. For example, the Swedish house Bagge af Berga came from Småland and was a mediaeval family. The most famous family member, Per Bagge od Berga, came to serve as an admiral during the Nordic Seven Years' War (Sjöblom 2016:67). Quartermaster Mats Holst probably came from Holstein (North of Germany). In addition, two of the eleven hired seamen had "Holst" as their surname.

Representatives from the whole country

The majority of the hired mariner volunteers were identified their origin. The hired personnel came from the large Swedish cities.

Table 3: The origin of the hired mariner volunteers.

City/Village	Location	Number
Stockholm	Coast	50
Uppsala	Coast	8
Öregrund	Coast	5
Örebro	Inland (lake Mälaren)	1
Gävle	Coast	33
Älvsborg	Coast	28
Västervik	Coast	10
Linköping	Inland (lake Roxen)	11
Lidköping	Inland (lake Vänern)	5
Nyköping	Inland/coast	13
Jönköping	Inland (lake Vättern)	2

Skara	Inland	6
Vadstena	Inland (lake Vättern)	3
Raumo (Finland)	Coast	9
Korpa (Finland)	Coast	10
Öland, Guneble socken (parish)	Coast	13
Öland, Kunle socken (parish)	Coast	9
Total		216

Source: RA, Skeppsgårdshandlingar 1564:I, vol. 10.1.

The table shows that most of the mariner volunteers originated from coastal cities or villages. Even so, there was a surprising number of hired mariners from inland villages. It needs to be said that many of these inland cities/villages are located near larger Swedish lakes (Mälaren, Vänern, Vättern and Roxen). An exception was Skara, a village located on the plains of Västgöta (Västgötaslätten).

The largest number of mariners originated from the capital city Stockholm. Many also came from the cities Gävle and Älvsborg. The rest of the villages (with a few exceptions) contributed to five to ten persons on average.

In addition to the origin of the hired mariner volunteers, many "seasonally employed" mariners had names reflecting their origin. For example, Calmar Nils originated from Kalmar and Michil Olender originated from Öland. The seaman Mats Håkansson from Linköping was noticed in the source marginal as originating from the county Värmland. These surnames with a "geographical" touch should not be confused with the two persons called "botnakarl" (man from Bothnia). A man called "botnakarl" was known to trade in Bothnian Bay which had nothing to do with their geographical origin. They could also be merchants from Stockholm or other cities trading with persons from Bothnian Bay. For instance, the hired seaman Jöns Botnakarl came from Stockholm. Maybe that was also the case for quartermaster Erik Botnakarl, but the sources do not reveal that fact because he was seasonally employed and not one of the hired mariners. As a conclusion, the main part of the mariners originated from coastal cities such as Stockholm, Gävle och Älvsborg. A fifth of the hired mariners came from inland cities located near lakes.

The survivors

The battle on 30th to 31st May in 1564 ended with close combat. The wind changed and *Mars*, without support from other Swedish warships, became surrounded by Danish *Byens Löve* and Lübeckian *der Engel* and *Peter und Paul*. A large stone gun exploded, and *Mars* caught fire. The Danish warship left the battle in order to avoid the blazing fire. The Swedish admiral surrendered to the Lübeckian admiral Friedrich Kneuel. Boarding and prize hunting started at the same time as the Swedish prisoners were moved to the Lübeckian warships. This was interrupted when the heavy fire ignited the gunpowder chamber. *Mars* exploded and went down with most of the crew together with looting Lübeckian mariners. The question is how many of *Mars* crew members survived the battle? Hövels Lübeckian chronicle mentions that 100 persons from *Mars* crew survived and were taken as prisoners (Hövel 1856). According to a list in the Swedish Royal Archive, 28 persons were, in 1565 released, from the prison in Lübeck (RA Flottans handlingar: Sjöexpeditioner 1560–1648. M 1848). These were:

Table 4: Names and roles of the survivors.

Role	Name	Role	Name
Pilot	Per Larsson from Stockholm	?	Bengt Sverinsson
Gunner	Olof Bottnakarl	Gunner	Michil Grott
Gunner	Siffred Mattsson	Gunner	Sven Persson
Gunner	Johan Olsson	Seaman	Simon Olsson
Seaman	Clemet Persson	Seaman	Hans Jacobsson
Seaman	Nils Jönsson	Seaman	Olof Jonsson
Seaman	Lasse Larsson	Seaman	Knut Siffredsson
Seaman	Per Mortensson	Seaman	Hans Ingemarsson
Seaman	Tomas Henriksson	Seaman	Per Mortensson *
Seaman	Bengt Hansson **	Soldier	Simon Mattson
Soldier	Staffan Larsson	Soldier	Nils Olsson
Soldier	Anders Olsson	Soldier	Jören Skomakare
Soldier	Olof Andersson	Soldier	Olof Olsson
Soldier	Jöns Olsson	Soldier	Anders Ingebrektsson

Source: RA Flottans handlingar: Sjöexpeditioner 1560–1648. M 1848. Note: The source lists the nine soldiers as "landsknekt (landsknecht). * = "Left behind in Stralsund". ** = "Captured on Mars and released from Lübeck on Palm Sunday 1565"

The prominent naval officers Jakob Bagge, Arvid Trolle and Christoffer Andersson, the master Mats Persson and supply secretary (*proviantskrivare*) Peter Poyss were all taken as prisoners to Copenhagen. Altogether, 33 prisoners are known by their name. Trolle died in prison. As Hövels chronicle pinpoints, as many as a hundred persons could have been captured, after surrendering to the enemy. Many may have died in prison in Lübeck and Denmark. Prisoners from *Mars* were released in the autumn of 1565 together with other prisoners taken during the battle of Bornholm on 7th July 1565 (RA. Räntekammarböcker Vol. 41, 1564:5, Vol. 42, 1565:2 och Varuhus och handling vol 37, 1566). This may have caused misunderstandings due to the total number of 168 released prisoners being wrongly identified as wounded from *Mars* when some of them were captured during the battle of Bornholm. (Sjöblom 2016: 332, note 87. Compare Peterson 2014:187–188 and Lager-Kromnow 1992:199, 342). It is possible that up to a hundred crew members were taken as prisoners and up to fifty of them survived and made it back to Sweden.

Conclusion

Sometimes, early modern warships are presented as a kind of a miniature of the contemporary society at that time (see discussion in Rönnby & Adams 1994). This should not be exaggerated since a ship is a very specialized society and the main purpose of an analysis, is to first and foremost, present an understanding of the living conditions on board a warship from a special period.

However, the ship was of course a part of a bigger society in a lot of ways. For example, the master on *Mars* was in fact also mayor of Stockholm. It is important to make more case studies of this kind to compare and contextualize with other research on the 16th century, for example concerning recruitment. It would also be interesting to see the conditions on board *Mars* compered to both earlier and later case examples.

Mars carried a crew of 672 persons. She had approximately 347 mariners and 325 soldiers. This text has tried to investigate their occupation and their roles. Compared to other large Swedish warships, it is possible that *Mars* had the capacity to take on board even more soldiers than Ekman's earlier calculation. Only 37 soldiers on *Mars* have been found in the payrolls and are known by their name. It should be possible in future research to compare payrolls for previous years in order to find out the large missing number of soldiers who can hypothetically be related to *Mars*.

In total, of the 672 persons, it has been possible to get information about 384 crew members (347 mariners and 37 soldiers) known by their names in the shipyard accounts in the Royal archives. The mariners were also divided into two groups according to how they were recruited. Firstly, the annually employed mariners consisted of conscripts. The soldiers were included in this group. The secondly group were the hired volunteers. The main part of the 216 hired volunteers were organized in groups after their origin. There were different kinds of occupations on the ship. *Mars* crew was led by three navy officers, 14 petty officers and ten pilots. The 32 gunners were responsible for the artillery and five persons for the food supply (including the highly paid supply secretary). The twelve craftsmen took care of the reparations and the two surgeons took care of the medical care. The chaplain was responsible for spiritual care and the drummer for the internal communication.

The admiral Jakob Bagge was experienced in war duties and crown bureaucracy, ennobled for his service. His companion, Arvid Trolle, originated from the Swedish nobility and was surprisingly even cousin to the Danish admiral. The master Mats Persson (Skulte) was previously mayor of Stockholm.

The hired mariners were identified by the part of the country from which they originated. The majority of the hired crew members originated from coastal cities/villages. Some of them also came from inland villages located near larger lakes. The largest number came from the capital city, Stockholm. The second and third cities of origin for the hired mariners were Gävle and Älvsborg. This is all in line with Martin Neuding Skoog's result from late medieval Sweden where burgers supported the Swedish realm as serving by themselves or using the military market to hire replacements (Neuding Skoog 2018:305–310; 359; 503). In some cases, the surname of the mariners reveals that they came from abroad (as Bagge or Holst). Among the hired mariners, eleven were hired German and six hired Danish seamen. These seamen were paid in accordance to the other hired mariners, which indicates an open market for recruitment, even though they had to fight against their motherlands.

For some people, life continued after *Mars* exploded and went to the bottom. Up to a hundred persons may have survived and were possibly taken as prisoners. It is unclear how many persons survived, but 32 persons were released and known by their name. It means that between 550 to 600 of *Mars*, large crew of 672 persons, followed the ship down to the bottom of the Baltic Sea. For those people, life ended on *Mars*.

References

Unpublished primary sources

Riksarkivet, Stockholm (RA)
Flottans handlingar: Sjöexpeditioner 1560–1648. M 1848
Räntekammarböcker vol. 41, 1564:5
Skeppsgårdshandlingar 1564:I vol. 10:1 and 4.
Varuhus och handling vol. 37, 1566

Primary works

Hövel, G. von, *Chronick von A. Fahne*. Cöln, 1856.

Secondary works

Barfod, J. H., 1995. Christian 3.s flåde – Den danske flådes historie 1533–1588. Marinehistorisk Selbskabs Skrift nr 25. København: Marinehistorisk Selskab.

Briand de Crévecoeur, E., 1959. Herluf Trolle. Kongens admirael og Herlufsholms skoles stifter. København: C.A. Reitzels forlag.

Ekman, C., 1942. Nordiska sjuårskrigets två första krigsår 1563–1564, avsnitt ur artikel: "Svenska Flottans sjötåg fram till Kalmarkriget. *Svenska flottans historia del 1 1521–1679*. Red Lybeck, Otto. Malmö: Allhems förlag.

Ekman, C., 1945. Erik XIV:s skeppsregemente. i *Tidskrift i Sjöväsende nr 10 1945*. Stockholm: Kungliga Örlogsmannasällskapet.

Ekman, C., 1946. Några data om Erik XIV:s sjökrigskonst. i *Tidskrift i Sjöväsende nr 2 1946*. Stockholm: Kungliga Örlogsmannasällskapet.

Glete, J., 2000a. *Warfare at Sea 1500–1650. Maritime Conflicts and the Transformation of Europe*. London: Routledge.

Glete, J., 2000b. Axel Zettersten och Svenska flottans historia. I: *Historia, Krig och Statskonst. En vänbok till Klaus-Richard Böhme*. (red) Zetterberg, Kent och Åselius, Gunnar. Stockholm: Probus förlag.

Glete, J., 2010. *Swedish Naval Administration 1521–1721. Resource Flows and Organisational Capabilities*. Leiden/Boston: Brill.

Hammar, A., 2014. *Mellan kaos och kontroll. Social ordning i svenska flottan 1670–1716*. Lund: Nordic Academic Press.

Höglund, P., 2020. *Skeppssamhället. Befattningar och status på örlogsskepp under 1600-talet*. Avhandlingsmanus (in prep).

Kloth, H., 1923. Lübecks Seekriegswesen in der Zeit des nordischen Siebenjährige

Krieges, 1563–1570: Ein Beitrag zur deutschen Seekriegsgeschichte im 16. Jahrhundert. *Zeitschrift des Vereins für Lübckische Geschichte um Altertumskunde*, nr 21, 1923, s. 1–51, 185–256; nr 22, 1925, s. 121–152, 325–379.

Lager-Kromnow, B., 1992. *Att vara Stockholmare under 1560-talet*. Stockholmsmonografier vol 110. Stockholm: Kommitten för Stockholmsforskning.

Mortensen, M. H., 1999. *Dansk artilleri indtil 1600*. Aa. København: Tøjhusmuseet.

Neuding Skoog, M., 2018. *I rikets tjänst. Krig, stat och samhälle i Sverige 1450–1550*. Aa. Bokförlaget Augusti.

Peterson, E., 2014. Wounded Veterans and the State. The Precursor of the Veteran's Home in Sweden (1560–1650). In: *Scandinavian Journal of History*. Vol. 39 Nr 2 may 2014, London: Routledge/Taylor and Francis Group.

Royen, P. C., Bruijn, J. R., and Lucassen, J. (eds.), 1997. *Those Emblems of Hell: European sailors and the maritime labour market, 1570–1870.* St Johns, 1997.

Rönnby, J. & Sjöblom, I., 2016. Havsguden från Västervik – om skeppet Neptunus och vasakungarnas nya stora kravlar. Red Palm, Veronica. *Västerviks historia II.* Västervik: Västerviks Museum.

Spens, E., 1942. Livet ombord och i land under äldre vasatid. i *Svenska flottans historia. Örlogsflottan i ord och bild från dess grundläggning under Gustav Vasa fram till våra dagar. Bd 1 1521–1679.* Lybeck, Otto (red.), Malmö: Allhems förlag.

Sjöblom, I., 2003. Makalös motgång. *Svenska slagfält.* Ericson, L., Hårdstedt, M., Iko, P., Sjöblom, I. & Åselius, G. Stockholm: Wahlström & Widstrand/Publisher Produktion, 2003.

Sjöblom, I., 2012. Analys av dokumenterad kanon – identifiering av vraket. I *Skeppet Mars (1564). Fältrapport etapp I 2011.* Rönnby, Johan (red.). Huddinge: Södertörns högskola, 2012.

Sjöblom, I., 2013. Dokumentation av eldrör och lavetter". I *Skeppet Mars (1564): Marinarkeologisk fältrapport etapp II 2012.* Rönnby, Johan (red.). Huddinge: Södertörns högskola.

Sjöblom, I., 2014. The Guns of *Mars* the Magnificent: Cannon Helps Provide Proof of a Wreck's Identity. I *Quest. The Journal of Global Underwater Explorers*, Vol. 15, Nr 4. High Springs, Florida, USA: Global Underwater Explorers, 2014.

Sjöblom, I., 2016. *Svenska sjöofficerare under 1500-talet.* Aa. Universus förlag: Malmö.

Stirland A., 2012. The Men on Mary Rose. In: *The Social History of English Seamen, 1485–1649* by Cheryl A. Fury (ed.). The Boydell Press: Woodbridge, 2012.

Zettersten, A., 1890. Svenska flottans historia 1522–1634. Stockholm.

Appendix

Officers and staff (including craftsmen)

Rank	Name	Salary	Rank	Name	Salary
Admiral	Jakob Bagge	-	Vice admiral	Arvid Trolle	-
Captain	Christoffer Andersson	-	Drummer	Anders Ingelsson	14
Office secretary	Bertil Eriksson	100	Surgeon	Hans Deÿbellth	20
Supply secretary	Per Poÿss	200	Master surgeon	Hans Bergh	50
Chaplain	Mr. ("Herr") Erik Larsson	20	Master	Mats Persson	-
Vice Master	Henrik Månsson	30	Vice Master	Per Jonsson	30
	Olof Siuordsson	16		Per Michilsson	16
Ship secretary	Anders Tydemansson	20 (hire)		Nils Svensson	12
	Staffan Knutsson	12		Per Rorsson	8
	Clemet Andersson	9		Knut Matsson	9
	Marcus Henriksson	9		Bertil Henriksson	9
	Mats Larsson	9		Mats Eskilsson	8
	Per Mortensson	8		Nils Persson	9
Supplier	Morten Persson	8		Jacob Matsson	8
	Pelle Persson	8		Greiss Siffredsson	9
Cook	Jacob Jonsson	8		Jöran Nilsson	10
	Nils Andersson	10		Per Larsson	7
	Mats Olsson	6		Morten Jonsson	7
	Jöns Larsson	6		Mats Thomasson	6
	Nils Esbiörnsson	6		Erik Larsson	6
	Hokon Håkonsson	6		Henning Matsson	6
	Lasse Pouelsson	6		Morten Olsson	3
	Nils Monsson	6		Erik Siffredsson	4
Carpenter	Olof Henriksson	22	Carpenter	Eskil Henriksson	18
Carpenter	Seffred Jonsson	12	Carpenter	Clement Pouelsson	12
Carpenter	Erik Larsson	12	Hooper	Seffred Hansson	18
	Olof Jacobsson	4		Sven Nilsson	4
Cook	Eskil Henriksson	12	Cook	Lasse Knutsson	10
Turner	Henrik Olsson	12	Sail maker	Per Olsson	12
Quartermaster	Per Ambjörnsson	40	Quartermasters (Ambjörnssons) valet	-	10
Quartermaster	Nils Nilsson	40	Quartermaster	Olof Eriksson*	40
Quartermaster	Eskil Michelsson	40	Quartermaster	Greis Helsing	40
Quartermaster	Erik Bottnekarl	40	Quartermaster	Lasse Tyckesson	40
Quartermaster	Mats Holst	40	Quartermaster	Erik Monsson	40

Note: * = Committed suicide ("Förgjorde sigh sielff"). Note: Persons with a blank square for their rank, could probably (in some cases) be connected to the previously mentioned rank.

Artillery

Rank	Name	Salary	Rank	Name	Salary
Gunner	Esbiörn Staffansson	34	Gunner	Calmer Nilsson	28
Gunner	Michil Olender	16	Gunner	Jacob Hwith von Hamborg	10
Gunner	Hans Henriksson	11	Gunner	Botvid Persson	10
Gunner	Benkt Biörnsson	11	Gunner	Sven Persson	10
Gunner	Povel Persson	12	Gunner	Hans von Hamborg	15
Gunner	Nicolaus von Fransos	15	Gunner	Jacob Skotte	20
Gunner	Erik Sågare	14	Gunner	Erik Svarvare	10
Gunner	Jacob Henriksson	10	Gunner	Seffuor Bagge	16
Gunner	Olof Persson	13	Gunner	Johan Olsson	10
Gunner	Anders Andersson	11	Gunner	Per Karlsson	12
Gunner	Olof Larsson	12	Gunner	Olof Henriksson	10
Gunner	Håkan Andersson	12	Gunner	Nils Eriksson	14
Gunner	Siffred Matsson	15	Gunner	Mats Matsson	14
Gunner	Erik Jonsson	12	Gunner	Jöns Larsson	10
Gunner	Per Olsson	14	Gunner	Mons Jonsson	6
Gunner	Jöran Matsson	8	Gunner	Nils Larsson	8

Hired mariners from Stockholm

Rank	Name	Salary	Rank	Name	Salary
Vice-master	Nils Eriksson	50	Seaman	Anders Jonsson	10
Seaman	Erik Henriksson	10	Seaman	Lasse Persson	10
Seaman	Lasse Jonsson	10	Seaman	Olof Jonsson	10
Seaman	Olof Larsson	10	Seaman	"Old" Mats Henriksson	10
Seaman	Henrik Michilsson	10	Seaman	Henrik Claesson	6
Seaman	Lasse Olsson	10	Seaman	Morten Michilsson	10
Seaman	Anders Persson	10	Seaman	Morten Olsson	10
Seaman	Jacob Bengtsson	10	Seaman	Olof Persson	6
Seaman	Per Larsson	6	Seaman	Henrik Larsson	10
Seaman	Jöns Michilsson	10	Seaman	Siffred Eriksson	10
Seaman	Markus Markusson	10	Seaman	Bengt Mortensson	6
Seaman	Nils Jörensson	6	Seaman	Olof Monsson	10
Seaman	Siffred Matsson	10	Seaman	Hans Larsson	10
Seaman	"Young" Mats Henriksson	10	Seaman	Jöns Botnekarl*	14
Seaman	Olof Eriksson*	12	Seaman	Jöran Eriksson*	12
Seaman	Erik Andersson	10	Seaman	Per Olsson	6
Seaman	Clemet Nilsson	6	Seaman	Simon Henriksson	10
Seaman	Per Henriksson	6	Seaman	Mats Knutsson	6
Seaman	Michil Mortensson	6	Seaman	Erik Jacobsson	10
Seaman	Siffred Olsson	10	Seaman	Ingvald Persson	10
Seaman	Frans Larsson	10	Seaman	Jacob Olsson	10
Carpenter	Herman Larsson	12	Carpenter	Tomas Henriksson	12
Carpenter	Olof Philpusson	12	Carpenter	Olof Andersson	10

* Located in Finland during the winter ("Dessa var i Finland över vintern"). Total: 46 hired mariner volunteers from Stockholm. Also, four hired pilot volunteers are noted in a table below.

Hired mariners from Gävle

Rank	Name	Salary	Rank	Name	Salary
Seaman	Olof Monsson	10	Seaman	Mons Håkansson	10
Seaman	Mats Tydemansson	10	Seaman	Hans Larsson	10
Seaman	Erik Muremestare	10	Seaman	Jöns Andersson	10
Seaman	Jöran Henriksson	10	Seaman	Ander Johansson	10
Seaman	Olof Eriksson	10	Seaman	Olof Persson	10
Seaman	Erik Nilsson	10	Seaman	Henrik Persson	10
Seaman	Björn Osvedsson	10	Seaman	Olof Svensson	10
Seaman	Per Olsson	10	Seaman	Jöns Persson	10
Seaman	Erik Olsson	10	Seaman	Joen Persson	10
Seaman	Per Olsson	10	Seaman	Nils Greisson	10
Seaman	Michil Matsson	10	Seaman	Olof Jonsson	12
Seaman	Otthe Nilsson	12	Seaman	Olof Skog	10
Seaman	Morten Ivarsson	10	Seaman	Olof Broddesson	10
Seaman	Clemet Nilsson	10	Seaman	Erik Nilsson	12
Seaman	Erik Persson	10	Seaman	Staffan Jonsson	10
Seaman	"Young" Erik Persson	10	Seaman	Joen Olsson	10
Seaman	Joen Broddesson	10			

Total: 33 hired mariner volunteers from Gävle.

Hired mariners from Öregrund

Rank	Name	Salary	Rank	Name	Salary
Seaman	Staffan Olsson	10	Seaman	Joen Bagge	10
Seaman	Erik Gunnarsson	8	Seaman	Lasse Jacobsson	10
Seaman	Sven Jonsson	10			

Total: 5 hired mariner volunteers from Öregrund.

Hired mariners from Uppsala

Rank	Name	Salary	Rank	Name	Salary
Seaman	Frans Larsson	10	Seaman	Erik Hunble	10
Seaman	Knut Michelsson	10	Seaman	Olof Olsson	10
Seaman	Nils Eriksson	10	Seaman	Nils Persson	X
Seaman	Joen Bagare	X	Seaman	Henrik Jacobsson*	5

* Henrik Jacobsson was mention by himself in the payroll list, but have been put together with the other hired mariner volunteers originated from Uppsala. Total: 8 hired mariner volunteers from Uppsala.

Hired mariner from Örebro

Rank	Name	Salary
Seaman	Anders Erkilsson	10

Total: 1 hired mariner volunteers from Örebro.

Hired mariners from Nyköping

Rank	Name	Salary	Rank	Name	Salary
Seaman	Simon Olsson	10	Seaman	Ivar Matsson	10
Seaman	Markus Marcusson	10	Seaman	Per Henriksson	10
Seaman	Lasse Olsson	10	Seaman	Olof Eriksson	10
Seaman	Jören Theysson	10	Seaman	Per Siffredsson	10
Seaman	Hans Jacobsson	10	Seaman	Per Jonsson	10
Seaman	Michil Jonsson	10	Seaman	Anders Larsson	10
Seaman	Per Siffredsson	12			

Total: 13 hired mariner volunteers from Nyköping

Hired mariner from "Fransoo"

Rank	Name	Salary
Seaman	"Old" Ivar	10

Hired mariners from Linköping

Rank	Name	Salary	Rank	Name	Salary
Seaman	Mons Håkansson	10	Seaman	"Flÿcke" Erik Larsson	6
Seaman	"Wernelandsbo" Mons Håkansson	10	Seaman	Germund Stensson	10
Seaman	Sven Grytgjutare (potfounder)	10	Seaman	Halfued Olsson	8
Seaman	Johan Persson	6	Seaman	Benkt Olsson	10
Seaman	Jöns Grytgjutare (pot founder)	10	Seaman	Nils Svensson	4
Seaman	Per Skute	X			

Total: 11 hired mariner volunteers from Linköping.

Hired mariners from Älvsborg

Rank	Name	Salary	Rank	Name	Salary
Seaman	Benkt Olsson	10	Seaman	Anders Wlkop	10
Seaman	Anders Eriksson	10	Seaman	Erik Jonsson	10
Seaman	Olof Jonsson	10	Seaman	Olof Nilsson	X
Seaman	Olof Birgersson	10	Seaman	Nils Olsson	X
Seaman	Sven Skräddare	10	Seaman	Hans Arvidsson	10
Seaman	Per Monsson	8	Seaman	Arvid Karlsson	6
Seaman	Anders Birgersson	10	Seaman	Anders Larsson	6
Seaman	Nils Gustafsson	6	Seaman	Anders Olsson	X

Rank	Name	Salary	Rank	Name	Salary
Seaman	Povel Nilsson	10	Seaman	Karl Jonsson	10
Seaman	Lasse Arnesson	10	Seaman	Anders Birgersson	10
Seaman	Sigge Torsson	10	Seaman	Per Arvidsson	16
Seaman	Per Henningsson	16			

Total: 23 hired mariner volunteers from Älvsborg. Also, five hired pilot volunteers are noted in a table below.

Hired mariners from Lidköping

Rank	Name	Salary	Rank	Name	Salary
Seaman	Nils Matsson	X	Seaman	Tord Gunnarsson	8
Seaman	Lasse Karlsson	6	Seaman	Joen Håkansson	10
Seaman	Nils Matsson	6			

Total: 5 hired mariner volunteers from Lidköping.

Hired mariners from Västervik

Rank	Name	Salary	Rank	Name	Salary
Seaman	Jöran Andersson	10	Seaman	Lasse Fiskare (fisherman)	10
Seaman	Johan Enevaldsson	10	Seaman	Benkt Nilsson	8
Seaman	Henrik Arnesson	10	Seaman	Per Mortensson	6
Seaman	Per Nilsson	X	Seaman	Segul Larsson	4
Seaman	Hans Persson	10	Seaman	Lasse Persson	10

Total: 10 hired mariner volunteers from Västervik.

Hired mariners from Oland Gumble socken (parish)

Rank	Name	Salary	Rank	Name	Salary
Seaman	Joen Persson	6	Seaman	Olof Michilsson	6
Seaman	Jacob Olsson	6	Seaman	Anders Nilsson*	X
Seaman	Per Larsson	6	Seaman	Mats Olsson	6
Seaman	Jacob Persson	6	Seaman	Olof Henningsson	6
Seaman	Jacob Jonsson	6	Seaman	Henrik Michilsson	6
Seaman	Mats Persson	6	Seaman	Joen Jonsson	6
Seaman	Henrik Jonsson	6			

* "Huggen ofärdig" (stabbed and crippled). Total: 13 hired mariner volunteers from Guneble parish.

Hired mariners from Oland Kunle socken (parish)

Rank	Name	Salary	Rank	Name	Salary
Seaman	Mats Tomasson	6	Seaman	Clemet Henningsson	6
Seaman	Bernt Henriksson	6	Seaman	Siffred Jonsson	X
Seaman	Joen Staffansson	X	Seaman	Morten Persson	6
Seaman	Lasse Jacobsson	6	Seaman	Finved Jonsson	6
Seaman	Jöns Gudmundsson	6			

Total: 9 hired mariner volunteers from Kunle parish.

Hired mariners from Korpa (Finish region)

Rank	Name	Salary	Rank	Name	Salary
Seaman	Mats Persson	8	Seaman	Rasmus Knutsson	6
Seaman	Morten Larsson	6	Seaman	Ivar Mortensson	6
Seaman	Lasse Wolmarsson	6	Seaman	Henrik Larsson	6
Seaman	Christoffer Olsson	6	Seaman	Rasmus Knutsson	4
Seaman	Erik Henriksson	4			

Total: 10 hired mariner volunteers from Korpa. Also, one hired pilot volunteers are noted in a table below.

Hired mariners from Raumo (Finish region)

Rank	Name	Salary	Rank	Name	Salary
Seaman	Jacob Jonsson	10	Seaman	Frans Mortensson	6
Seaman	Jacob Clemetsson	6	Seaman	Per Jonsson	10
Seaman	Jöns Andersson	8	Seaman	Olof Henriksson	8
Seaman	Jacob Jonsson	6	Seaman	Per Henriksson	6
Seaman	Henrik Larsson	6			

Total: 9 hired mariner volunteers from Raumo.

Hired mariners from Germany

Rank	Name	Salary	Rank	Name	Salary
Seaman	Hans Stenck	10	Seaman	Joakim Holst	10
Seaman	Petter Rodeck	10	Seaman	Mygge von Stöde	10
Seaman	Hans Nymeier	10	Seaman	Henrik Weffere	10
Seaman	Hans Rothmer	10	Seaman	Kaeth von Bromen	10
Seaman	Herman Holst	10	Seaman	Hans Webuer	X
Seaman	Larens Parmenssel	6			

Total: 11 hired mariner volunteers from Germany.

Hired mariners from Denmark

Rank	Name	Salary	Rank	Name	Salary
Seaman	Olof Duss	10 + 4*	Seaman	Söffring Tordsson	10 + 4*
Seaman	Olof Bagge	10 + 10*	Seaman	Pouel Nilsson	10 + 10*
Seaman	Sven Bagge	10 + 10*	Seaman	Hans Bagge	10

* "Restantie 1563" (payed salary claim from 1563). Total: 6 hired mariner volunteers from Denmark.

Hired mariners from Skara

Rank	Name	Salary	Rank	Name	Salary
Seaman	Lasse Andersson	6	Seaman	Lasse Persson	6
Seaman	Joen Håkansson	8	Seaman	Hans Jonsson	X
Seaman	Anders Larsson	4	Seaman	Mons Nilsson	4

Total: 6 hired mariner volunteers from Skara.

Hired mariners from Jönköping

Rank	Name	Salary	Rank	Name	Salary
Seaman	Nils Jonsson	8	Seaman	Olof Davidsson	8

Total: 2 hired mariner volunteers from Jönköping.

Hired mariners from Vadstena

Rank	Name	Salary	Rank	Name	Salary
Seaman	Hans Henningsson	4	Seaman	Christoffer Jacobsson	4
Seaman	Anders Jonsson	4			

Total: 3 hired mariner volunteers from Vadstena.

Hired pilots

Origin	Name	Salary
Stockholm	Jöns Olenninge	50
Stockholm	Per Grönskalle	50
Stockholm	Per Larsson	50
Stockholm	Morten Jonsson	50
Älvsborg	Clas Assarsson	30
Älvsborg	Birger Olsson	30
Älvsborg	Björn Olsson	30
Älvsborg	Anders Olsson	30
Älvsborg	Tord Bagge	30
Korpa	Mons Eriksson	20

Total: 10 hired pilot volunteers from different parts in Sweden.

Hired mariners without origin

Rank	Name	Salary	Rank	Name	Salary
Seaman	Michil Simonsson	10	Seaman	Mats Andersson Guty	10
Seaman	Bengt Siggesson	10	Seaman	Mats Nilsson	10
Seaman	Lasse Broor	10	Seaman	Mats Jacobsson	10
Seaman	Jacob Olsson	10	Seaman	Henrik Simonsson	10
Seaman	Bengt Hansson	10	Seaman	Simon Persson	8
Seaman	Sven Jonsson	10	Seaman	Nils Skaffare	10
Seaman	Lasse Nilsson	6			

Total: 13 hired mariner volunteers without notified origin in the payroll list.

Infantry

Rank	Name	Salary	Rank	Name	Salary
Provost (prefekt)	Marcus Olsson	24	"Senior" file master (Övre rotemästare)	Michill Joensson	12
Soldier	Nils Olsson	10	Soldier	Birger Smålänning	10
Soldier	Erik Olsson	10	Soldier	Jöns Siffredsson	10
Soldier	Gregelz Larsson	7	Soldier	Staffan Andersson	7

Soldier	Olof Larsson	7	Soldier	Per Larsson	7
Soldier	Mickill Persson	5	Soldier	Per Eriksson	5
Soldier	Erik Jopsson	6	Soldier	Erik Hobborsson	6
Soldier	Erik Siegelsson	6	Soldier	Per Nilsson	6
Soldier	Nils Nilsson	6	Soldier	Oluf Gregelsson	6
Soldier	Anders Eriksson	6	Soldier	Henrik Matsson	6
Soldier	Morten Helsing	10*	Soldier	Jöns van Hoessen	10*
Soldier	Per Marsvenn	10*	Soldier	Nils Persson	10*
Soldier	Lage Persson	10*	Soldier	Mats Nilsson	9
Soldier	Pouell Persson	8	Soldier	Jörgen Michilsson	8
Soldier	Lasse Andersson	8	Soldier	Nils Olsson	8
Soldier	Urban Clemetsson	8	Soldier	Marcus Nilsson	8
Soldier	Hans Hansson	8	Soldier	Anders Andersson	8
Soldier	Olof Staffansson	8	Soldier	Olof Persson	8
Soldier	Olof Olsson	8			

* "Restantie 1563" (payed salary claim from 1563). These soldier probably received salary only for 1563. Total: 37 persons in the payroll from infantry. Source: RA, Skeppsgårdshandlingar 1564:I vol 10:4. Claes Jöranssons löneregister över skeppsknektarna., 33v–34r

Stories from Historic Lake Champlain:
The Impact of War on the People Who Fight in it as Seen Through the Lens of Shipwreck Archaeology

ART COHN

Introduction

In the fall of 1776, an American naval squadron prepared to engage the British Naval forces for control of strategic Lake Champlain. On October 11, a three-day contest began that became known as the Battle of Valcour Island and it resulted in control of the lake being passed from the American rebels back to the British. This significant naval contest, often associated with the American commander Benedict Arnold, is linked to its contribution just one year later to the American victory at the Battles of Saratoga. The stories of the individual casualties of the engagement are little recorded or remembered. However, through the chance discovery linking a government pension application to a stone cemetery marker, we are now aware of the circumstances and impact of this naval contest on the lives of Sergeant Jonas Holden and Lieutenant Thomas Rogers. They enlisted and served together on the American gunboat *New York* and their story helps illustrate that although this contest was between rival nations, it was fought by individual men, each with his own personal story.

Lake Champlain

Most significant historic naval conflicts took place on the world's oceans and logically, that is where we would expect to find most of the submerged warships that comprise the focus of this book. However, from shortly after the discovery of the New World, up until the mid-19th century, Lake Champlain was an internationally-known waterway that competing European nations coveted for its strategic importance. The long, narrow lake, bordered on its western side by the state of New York and on the eastern side by the state of Vermont, stretches north and south for more than 120 miles (Figure 48). It was named during a brief visit by the French explorer Samuel de Champlain in 1609. As a navigable link in the inland waterway that connects Canada with the Hudson River, the north end of the lake connects in the province of Quebec, Canada with the

Richelieu River and is navigable for twenty miles, to St Jean sur Richelieu and the Chambly Rapids.

Prior to the 19th century, Lake Champlain was not directly connected for continuous navigation to the natural waterways to its north or south. In 1823, the completion of the Champlain Canal connected Lake Champlain at its southern end to the Hudson River. Then, in 1843, despite concern by Canada's British military planners about providing the US with a potential invasion route, the Chambly Canal was completed. This 12-mile canal circumvented the Chambly Rapids, providing a navigable route all the way north to the St Lawrence River. With the completion of these two canals, it became possible to take a vessel from New York City north into Canada, a route that remains open to this day (Figure 49).

As a key strategic route, Lake Champlain was the site of multiple episodes of military action, including rival French and British fleets during the Seven Years' War, rival American and British fleets during the American Revolution, and rival squadrons of warships which helped define the outcome of the War of 1812 (Crisman 2014). Although it was not known at the time, the War of 1812 would be the last time Lake Champlain would hear cannons fired in anger. With the opening of the canals, the lake began its transition from a contested strategic military waterway into a dynamic commercial highway. For the next century and a half, Lake Champlain would help define the economic and demographic characteristics of the region and the nation.

Over the past four decades, rapid advancements in underwater survey technology have fuelled the discovery of a remarkable number of shipwrecks as a well as a wide variety of submerged cultural artefacts. Not surprisingly, many of these underwater sites are of military origin. While these artefacts can serve to confirm the broad chapters of nation-versus-nation international conflicts, they can also tell the poignant and intimate stories of some of the less well-known people who became casualties. The combination of nautical archaeology and archival research into these long-lost warships and the people who fought life and death struggles on this remote mountain lake provides powerful insight and appreciation into the true costs of the conflict.

Battles

For the first three years of the American Revolution, the Champlain Valley was the scene of many incursions north and south by the combatants. Just three weeks after the first shots were fired at Concord and Lexington on April 19, 1775, a small force of "Green Mountain Boys," led by Ethan Allen and joined by Benedict Arnold, a Connecticut officer holding a Massachusetts commission, seized the forts at Ticonderoga and Crown Point. Equally important, Benedict Arnold led a force to capture the only two large warships then on the lake. Knowing the significance of gaining control of the waterway, Arnold then reported to Congress *"We are Masters of Lake Champlain"* (NDAR, Vol 1, 1964).

Although the goals and methods of the struggle were still unfolding, the Rebel planners decided to invade British Canada to seize the last British stronghold in North America. Two armies were dispatched, one travelling up the Lake Champlain corridor, and a second force, led by Benedict Arnold, marched through the Maine and Canadian wildernesses. The two armies, working independently of each other, suffered many hardships in their efforts to further their military objectives. After months of travel, siege and starvation, the two armies met in front of the walled fortress city of Quebec. It was early winter, and the cold, snow and lack of supplies took its toll on the citizen soldiers. A failed New Year's Eve attempt to surprise and take the city doomed the campaign, and when a British relief convoy dropped anchor at Quebec in the spring of 1776, what remained of the rebel army began a demoralized retreat from Canada that didn't stop until they were back at the relative safety of Lake Champlain. Primary accounts record that the fleeing forces stopped at Isle Aux Noix, a low-lying island in the Richelieu River. Here, it is recorded that many of these men, sick with smallpox, could go no further and died. These casualties of war died far from home and family and were buried in unmarked mass graves that to this day have not been located. Dr Samuel Meryick, surgeon with the Massachusetts regiment wrote, *"Great numbers could not stand, calling on us for help, and we had nothing to give them. It broke my heart and I wept till I had no more power to weep"* (Clark 1964, NDAR, Vol 5, 1970).

The Americans' safety that spring was a result of holding naval superiority over Lake Champlain. This had been achieved due to the capture of the only large vessels on the lake the previous season. Now, in June of 1776, as the fresh British force advanced to St Johns, and the Americans fell back to Crown Point and Fort Ticonderoga, it became clear that the campaign of 1776 would be a contest for naval control of the Lake Champlain invasion route. To that end, the British established a shipyard at St Johns in the north and brought Royal Navy officers and men, supported by their Hessian allies, to assemble a fleet of fighting ships to take back control of the lake. The Rebels, led by the controversial General Benedict Arnold, established a shipyard at Skenesborough, now Whitehall, N.Y., near the southern end of the lake, to build warships to strengthen their tenuous naval advantage (Figure 49).

The combatants' efforts came to a climax on October 11, 1776 when the American and British fleets met at the crucial, but little remembered Battle of Valcour Island. During a three-day contest that extended over more than 70 miles of Lake Champlain, the rival naval squadrons fought a series of intensive engagements. When the smoke had cleared at the end of the third day, the Americans had lost eleven of their fifteen warships as well as control of the lake. The superior British fleet was now firmly in command of the lake corridor, but with the weather turning cold and content with their regained status, they chose to halt their invasion and withdrew back to Canada for the winter (Hatch 1979).

In the spring of 1777, a confident British army, now under the command of General John Burgoyne, returned to the rebelling colonies via Lake Champlain. Their goal was nothing less than to divide the Colonies and end the war. Burgoyne's initial success on Lake Champlain slowly gave way to setbacks as his army moved south towards the Hudson River. The 1777 campaign ended in October, one year after the Battle of Valcour Island, with the profound and shocking British defeat at the Battles of Saratoga, known as the "turning point of the Revolution" (Darley 2013, Ketchum 1997).

Nautical archaeology

"Where history happens, people leave their stuff behind"

For the past three decades my colleagues and I have used historic records to help locate and document the underwater archaeological remains of this decisive 1776 naval engagement. This effort has led to the discovery of artefacts and a portion of a vessel within Arnold's Bay, Vermont, the twenty-two intact footings belonging to the "Great Bridge," (Cohn et al. 1995) built upon the winter ice in 1777 to span the lake between Fort Ticonderoga and Mount Independence, and in 1997, as part of our "Whole Lake Survey," the discovery in the deep waters of Lake Champlain of the intact, upright remains of the gunboat *Spitfire*. On June 6, 2017, the *Spitfire* Management Project marked the twentieth anniversary of the gunboat's discovery with the formal release of management recommendations (Lundeberg et al. 2017). These recommendations, which call for the *Spitfire*'s recovery, conservation and public exhibition, were delivered to the US Naval History and Heritage Command and a deliberative process has begun to evaluate them.

The Battle of Valcour Island, when it is remembered, is often interpreted in sweeping terms, recounting an engagement between British and American naval squadrons that proved to become one of the most important of the American Revolution. History has well remembered principals such as Benedict Arnold and Sir Guy Carleton, and American vessels such as *Liberty* and *Royal Savage* fighting British vessels with names like *Inflexible* and *Thunderer*. But perhaps the best example of the impact of "War on Board" was the chance discovery of a cannon fragment beneath the lake's silty bottom at the site of the battle. The story of this artefact provides a direct connection to some of the naval contest's lesser known participants. The cannon's history serves to remind us that casualty counts are made up of individuals whose lives are ended or changed in profound ways. It has also served to remind us that each of the casualties has a circle of family and friends that are also impacted by the loss.

The Valcour Bay Research Project (VBRP)

In 1999, New York State Police diver Ed Scollon was testing a new metal detector at the site of the Battle of Valcour Island. As part of the state police dive team, Ed was regularly called out to help recover victims of drowning or conduct underwater searches for evidence after accidents or crimes. Today, the lake bottom where the battle took place is a featureless, relatively flat, muddy landscape. Hiding under 50 to 60 feet of cold, fresh water, the site presents few obvious clues to the momentous events that once took place there. However, as a police diver, Ed was keenly aware that for decades, first hard hat and later SCUBA divers regularly visited the location to hunt for souvenirs.

As Ed experimented with the new detector to search the non-descript bottom, the detector began to sing out loudly that there was dense metal somewhere under the mud. To verify the target, Ed began hand-fanning the silt to expose the source of the noise. Although the detector was unfamiliar, the indication was that it had located something containing a significant mass of metal, but after patient digging, Ed was unable to find the object. After defining the extent of the anomaly, Ed set the detector down and continued to dig by hand until, more than three feet below the plane of the lake bottom, he reached what seemed like a circular jagged metal fragment. Ed traced the object to be about five feet long and at the deepest end, more than five feet under the silt. After feeling the mass, thickness and shape of the object, Ed began to believe he might have located a cannon. A cannon from the Battle of Valcour Island, even a broken one, would be a significant discovery and the excited diver called a diving buddy, Dan Carpenter, to help him recover the object. Once on site, Dan took stock of Ed's description and suggested that he call this author to discuss the archaeology of the situation before carrying out any recovery activities.

I received Ed's call from a boat over the site of the discovery and he related to me what he had done, what he thought he had found and his intention to recover the presumed cannon to protect it from the many souvenir hunters who regularly dove the site. I counselled caution and patience and suggested that the cannon, if that was indeed what it proved to be, had been there for over 230 years and would probably be okay for another day or two. After some discussion, it was agreed that it would be problematic for Ed, as a New York State trooper, to recover the object without a New York State permit. Instead, he was invited to come to LCMM to talk about management options. At that meeting, we discussed launching a new in-water research project to archeologically map the submerged battle site, with the hope that it might reveal more of its secrets and offer new historical insights. It might also serve to engage area divers in a formal, permitted archaeological project that could slow or even stop the damage to the site from casual collecting. Ed, passionate about the history, was very willing to collaborate with LCMM on such a project.

By mapping and comparing the archaeological results with the known historical record, we hoped to gain a better understanding of historical events. Using the "cannon" discovery as the zero point, the bottom was divided into fifty-foot square survey areas. These squares were further subdivided into survey transects every three feet and systematically examined by diver teams using metal detectors to locate and map the artefact scatter from the battle.

The cannon fragment's jagged, fractured metal communicates that at some point in the weapon's life it failed and exploded, but when and under what circumstances? The odds that research would ever be able to find an account so specific as to shed light on the object and its story was a long shot, but in fact, that is exactly what occurred (Cohn et al. 2007).

Two years before the cannon's discovery, the LCMM team, responding to the invasion of zebra mussels, initiated a ten-year project to systematically examine the entire bottom of Lake Champlain. In 1997, the second year of the Whole Lake Survey, a sonar target was located which proved to be the last unaccounted-for vessel from Benedict Arnold Revolutionary War fleet. The shipwreck was determined to be one of the eight 54-foot long gunboats from the American fleet, but the specific identity of the gunboat could not be determined by the known historical record and therefore the shipwreck was first named the *Missing Gunboat*. The discovery, however, stimulated a new round of historical research with the goal of identifying which gunboat it was (Figure 56).

Townsend document and pension record

Perhaps the most informative new evidence to come to light was what we have come to call the "Townsend Document" (Figure 53) because it was provided by John Townsend, a historic book dealer from Connecticut. This document, entitled "Return of the fleet belonging to the United States of America on Lake Champlain…" was so specific as to type of "Vessels," their "Names," "by Whom Commanded' and "Fate," that the Missing Gunboat was conclusively identified as the gunboat *Spitfire*.

A second document, newly-discovered by researcher George Quintal, is a pension record application, located in the National Archives has led to the discovery of the exact circumstances as to how the cannon fragment came to rest for more than two centuries in protective suspension within the silty bottom. The account was a pension record for Sergeant Jonas Holden, who as an elderly man, needed his country's assistance. Over the next twenty or so years Jonas filed the required sworn statements to make his claim and stated that he was present and injured at the Battle of Bunker Hill *"where the deponent was wounded by a musket shot through the thigh & was carried off the ground"* (6 April 1818). Jonas healed well enough to march north to Fort Ticonderoga in 1776 and, *"The next was on Lake Champlain under Arnold, on board a gondola, where I was again wounded on the right arm and side, by the bursting of a cannon"* (21 February 1835). This reference to the "bursting of a cannon" led researchers to Westford, Massachusetts, Jonas's home at the time of his enlistment, and to the remarkable discovery of the fate of his fellow townsman and friend Lt Thomas Rogers.

In 1776, Lt Rogers, and his brother Sartell were dispatched to the American fleet then fitting out on Lake Champlain to face the British. The three Westford men were assigned to serve upon the gunboat *New York*, under the command of Captain John Read, and aboard this gunboat they fought the British at the Battle of Valcour Island on October 11, 1776 and escaped during the night of October 12. The *New York* was the only gunboat out of the eight to survive the three-day engagements and to return to Fort Ticonderoga. We also learn that Sgt Holden claims throughout his requests for a pension that in detailing his wounds, he repeatedly reports that he was injured on his right arm and side during the battle by the bursting of a cannon. Could the cannon fragment found in 1999 be part of the same cannon that caused Sgt Holden's wounds? The answer to this question was to be found within the details of the Townsend Document.

The Townsend Document, written just ten days after the battle, had already provided the crucial details that led to the conclusive identification of the Missing Gunboat as the *Spitfire*. This identification had been made by comparing the dozens of known primary accounts of the Battle of Valcour Island with the new information provided by the document, specifically, "*The Fate of the Fleet*" column, which provided the known status of each vessel which had permitted the *Spitfire*'s identity to be confirmed. In addition to this important piece of information, the Townsend Document also provided a minutely-detailed inventory of the number and size of the cannons aboard each vessel. Most "returns", or descriptions of the eight gunboats' armament typically reported that they were each equipped with a 12-pounder in the bow and two 9-pounders mounted mid-ship. However, the Townsend Document breaks the cannon inventory down to very specific numbers and informs that only one of the eight gunboats was equipped with 6-pounder cannons. The Townsend Document lists the 6-pounders as being aboard the gunboat *Success*, which was an earlier name given to the gunboat *New York*. In the return, the gunboat identified as *Success* is listed as being under the command of "*Captain Reed*" whose "Fate" was that she was the only gunboat that "*Arrived Safe in Port.*" Captain Reed (or Read) was the Captain of *New York* and the *New York*, as confirmed by multiple primary accounts, was the only gunboat to make it back to Fort Ticonderoga in the aftermath of the battle. Hence, we believe it is accurate to conclude that since the *New York* was the only gunboat noted to be carrying a six pound cannon and the *New York* was the vessel to which the three Westford men were assigned to serve, that if the cannon fragment was determined to be from a 6-pound gun, it would be safe to conclude that the cannon found was the cannon that exploded aboard the gunboat, injuring Sgt Holden.

Once the VBRP began its systematic examination of the lake bottom surrounding the original cannon fragment, several more chunks of the cannon were located, identified and mapped. On June 30, 2001, in commemoration of the 235th anniversary of the Battle of Valcour Island, a plan was developed and permitted by both the State of New York and the US Navy to recover several significant diagnostic and exhibit-quality artefacts which had been discovered during the first three years of the VBRP's archaeological study. The original large cannon fragment was selected for recovery, along with several smaller fragments located during the study. The cannon pieces and their far-flung distribution mapped by the archaeology was testimony to the violence of the event, which must have taken place during the battle.

The artefact recovery was a highly engineered production. The US Coast Guard, Station Burlington's Buoy Tender provided the controlled lifting platform. Vermont Senator Patrick Leahy and New York Senator Hillary Clinton joined with 300 citizens, half from New York and half from Vermont, aboard the Lake Champlain Transportation Company's ferry *Adirondack* for the lifting of the cannon by a Barrett's Tree Service crane and gentle placement on the ferryboat's deck (Figure 51). A quick examination of the cannon muzzle diameter confirmed that the recovered cannon was indeed a 6-pound gun and therefore must have been the very gun described by Sgt Jonas Holden as the one that injured him and killed his comrade-in-arms and fellow townsman Lt Thomas Rogers.

The traumatic incident of the cannon exploding on a crowded deck filled with men all about it occurred during the heat of the October 11 fighting and was not described in Commodore Arnold's first after-action report in a letter to General Horatio Gates written from Schuyler Island. Arnold was writing during his dramatic attempt to escape and provided a summary rather than specifics. He wrote that, "…*the* New York *lost all her Officers except her Captain…the whole* [in the fleet] *killed & wounded amounts to abt Sixty*" (NDAR, Vol 6, 1972). The report was designed to inform Gates, the officer-in-charge, of the material circumstances of the engagement and therefore names and specific circumstances affecting the individuals involved would not be expected to be included. At least for now, the men who died or were wounded would be left nameless. In the case of the officers of *New York*, they might have remained anonymous if not for the discovery, more than two centuries later, of the broken cannon under the mud of Valcour Bay.

The pension application of Sgt Jonas Holden, initiated in 1818 to relieve him of his poverty more than four decades after his military service, takes us deeper into the details of what happened on the day he was wounded in that engagement. Jonas's pension statement reports that he had enlisted in time to fight at Concord, got wounded at Bunker Hill and had healed enough by the start of the 1776 campaign to enlist again for the fight to control Lake Champlain. Wounded again in that engagement, his pension record reveals that once he healed from those wounds, he enlisted again to serve his country and was present in the army that pressed Lord Cornwallis to surrender at Yorktown in 1781.

We also learn from the Jonas Holden's pension record about the death of Thomas Rogers in that same explosion, whose military and life record dies with him at the Battle of Valcour Island on October 11, 1776. Alerted to this tragic event, it led to the discovery of a memorial stone in the Old Cemetery in Westford, Massachusetts; a remarkable document of the impact of Rogers loss on his family (Figure 55).

Momento mori. The words transcribed from the memorial stone marker erected "*…to the memory of Lieut. Thomas Rogers by Mrs. Molly his Sorrowful widow*" which was found in the Old Cemetery of Westford, Massachusetts. The memorial records that "*he was killed by the Splitting of a Cannon on the 11th of Oct. 1776 in the Continental Army in the service of his Country and in the caus of Liberty.*"

That Mrs. Molly would have reflected on the loss of her husband in this tangible way is a powerful reflection of the loss. Life in the 18th century was often harsh, and research informs us that Thomas and Molly had already suffered the death of their first child, also named Molly, during the summer of 1775. Young Molly was one of 23 Westford children who died at that time from what has been speculated as being a camp disease brought home by one of the town's soldiers encamped at the siege of Boston. When Thomas left for Lake Champlain in 1776, Mrs Molly was pregnant with their second child. This child, also to be named Molly, was born three months after her father's death and this child's life would also prove to be short-lived. On September 11, 1778, at the age of 20 months, young Molly also died. Mrs. Molly, now a widow who had lost two daughters before they had reached their second birthday, resolved to memorialize her husband Thomas and his tragic loss in the "*cause of Liberty*" by erecting a memorial stone to his memory. She erected the stone to be placed in-company with their two infant daughters, and like many a "sorrowful widow" or mother, father, sister or brother that lost a loved one to war, tried to heal and move on with life. It seems inescapable that Molly had this memorial stone erected to make sure that Thomas and their sacrifice would not be forgotten. The hand-carved stone and the broken cannon combine to provide the details of this little-known incident in this almost forgotten naval battle and demonstrate the power of the historical and archaeological record to reveal otherwise lost stories from earlier times.

At war's end, Lt Rogers was gone, Jonas Holden had risen to the rank of Lieutenant, healed and moved to Wallingford, Vermont and Mrs. Molly remarried. In 1783, some seven years after Thomas' death and five years after the loss of their second daughter, Mrs. Molly married William Munroe, another active American patriot during the struggle for independence. William had been present at Lexington and Concord and the Battle of Saratoga and was, in fact, the owner of a tavern in historic Lexington, Massachusetts. On what became the first day of the American Revolution, the shocked British force occupied the tavern as a resting place and make-shift hospital. It is quite possible that William had served with Thomas and that Molly knew him from that common bond. While William lived until 1827 and the age of 85, Molly died in 1799 at the age of 44. The record indicates that Molly and William had no children together, but little is currently known about the quality of Molly's life after her second marriage. It can only be hoped that in the aftermath of her multiple losses, the erection of the hand-carved, stone memorial put Molly on a path of healing and potential happiness. The historic Munroe Tavern still stands today as a Lexington Historic Site, the memorial stone still stands in the Westford cemetery, and the fragments of the cannon are contained within the traveling exhibition "A Moment in Time." All serve as a touchstone to the origins of the national story and a connection to Thomas and Molly Rogers' poignant story of life and death aboard ships of war (Figure 54).

Today on Lake Champlain, the wooden warships, steamboats and commercial craft of yesterday have been replaced by modern steel ferries and recreational craft. The armies and navies of French, British, American, and Hessian soldiers and sailors, supported by the unfortunate Native Peoples who got drawn into the conflict, have been replaced by armies of visitors coming to buy maple syrup, bask in the glow of our multi-coloured fall foliage and ski, walk, bike and hike in our beautiful mountains. They also come to visit an interesting collection of historic sites, like Saratoga National Historical Park, Fort Ticonderoga, Mount Independence, Fort Crown Point/ Fort St Frederic and Fort Chambly, all of which provide strong insights into the lake's military past. Today, instead of positioning lookouts to keep a vigilant watch for the enemy, visitors to Lake Champlain look west to watch some of the most glorious sunsets on the planet. Amazingly, what our generation has only recently discovered is that beneath Lake Champlain's cold, deep, fresh-water is a collection of remarkably intact wooden historic watercraft that connect us to an earlier time when cannon, musket and sword were the tools of the trade.

Figure 48: Lake Champlain in the fall looking north. The 120-mile long, navigable waterway has been a natural transportation corridor for thousands of years. Historic Basin Harbour, Vermont is centre right. New York's Split Rock Mountain is on the left (Photo by Eric Bessette, Shadow and Light Design)

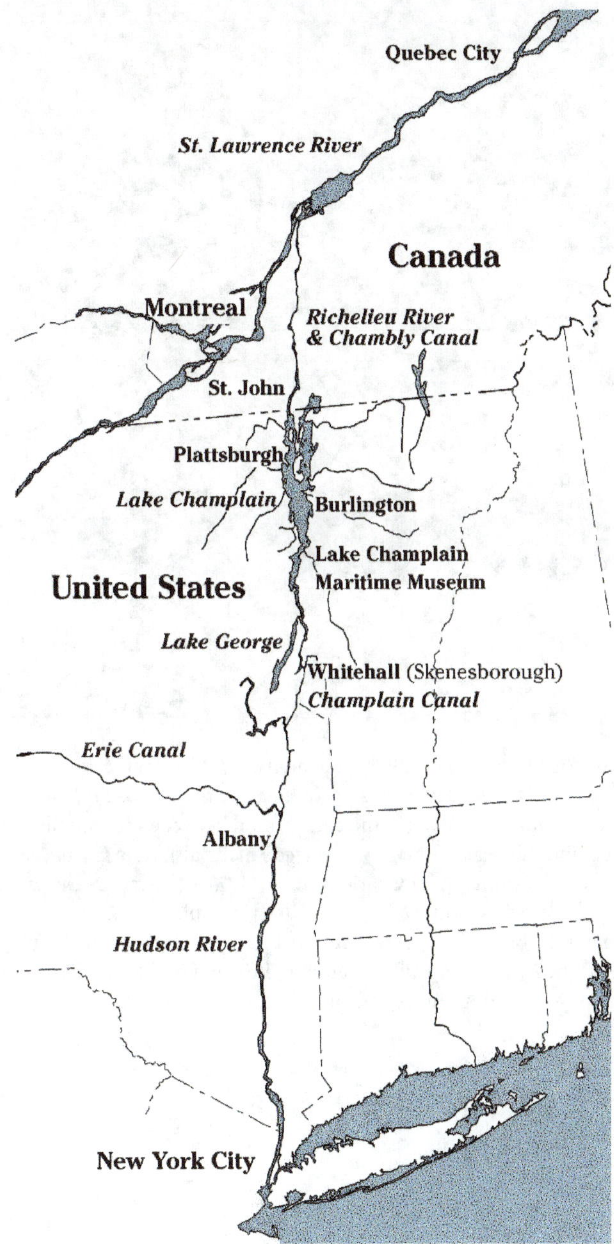

Figure 49: Where in the world is Lake Champlain? A map of Quebec, Canada to New York City illustrates Lake Champlain's maritime connection to Old World Countries and New World powers. (LCMM)

Figure 50: Top: A View of the New England Arm'd Vessels at Valcour Bay on Lake Champlain, 11 October 1776. The vessels from left to right: *Revenge, Washington, Philadelphia, Congress, Spitfire, Lee, Royal Savage* (foreground), *Boston* (in the background between the topsails of the *Royal Savage*), Jersey (partly hidden behind the peak of the *Royal Savage*'s mainsail), *New Haven, Providence, Connecticut, New York, Enterprise,* and *Trumbull,* by Charles Randle, 1777 (courtesy National Archives of Canada). Bottom: A View of His Majesty's Arm'd Vessels on Lake Champlain, 11 October 1776. The vessels are shown sailing south before the battle. The vessels from left to right: *Carleton, Inflexible,* a cutter-rigged gunboat, *Maria, Loyal Convert, Thunderer;* and several small British gunboats in the background, by Charles Randle, 1777 (courtesy of National Archives of Canada)

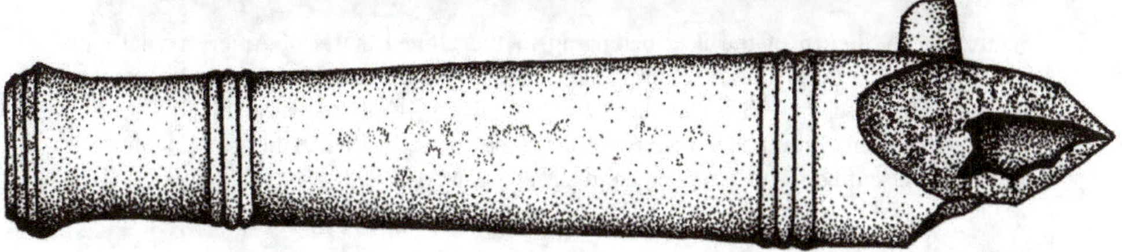

Figure 51: Top: The cannon fragment in-situ just before recovery. Bottom: An archaeological plan of the recovered cannon fragment (LCMM)

Figure 52: The cannon fragment is transferred after recovery from a U.S. Coast Guard, Station Burlington buoy tender to the ferry *Adirondack* where VBRP team members guide the cannon to the deck (LCMM)

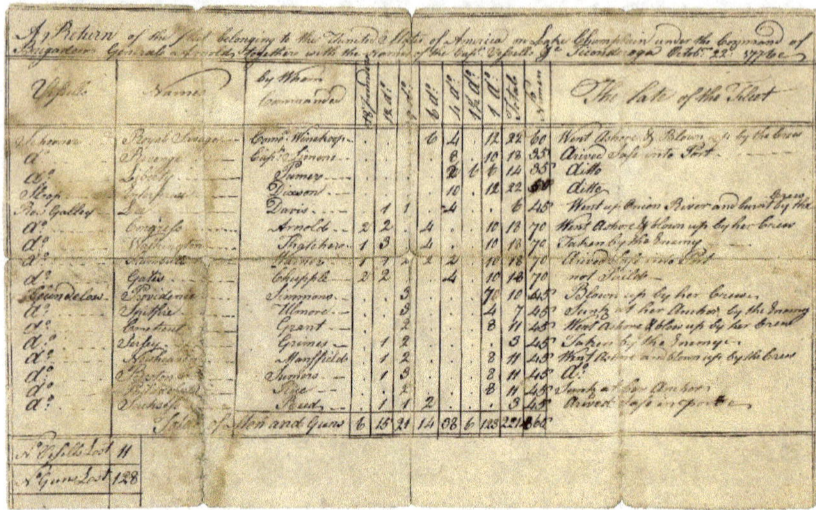

Figure 53: "A Return of the fleet belonging to the United States of America on Lake Champlain under the command of Brigadier General Benedict Arnold together with Names of the Capt. Vessels. Ft. Ticonderoga October 22, 1776." Now known as the Townsend Document, this important document was first loaned and then gifted to the Lake Champlain Maritime Museum by John Townsend and family (LCMM)

Figure 54: "A Moment in Time," by marine artist Ernie Haas, uses the archaeological record to recreate the explosion on board the gunboat New York during the Battle of Valcour Island (LCMM)

Figure 55: Memorial stone, Westford Massachusetts

Figure 56: 'The Missing Gunboat Found,' by marine artist Ernie Haas, was based on video and still images taken by a remote operated vehicle (ROV). Occasionally history and archaeology combine to help transport us back to past events. The intact gunboat, now identified as *Spitfire*, well preserved in the deep waters of Lake Champlain, provides a powerful connection to the men and families whose lives were impacted by the events of the conflict (LCMM)

References

Clark, W. B., W. J. Morgan & M. Crawford. (eds.). *The Naval Documents of the American Revolution*. 13 Volumes, Washington: Government Printing Office, 1964 to date.

Cohn, Arthur, B. *1992 Fort Ticonderoga-Mount Independence Submerged Cultural Resource Survey*. Lake Champlain Maritime Museum, Basin Harbour, Vermont. 1995.

Cohn, Arthur B., Kane, A. I., Sabick, C. R. & Scollon, E. R., *Valcour Bay Research Project: 1999–2004 Results from the Archaeological Investigation of a Revolutionary War Battlefield in Lake Champlain*. Lake Champlain Maritime Museum, Basin Harbour, Vermont. 2007.

Crisman, Kevin J. ed., *Coffins of the Brave; Lake Shipwrecks of the War of 1812*. Texas A&M University Press, College Station, Texas. 2014.

Hatch, Robert McConnell. *Thrust for Canada: The American Attempt on Quebec in 1775–1776*. Houghton Mifflin Company, Boston. 1979.

Darley, S., *The Battle of Valcour Island*. Published by the Author. 2013.

Ketchum, R. M., *Saratoga: Turning Point of America's Revolutionary War*. Henry Holt and Company. New York. 1997.

Lundeberg, P. K., Arthur B. Cohn, Jennifer L. Jones. *A Tale of Three Gunboats: Lake Champlain's Revolutionary War Heritage*. Lake Champlain Maritime Museum, Basin Harbour, Vermont. Smithsonian National Museum of American History. 2017.

The Townsend Document. Lake Champlain Maritime Museum, Basin Harbour, Vermont.

Revolutionary War Pension and Bounty Land Warrant Application Files, National Archives, Roll 1306 of M804.

Mercurio (1812) – Artefacts from a 'Cosmopolite' Warship of the Early 19th Century.

CARLO BELTRAME

The battle

On the night between the 21st and the 22nd of February 1812, the brig *Mercurio* was sunk by the British brig *Weasel*, off Punta Tagliamento, north of the city of Venice. The *Mercurio* was part of a squadron escorting the 80-gun French vessel *Rivoli*. *Mercurio* was built, in 1806, in Genova for the French Navy, but between 1809 and 1810, it was transferred, under Napoleons command, to the fleet of the kingdom of Regno Italico (Beltrame, 2007; 2010).

The 80-gun-ship *Rivoli* was one of the first vessels built by Napoleon to try to take control of the Adriatic which was in the hands of the British. The escorting squadron was commanded by admiral Barrè and, in addition to *Mercurio*, *Rivoli* was accompanied by the French brig *Jena* and the Italian brig *Mameluck*.

Rivoli and the other ships left harbour and set out into the Adriatic night on 21st February. Soon a British squadron, commanded by Captain John Talbot, accompanied by the 74-gunned *Victorius* and the brig *Weasel*, began to follow the squadron escorting the *Rivoli*. After a while *Weasel* reached the *Mercurio* which was slower than the other ships. After a 40-minute-battle *Mercurio* exploded and sank at 5 o'clock in the morning.

Only three men on *Mercurio* survived and were saved by the English ship after the explosion.

The battle continued for six hours. The two other French brigs escaped while, off the small city of Grado (which gave the name to the battle), the British squadron captured the *Rivoli*, inflicting a heavy loss on the French fleet (Beltrame, 2007; 2010).

In 2001, the remains of the *Mercurio* were discovered by a fishing trawler seven nautical miles from Punta Tagliamento (from the border between the Veneto and the Friuli Venezia Giulia regions), at a depth of 17 metre and in the same year a project of excavation began (Figure 58). During the seasons of investigation, organized on the site in 2001 and from 2004 to 2011 (Beltrame, 2007; 2009; 2010 and references), part of the bow area and the sternpost of the hull were documented and about 2000 items were found (excluding 700 lead musket shot and a group of 300 items composed by nails, bolts and fragments of copper sheeting).

The port bow area, which corresponds to where the excavations were carried out deeper in the sand, has preserved every kind of object – many of which were made of wood and leather – in excellent conditions. Due to the position of the ship, the hull on the port side is well preserved almost up to the deck, and part of the orlop deck is visible.

Due to the conditions of preservation of the items and the hull, and because of the extraordinary presence of skeletal remains, this site may be considered as one of the best preserved underwater archaeological contexts along the Mediterranean coastline.

In the Mediterranean, the study of shipwrecks from the 18th and 19th centuries has been neglected in comparison to that of Antique shipwrecks. One of the reasons is due the abundance of information about this period. We have indeed access to many historical sources on battles, life aboard the vessels and naval architecture from this period. Some plans and models of the ship made during their lifetime are also available. There is, however, an unawareness, although a relative wealth of information, that archaeological investigation can still tell us much more. Archaeology is indeed able to contextualize, improve and correct the historical data.

The study of the *Mercurio* is a good example of how the potential for an archaeological investigation to contributes to the knowledge of a post-Medieval marine context.

The discovery of the sternpost, far from the rest of the ship, has demonstrated that the cause of the sinking was the explosion of the powder magazine, as testified by some written sources. The explosion of the powder magazine indeed, located in the stern, cut the ship in two at this point.

The crew and personal belongings

The extraordinary presence of many skeletal remains in the port side area, also under wooden structures probably belonging to the deck, demonstrates that some of the crew, for unclear reasons (perhaps because they were wounded?), were below deck while the ship was in battle.

Furthermore, these human remains, thanks to recording by intra-site GIS (Beltrame and Manfio, 2014), have been tentatively associated with the numerous remains of uniforms, mainly buttons, shoes and some arms (Figure 58). The most interesting association is one of a metal pendant, with the image of Saint Anne (Figure 59), alongside the remains of a man who could have been the cadet Tommaso Locatelli, who attended the College of Saint Anne in Venice (Donadel pers. inf. 2016). Locatelli's age of 20 at the time of death would correspond indeed to the 16–20 years attributed by the anthropologists to the two skeletal remains (SK 1 and SK 4) located close to the medal (Bertoldi, Beltrame and Sisalli, 2014) (Figure 60).

Although the study of the objects belonging to the mariners (uniforms and personal items) has not led to other reliable associations with human remains, it has revealed an unexpected variety of geographical provenances of these items.

Donadel's studies (in press) have demonstrated that the pistols model from 1786 was probably made at "la Tule" in France while the only short musket, model 1786 of a French Hussar type, was probably made in Brescia, between 1802 and 1805, for the Republica Italiana (the state founded by Napoleon in the North of Italy which then became the Regno Italico), as indicated by the stamped initials. It was made from a Hussar cold steel, and in addition there was a sword of Austro-Hungarian type, made at Kligenthal (actual Germany) (Figure 61), while another sword (*a sabre de bord*) was of French production and a third one (*sabre briquet*), although a French model, was made in Brescia.

Gunflints were produced with stone from the Baldo mountain, located close to Trento (Figure 62). In the city of Avio, close to the Garda Lake, 170 km from Venice, there was a workshop for the manufacturing of this widely diffused flint which, in this case, has been preferred to the better-quality French "du Berry" gunflints (Biagi, Starnini and Beltrame, 2016).

The majority of the 388 buttons found in the site wreck were made of an alloy of tin and lead. They were used both by sailors and by officers of the navy of the Regno Italico and may have been made in Italy, however, regarding this category of objects, there may well be exceptions.

Ninety per cent of the buttons belonged to marine artillery-men, some to navy officers, one to the Garde Impériale of the Italic Kingdom. Two copper buttons belonged to the African King's Corpes (*Corpo Reale Africano*) (Figure 62) and one belonged to the 7th French regiment of Artillery; finally, five buttons were produced in London while an additional two buttons present a typology used in the British navy (Donadel, in press) (Figure 63).

The numerous shoes preserved present close similarities to the French models but could have been bought at a local market (Donadel, in press).

Among the personal objects, some copper coins were found: some belonged to the Regno d'Italia, two *Lire Venete* (Figure 65) and two Kreuzer were minted by the Austrian Empire while the others were Baiocchian, one made in Ferrara and five made in the State of the church, in Rome. (Figure 66).

Some jewels were also found. Some of them, including a gold wedding ring (Figure 67), could have well been produced in Sardinia where there is a strong tradition of jewellery.

The study of the objects in the galley has made it possible to distinguish between pottery for the officers and pottery for the sailors. Among the first category, there is a plate of majolica from the Castelli d'Abruzzo (Figure 68) while a coffee cup is of china. An object was identified as one of the very first tin-cans of food hermetically conserved, testimony of a lucky invention which changed among others the military supply. Our tin-can indeed could have been produced during the first experiments, begun only in 1810 after Durand's invention, and it could have been embarked on the brig as canned food for the long voyages (Manfio, 2014).

Much less heterogeneous than the personal belongings, is the origin of the ship's equipment. *Mercurio* was mainly armed with 16 (the number is not sure) 24-pounder iron carronades and with two 8-pounder iron guns made in the Du Creusot French foundry. The recovered bronze swivel gun, which belongs to a type of artillery piece not documented by the archival sources because of its small dimensions, is signed by the founder Michel Brezin of Paris. Two brass flintlocks, belonging to a sort of blunderbuss or a big musket, are other arms not documented in the archives and which were also produced in Paris (Figure 69).

The "cosmopolitan" dimension of *Mercurio* emerging from the analysis of the numerous personal objects from the wreck does not strictly to match the one indicated by the crew list (in Archivio di Stato di Venezia). The hundreds of items indicate places of manufacturing and provenance of the mariners.

The crew list of 87 men shows the provenance of the officers and the sailors being mainly from Venice (43%), which is the location of the fleet, six men from both the Dalmatian and the Illyrian area (14%), a zone which had a long nautical tradition in common with Venice from the beginning of the Republic of Saint Mark, and three men from France, the nation which controlled the Regno Italico and which shared the fleet with this small reign. Four men come from Chioggia, which is a small city located in the southern lagoon of Venice with a long tradition in common with Venice and inhabited by seamen and fishermen. In addition, four men come from the hinterland of Venice, which traditionally supplied the city with sailors, while another fifteen men come mainly from the Emilia region, but in general from the Regno Italico territory, which extended to the central and eastern part of Italy and along a part of the Adriatic western coast (Figure 71).

On the list, there are also less obvious presences such as one from Corfu, an island which has been Venetian for many centuries, one from Istria, a region which was strongly connected to Venice, one from the Liguria region, part of the Napoleonic Empire, one from St Petersburg, one from the Tirolo region, one from Belgrade and finally one from Constantinople.

Discussion

The introduction in the Army of distinguished corps, such as the artillery-men, the use among the soldiers of a standardized uniform – in the case of the crew from the Regno Italico Navy the use of a uniform *"même que dans la marine française"* (Boeri, Crociani e Paoletti, 1996, 94) differentiated only in the green colour of the jacket and in the embroidery that was in silver and not in gold (Donadel, in press) – and the innovative solutions, such as conserving the food hermetically on board, tell us of a period of innovation, experimentation but also homogenization both in the Army and in the Navy.

Although this ship belonged to the fleet of a city-state which, until few decades earlier, was one of the most important sea thalassocracies of the Mediterranean with a millennium of history aboard it, we do not find any trace of the Saint Mark's winged lion which marked every arm or object of the Venetian stately ships. These items indeed testify the will of the Napoleon Empire, which did not appreciate any reference to the past of the occupied nations, breaking with the very long naval history of the Serenissima, and imposing a strong standardization (Craik, 2005) in the uniforms following new French models.

Although the trend of the Napoleonic Navy was to generalize a standardization of uniforms and arms for the crew, archaeological evidence from the *Mercurio* shows an evident heterogeneity on the origins of both the personnel and of the objects (Figure 70). The crew indeed, as documented on the list, did not only consist of Venetians, offering a panorama which is expanded by the presence of objects from the centre of the peninsula and from outside the Alps.

Gunflints made in Trento, instead of using better-quality French gunflints, arms made in Brescia, and buttons (and possibly shoes) made regionally, in coexistence with other small arms, and the entire artillery made in France, are evidence of the relative independence of the supplies from France by the fleet of the Regno Italico which bought them from North Italian sellers, probably penalizing the quality and of course, at least in part, still following a practice applied in Venice in a millennium of nautical tradition.

Conclusions

The archaeological evidence emerging from this shipwreck is very rich because of the lucky conditions of preservation both in quantity and in quality. It forms a sort of kaleidoscope of the society aboard a military ship of that period. The high level of preservation of the archaeological evidence of this site, make it possible to present a situation quite close to the original conditions of the context, revealing a "complexity" which can almost be problematic regarding interpretation. This is seen regarding association among the objects: it will probably never be possible, for example, to say if the infantry buttons or the British buttons belonged to a particular sailor or if they were simply used in place of service uniforms.

The presence of this complexity, despite the strong trend in standardizing the arms, the uniforms and consequently the supplies happening in this period, is very interesting. It seems that this standardization is still not complete and, as the archaeological evidence shows it still presents numerous exceptions.

However, the study may also inspire more general considerations about information collected from the archaeological record. If, during the investigation of a shipwreck that sank in a period which should have applied standardization and centralized supplies, we still find quite a heterogeneous situation, as shown in the complex archaeological evidence, then what can we expect from shipwrecks that sank earlier, before the process of standardization of the Napoleonic period? What are we able to understand of the original context, before the formation processes of the archaeological record?

Is the complexity of *Mercurio* a peculiarity of this period or of this type of ship? Or may we suspect, on the contrary, that this condition – emerging thanks to the "narrow meshes" of the interpretative filters offered by the quality and the quantity of the historical sources (written documents, handbooks and drawing), allowing identify most artefacts precisely and provide a contextualization of these items in a well-known historical panorama – is present also in more ancient contexts? Are we sure that the apparent simpler panorama, offered by contexts of more ancient periods, is not only an "illusion"?

Can we suspect that a similar complexity does not emerge from other contexts both because of the poorer availability of traditional sources, which offer a weaker control to its trustworthiness, and of poorer conditions of preservation? For example, can we assign to which nation we would have attributed the shipwreck of the *Mercurio* after a simple pre-disturbance survey, producing only a selection of objects coming from so heterogeneous a panorama? Do we think that, in the presence only of French artillery, coins minted in Rome and English buttons, we would have identified the flag of the small Regno Italico?

An historical shipwreck like the *Mercurio* is a good context to stimulate this kind of theoretical doubt which should, perhaps, pervade the investigation of many other kinds of archaeological sites.

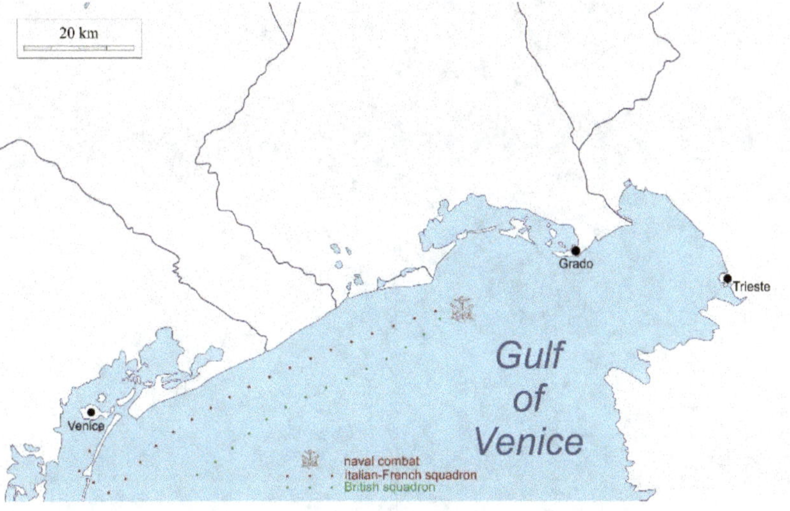

Figure 57: Routes of the squadrons and location of the shipwreck of the *Mercurio*

Figure 58: Intra-site GIS of the *Mercurio* shipwreck showing the position of the skeleton remains (elaborated by S. Manfio)

Figure 59: Pendant with the image of Saint Anne and the Baby

Figure 60: Remains of skeleton SK 1

Figure 61: Hussar sword of Austro-Hungarian type, made at Kligenthal

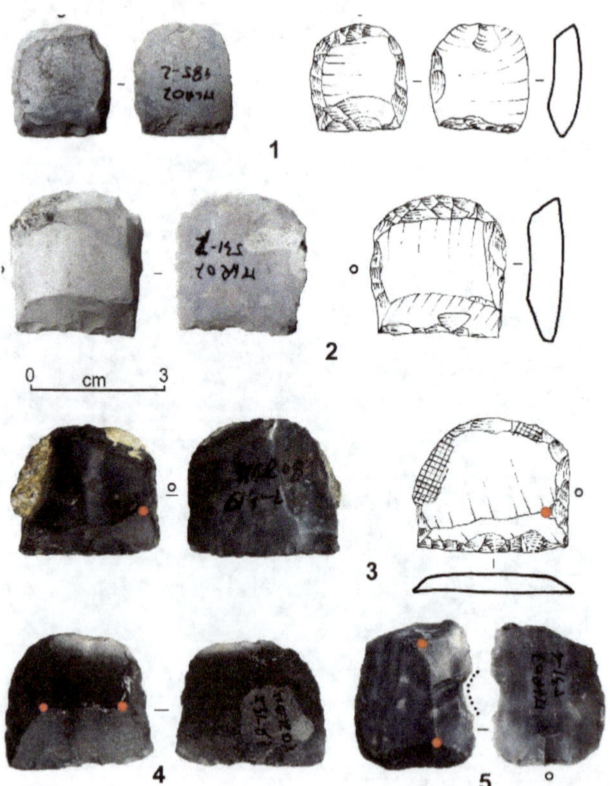

Figure 62: Gunflints produced with stone from the Baldo mountain, located close to Trento (from Biagi, Sternini and Beltrame, 2016)

Figure 63: Copper button belonging to the African King's corpse (*Corpo Reale Africano*)

Figure 64: Button of probable English production

Figure 65: *Lira Veneta* minted in Vienna

Figure 66: Copper *Baiocchi* minted in Rome

Figure 67: Gold wedding ring probably made in Sardinia

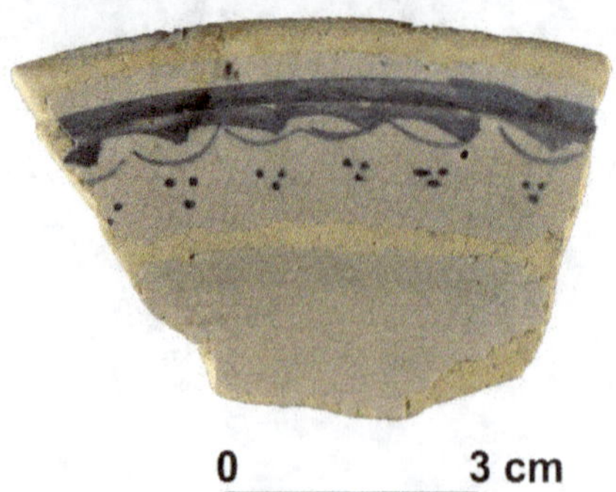

Figure 68: Fragment of plate of maiolica from Castelli d'Abruzzo

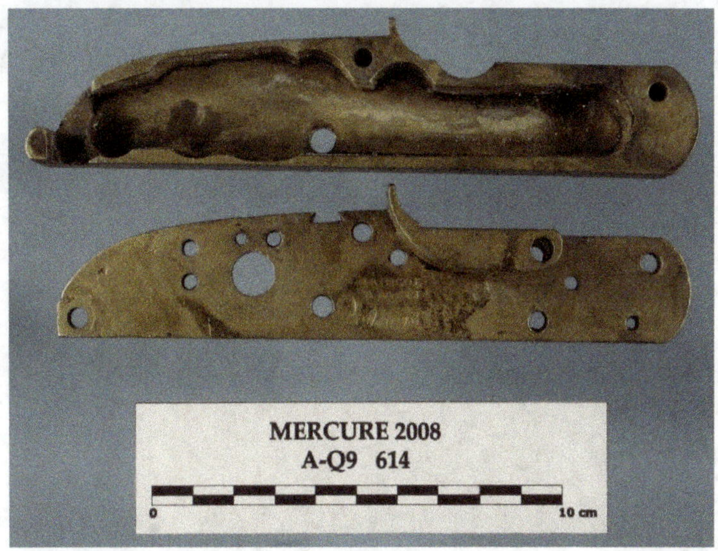

Figure 69: Brass flintlock belonging to a sort of blunderbuss or a big musket produced in Paris

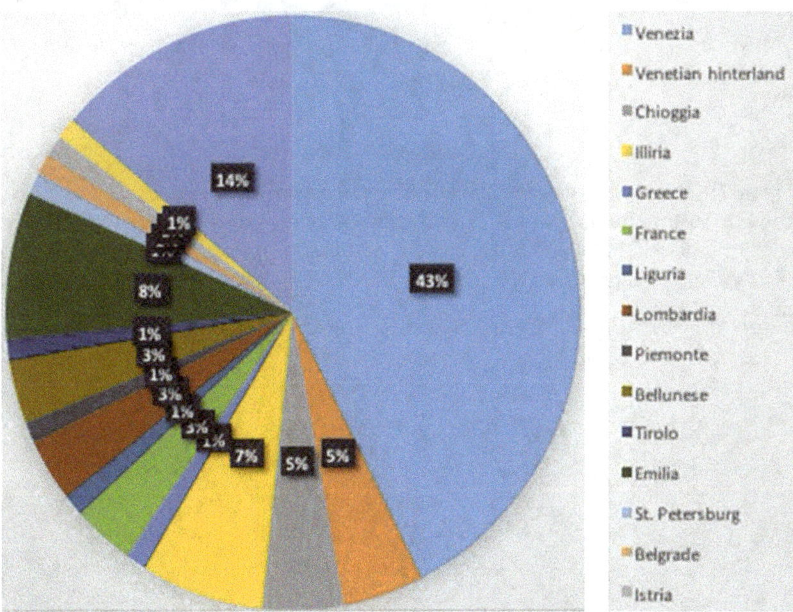

Figure 70: Pie chart showing the various proveniences of the *Mercurio* crew

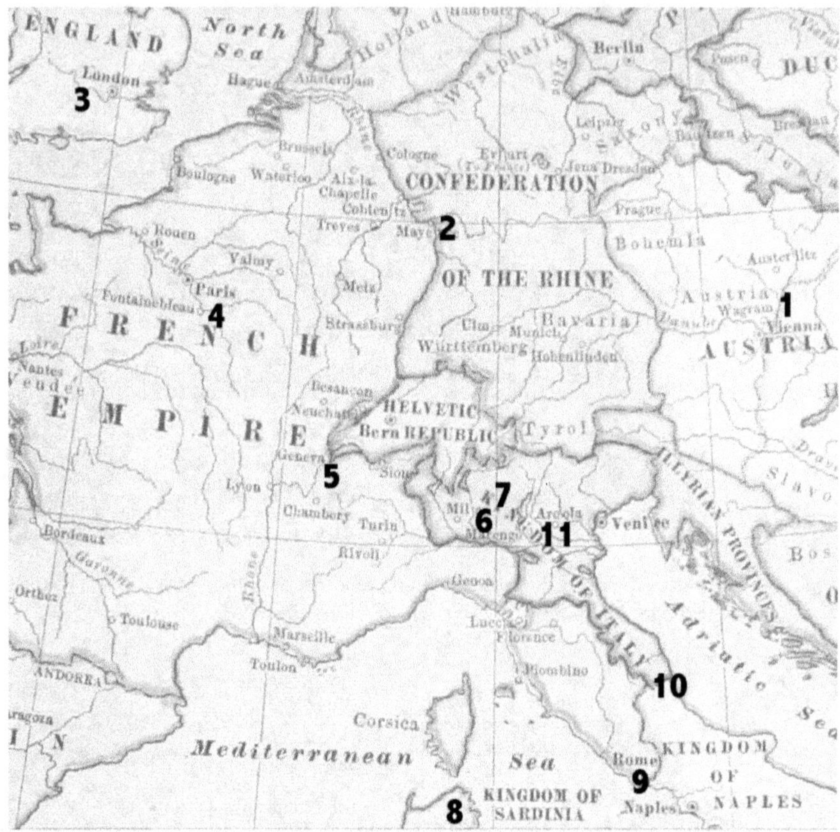

Figure 71: Provenance of some objects found in the shipwreck. 1. Lire venete and Kreuzer coins; 2. Austro-Hussar sword; 3. Seven buttons; 4. *Sabre de bord* and heavy and swivel artillery; 5. Pistol model 1786; 6. Musket model 1786 and sabre briquet; 7. Gunflints; 8. Gold ring (*fede sarda*); 9. Coins (Baiocchi) minted in Rome; 10. Dish of maiolica; 11. Coin (*Baiocco*) minted in Ferrara

References

Beltrame, C., 2007. Il Mercure. Il relitto del brick del Regno Italico affondato nel 1812 nella battaglia di Grado, in L. Fozzati, ed., *Caorle archeologica. Tra mare, fiume e terra*, Venezia, 137–146.

Beltrame, C., 2009. The excavation of the brig Mercure of the Regno Italico (1812). Why to investigate a military vessel from the beginning of the 19th century?, in R. Bockius, ed., *Between the Seas. Transfer and Exchanges in Nautical Technology. Proceedings of the Eleventh International Symposium on Boat and Ship Archaeology, Mainz 2006*, Mainz, 249–256.

Beltrame, C., 2010. Elementi per un'archeologia dei relitti navali di età moderna. L'indagine di scavo sottomarino sul brick *Mercurio*, in, ed., S. Medas, M. D'Agostino and G. Caniato, *Archeologia, storia, etnologia navale, Atti del I convegno nazionale, Cesenatico 2008*, Bari, 55–61.

Beltrame, C. and S. Manfio, 2014. *Alcune proposte metodologiche per l'impiego di un GIS intra-site nella documentazione di un relitto: l'applicazione sul brick Mercurio (Punta Tagliamento, Italia)*, Archeologia e calcolatori, 25, 43–59.

Bertoldi, F., Beltrame, C. and Sisalli, C., 2014. Human skeletal remains from the shipwreck of the brig *Mercurio* (1812), in, ed., C. Beltrame, *Archeologia dei relitti postmedievali. Archaeology of post-medieval shipwrecks*, Florence, 143–154.

Biagi, P., Sternini, E. and C. Beltrame, 2016. *The Mercurio gunflints: a techno-typological and cultural assessment*, Antiquaries Journal, 96, 1–27.

Boeri, G., Crociani, P. and C. Paoletti, 1996, *Uniformi delle Marine Militari Italiane nell'Età Napoleonica*, Rome.

Craik, J., 2005. *Uniforms exposed: from conformity to transgression (dress, body, culture)*, London/Oxford.

Donadel, S., 2019. *Crew, Uniforms and weapons*, in C. Beltrame, *The Mercurio. A Brig of the Regno Italico Sunk During the Battle of Grado (1812)*, Turnhout, 155–188.

Manfio, S., 2014. *La cucina del relitto del brig Mercurio (1812)*, in, ed., C. Beltrame, *Archeologia dei relitti postmedievali. Archaeology of post-medieval shipwrecks*, Florence, 157–175.

Archival sources

Ruolo di bordo del brick armato Mercurio, saltato in aria la notte del 22.2.1812 nelle acque di Ligniano e Buso, alle ore 4, cannoni n° 16 da 24 e 2 da 6, armato il 17.6.1810 a Venezia, Archivio di Stato di Venezia, Ufficio Generale di Iscrizione Marittima, Commissariato agli Armamenti, b, 104

On War on Board
– Some Reflections

JOHAN RÖNNBY

Is war natural?

In this book we have met many and varied examples of warfare at sea. A question underlying all studies dealing with war is of course why we are fighting each other at all. Can war be explained or at least understood?

Aggression as such is sometimes seen as a part of very old psychological and biological abilities for dealing with threats and danger, behaviour which we are said to share with our primate relatives (Eibl-Eibesfeldt 1993, 1998). But a simple biological explanation for war soon runs into trouble, for solving problems with violence is not always the natural choice among different kind of today's living primates, so what kind of "monkeys" the early hominids really were is debatable (see Berg & Douglas 2015).

An old question in many studies of war, whether articulated or not, is the question of a certain human nature. Some explanations claim that war and violence result from egotistical hostility that is fundamental to humans. The 17th century philosopher Thomas Hobbs wrote in his famous book *Leviathan* from 1651, that man's natural state was "a war of every man against every man". To handle and control this embodied danger is, according to Hobbs, necessary and that is the task for a state and a ruler (Hobbs 1976, see also for example Dawson 1996; Malesivic 2010).

Following Hobb's theme of man's natural violence, culture and civilization can be seen as a way of avoiding conflict. In such a perspective it has been argued that the Enlightenment and general cultural development during the Modern period have actually made the world more peaceful. A modern best-selling book arguing for such a perspective is Steven Pinker's *The Better Angels of Our Nature* (2011).

However, there have been and still are other views regarding human nature. A classic example is found in the writing of Jean-Jacque Rousseau (1712–1778). His view was the opposite to that of Hobbs. Rousseau claimed that it was in fact civilization which debased people and made them evil. In our original, natural state we humans were actually benign and innocent.

An interesting example of a way of avoiding any idea of fixed, 'hard-wired' character traits but still argue that humans are not born violent, is found in the Russian aristocrat, scientist and anarchist Pjotr Kropotkin's book *Mutual Aid* from 1902. He argues there that, typical for humans (and other species), is a fundamental instinct for cooperation. The ability to work together and to help your neighbour is according to Kropotkin, the most important factor for survival. That, he maintains, is the actual core factor in evolution, not the competition between individuals that Charles Darwin had observed on the small islands of the Galapagos. Pjotr Kropotkin based his idea originally on extensive fieldwork in Siberia. In this harsh environment, animals well as humans had to cooperate and care about each other if they wanted to survive. To kill fellow humans in battles and war is from this perspective, something very odd and in opposition to the empathic and helpful nature evolution has equipped us with for mutual human survival. We therefore actually dislike fighting and conflict (Kropotkin 2012, see also Dawson 1996: 11, Berg 2012:320–21).

Explaining war?

If one does not want to explain war simply as inevitable given the fixed, aggressive and predatory nature of humans, the explanation for actual warfare must be found somewhere else outside the human mind.

Following this line, war has sometimes been explained as a simple response to social stress caused by ecological factors, lack of food or overpopulation. A well-known argument of this kind was set out by Robert Malthus (1776–1834) in "An Essay on the Principle of Population".

Using archaeological data as a way of analysing warfare in a long-term perspective, some authors have seen it as part of cultural change and social evolution, claiming that the first evidence for warfare can be found far back in Palaeolithic times, probably in connection with more advanced tool technologies for hunting (Dawson 1996:26ff).

More common however, is to link the first systematic warfare to the late Stone Age. During the Neolithic period, people became increasingly sedentary and accumulated more possessions. The ability to accumulate surplus in various forms led to the possibility of appropriating such surpluses from one's neighbours, leading to new forms of organized conflict. Step by step over time humans got more and more "entangled" with their possessions and with the tools they needed to obtain and protect then (see Hodder 2012, Hagberg & Widman 2016, Adams & Rönnby this volume). From military contexts, well-known ideological constructions such as "honour, glory and duty" could also have arisen in connection to both raiding and defence as a new self-reinforcing part of this material entanglement.

The fact that wars often concern women, or in any case claims to do so, can also be explained by this perspective. In a hierarchical patriarchal society, women also become commodities that need both protection and can be conquered. The classic example is, of course, Homer's *Iliad* (see Kallifatides 2018).

Arguing this way is rather close to a classic Marxist explanation of history, i.e., conflict resulting from material surplus in society. What classic historical materialism adds is the concept of class struggle and also an idea of law-based dialectical evolutionary change (see, for example, Wigforss 1970 ,Cohen 2001).

As a comprehensive answer to why we fight, there are attractions in models that stress conflict in relation to possessions and surplus. One then does not have to link the explanations to a predestined, good or bad, human nature. If war can be explained by the distribution and inequality of wealth and things, it is also possible to do something about it! A fairer world would mean less war.

A general explanation like this is of course however a simplification and it hardly makes a participant in, or a researcher of a specific war, much the wiser about the particular circumstances or causes. General models of human behaviour are helpful and worth considering but they remain just that: models, and should not be confused with the complexity and unpredictability of real life.

The historian Alf Johansson has similarly warned against seeking simple monocausal explanations for modern wars. War is, according to him, a multidimensional phenomenon. It includes for example psychology and human aspiration but also international politics and economic structures (Johansson 1988: 370ff).

The interest in war

Coming close to the end of another book dealing with war it seems relevant to reflect on where the great interest in the subject comes from. A common rationale and justification for the interest in and the importance of war studies respectively is to simply state that it is a human phenomenon that has always existed, and which has had a great influence on individuals as well as collectives for thousands of years. Written history and of course the archaeological record (liberally scattered with evidence of contested land divisions, fortifications, weapon technologies and traces of battles back to early Stone Age) makes it difficult to contradict this.

However, if one scrutinizes this closely it becomes obvious that conflict and violence are not normal conditions. Even if organizing and preparing for war both technologically, and ideologically closely follows human history, in fact battle, i.e. occasions where people actually kill each other were very rare events. The warship *Mars* (1564) for example, mentioned several times in this book, sinks during a war known as the Nordic Seven Years' War (1563–1570). It is a concentrated period of warfare in Scandinavia known for bloody battles, major naval operations and great suffering for civilians. Maritime warfare and fleet actions played an important role during these years but even during this extremely tense period (see Ekman & Unger 1942: 168–191), the actual days and hours where humans were involved in direct fighting aboard ship is calculated at less than some weeks. That means that during the seven years of warfare the actual duration of all combat was less than one percent of the time.

But still, even if actual combat resulting in fatalities is rather rare, the fascination and depictions of violence and killing are visible around us all the time. The news is full of reports from wars in various places, and we meet it daily in popular stories, literature and pure entertainment. If one studies the shelves of magazines in a news agent's store, a surprisingly large number of them deal with war in history. There seems to be an unquenchable appetite for the violent adventures of Roman legionaries, Viking warriors or the air aces of the two World Wars. And this is just the historical part of the shelf, besides these there are also a large number of popular magazines which deal with weapons, military training and mercenaries.

The war hero

Even in texts and other forms of expression that purport to be objective witness testimony or research studies, one can often sense a rather unpleasant fascination for violence and the mechanisms connected to war. Recurring themes are the life-enhancing, euphoric feeling of being close to death, the special comradeship of soldiers ("brothers in arms") and the technical ingenuity regarding the tools for killing. Not least among these sentiments is the warrior, the hero and his extraordinary qualities which enjoy a continuity through our interest in war. It is the same story regardless of whether he is called Hercules, Sigurd Fafnesbarne, Sir Lancelot, Braveheart or Rambo. The fact that the hero is often pictured as a complicated person just reinforces the status. Not just a super warrior, but a human super warrior in whom we can recognize ourselves (see for example Rathsack 2009, Kyhle 2015).

The image of the hero is also obviously very much linked to masculinity. Svetlana Aleksijevit's highlights the phenomenon in her book about Soviet female fighters during WWII. They were first hailed as heroes and were celebrated for their extraordinary achievements as snipers or fighter pilots, yet after the war they became invisible and were forgotten. They themselves also preferred to hide their stories and their decorations when they returned home. What they had done and had been during the war did not fit with the norms of society at that time. A female war hero was greeted not with gratitude or admiration but with hostility and suspicion, not least by fellow women (Aleksijevits 2012).

During early modern times, masculinity of the male war hero was expressed both by attributes and clothes (see Stadin in this volume) but it is also woven into the societal regulations about how to behave and into general attitudes regarding being a brave man or being a coward. The importance of behaving in a "manly" way on board a warship was a part of this (see Hammar in this volume). The concept of masculinity during war has throughout history also had a dark side of abuse and rape. The complex subject of gender, sex and violence during war has been discussed from an early modern example by Maria Sjöberg (2016: 87–108).

Where we do not want to be

How should our longstanding fascination and obsession with war, killing and hero warriors be explained, when war and battles as discussed above seem to be rather rare events? Is this in fact a good argument for Thomas Hobbs' old idea about our basic "wolf-like" nature? The real, evil side of our nature which is just covered by a veneer of 'civilization' and held in check by laws and regulations? Do we actually like war?

Not necessarily so. A first point regarding this is that human interest in and preoccupation with war, rather than being held back by culture and power structures, are instead often driven and encouraged by ideological structures and power-holders in society. Especially if one uses the most common definition of war, which stresses it as an organized systematic form of violence. The glorification of war and fighting heroes has been a favourite theme for rulers and potentates over the centuries. One finds it for example in Homers famous descriptions of Achilles and Hector during the battle of Troy (for an interesting alternative interpretation of the *Iliad* as an anti-war book, see Kallifatides 2018:201).

Stories about war have held groups and states together, allowing soldiers to leave their homes and families and be part of regiments, armies and boat crews without excessive protests. It has also made the killing acceptable and even appreciated in some societies. Payment, military hierarchy, and reward have made warfare and training for war a way of life and a profession with a career structure. War industries and profit from both manufacturing and selling equipment for war has long been an important component of maintaining power regimes and of national economies at least since the early modern period and the formation of the new states during the 15th and 16th century.

The organized societal transformation process to prepare humans for war, to make them into warriors also has a surprisingly similar history on different places and reveals perhaps how the soldier's mentality and identity is a construction. The initiation of young ancient Spartans during the 5th century BC and new Arctic Swedish rangers in the 1980s have a lot in common (see Haldén & Jackson 2016). Maybe such a preparation, such a transformation is necessary for ordinary humans in order for them to function in war? This process is then necessary regardless of whether one is to fight for an aggressive dictator or in the civil defence of a peaceful democracy.

A lot of research into the subject of killing further suggests that we are actually rather bad as killers. We are neither psychologically nor physically particularly effective unless we are trained and prepared for it. To make unwilling soldiers actually strive to kill the enemy has been a central problem for officers and military leaders throughout history (see Grossman, 2004 2009, Bourke 1999:57ff).

If one therefore chooses to believe Prince Kropotkin that humans are good, or at least that we are not predestined for fighting and killing, it can be argued that most human beings throughout history and all over the world prefer to use their social capacity to avoid direct conflict. They favour, if they have a choice, to cooperate and interact peacefully instead of using their skills and creativity for warfare.

This book about warfare and ships during the early modern period can then be seen as an examination of aspects and circumstances that contributed to the fact that it went so wrong on some occasions. A collection of examples of material culture, symbols, economic constraints, ideas, beliefs and ideological structures that are needed for making something so counterproductive and devastating for humans as warfare and bloody sea battles happen.

Because to be on board a ship at war is not where we want to be.

References

Aleksijevitj, S., 2012 [1985]). *Kriget har inget kvinnligt ansikte: utopins röster.* Stockholm: Ersatz.

Berg, L., 2012. *Gryning över Kalahari: hur människan blev människa.* Uppdaterad utg. Stockholm: Ordfront.

Berg, L., 2014. *Ut ur Kalahari: drömmen om det goda livet.* Stockholm: Ordfront.

Berg, L., 2011. *Skymningssång i Kalahari: hur människan bytte tillvaro.* Stockholm: Ordfront.

Berg, L., & Douglas, C., 2015. *Vårt inre Afrika: upptäcktsresor.* Stockholm: Ordfront.

Bourke, J., 1999. *An intimate history of killing: face-to-face killing in twentieth-century warfare.* [New York]: Basic books.

Dawson, D., 1996. The Origins of War: Biological and Anthropological Theories. *History and Theory,* Vol. 35, No. 1 pp. 1–28. Wesleyan University.

Dupuy, T. N., 1990 [1984]. *The evolution of weapons and warfare.* New York, N.Y.: Da Capo Press.

Eibl-Eibesfeldt, I., 1993. Aggression och krig något mänskligt? In: Berglund, Björn E., Rowley-Conwy, Peter & Burenhult, Göran (1993). *Bra böckers encyklopedi om människans historia. 1, Mänsklighetens gryning: de första människorna i Afrika och Europa.* Höganäs: Bra böcker.

Eibl-Eibesfeldt, I. & Salter, F. K. (ed.), 1998. *Indoctrinability, ideology and warfare: evolutionary perspectives* . New York: Berghahn.

Ferrill, A., 1997. *The origins of war: from the Stone Age to Alexander the Great* . Rev. ed. Boulder, Colo.: Westview.

Lybeck, O. (red.), 1942. *Svenska flottans historia: örlogsflottan i ord och bild från dess grundläggning under Gustav Vasa fram till våra dagar. Bd 3, [1815–1945].* Malmö: Allhem.

Grossman, D. & Christensen, L. W., 2004. *On combat: the psychology and physiology of deadly conflict in war and peace.* [S.l.]: PPCT research publications.

Grossman, D., 2009. *On killing: the psychological cost of learning to kill in war and society.* Rev. ed. New York: Little, Brown and Co.

Hagberg, B. & Widman, M., 2016. *Att döda en människa: på spaning efter det första kriget.* Stockholm: Norstedt.

Haldén, P., & Jackson, P. (ed.), 2016. *Transforming warriors: the ritual organization of military forces.* New York, NY: Routledge.

Hobbes, T., 1976. *Leviathan* . London: Dent.

Hodder, I., 2012. *Entangled: an archaeology of the relationships between humans and things.* Malden, MA: Wiley-Blackwell.

Johansson, A. W., 1988. *Europas krig: militärt tänkande, strategi och politik från Napoleontiden till andra världskrigets slut.* Stockholm: Tiden.

Kallifatides, T., 2018. *Slaget om Troja.* Albert Bonniers Förlag.

Kropotkin, K. P. A., 2012 (1904). *Mutual aid: a factor of evolution.* Radford: Wilder Publications.

Kyle, C., McEwen, S. & DeFelice, J., 2015. *American sniper: den amerikanska militärens dödligaste prickskytt* . [Ny utg.] Stockholm: Bonnier pocket.

Malesevic, S., 2010. *The sociology of war and violence.* Cambridge: Cambridge University Press.

Malthus, T. R., (1969). *Om befolkningsfrågan samt debatten kring denna.* Stockholm: LT.

Pinker, S., 2011. *The better angels of our nature: why violence has declined.* New York: Penguin Books.

Rathsack, T., 2009. *Jägare: bakom fiendens linjer.* Stockholm: Fischer & Co ces. New York, NY: Routledge.

Sjöberg, M., 2016. Transformation into manhood. Sex violence, and the making of warriors, women and victims in early modern Europe, In: Haldén, Peter & Jackson, Peter (ed.). *Transforming warriors: the ritual organization of military forces*. New York, NY: Routledge.

Wigforss, E., 1970 (1908). *Materialistisk historieuppfattning. Industriell demokrati* . [Ny utg.] Stockholm: Tiden.

Ångström, J., 2016. Transforming into nature: Swedish Army Rangers rites of passage. in: Haldén, Peter & Jackson, Peter (ed.) (2016). *Transforming warriors: the ritual organization of military forces*. New York, NY: Routledge.

The Authors

Jon Adams, PhD, Professor of Maritime Archaeology at the University of Southampton and the Director of Southampton's Centre for Maritime Archaeology, CMA. He has a special interest in ships as manifestations of innovation and social change, and the practice of archaeology in the coastal zone and under water. Adams was Deputy Director of the *Mary Rose* Project and has since then been involved in numerous other research projects and fieldworks, several of them in the Baltic. He is currently directing a large international project concerning shoreline displacement and deep-water shipwrecks in Black Sea.

Carlo Beltrame, PhD, Associated Professor of Maritime Archaeology at Univeresità Ca' Foscari Venezia. His research has focused on shipwrecks dated from the Antiquity till the Modern. He is specialized in the techniques of ship construction, in the life aboard the ships and in the techniques of documentation of the underwater sites.

Arthur Cohn, JD, Director Emeritus of the Lake Champlain Maritime Museum, has spent four decades as an advocate for the development of public policy for the protection of Underwater Cultural Heritage. He has participated in dozens of shipwreck survey and documentation projects and is the Principal Investigator for the Spitfire Project.

Niklas Eriksson, PhD, Associate Professor and Researcher at the Department for Archaeology and Classical Studies, at Stockholm University. He has been involved in many archaeological surveys and published a number of books and articles on different historical and maritime archaeological topics, from ship architecture and sculptures to history of maritime archaeology. Right now, he is preparing a manuscript on sailing routes.

Matilda Fredriksson, MA in Osteoarchaeology. Working as a curator at the cultural heritage unit at the Swedish National Maritime and Transport Museums. Currently active as an independent researcher in the project 'Skeppet *Mars* 1564'. Her research interests lie mainly within the field of marine osteoarchaeology and forensic taphonomy.

AnnaSara Hammar, PhD and a Research Fellow at the Centre for Maritime Studies at Stockholm University, Sweden. She is a naval historian and her research has mainly focused on social order and the creation of hierarchies among officers and men in the early modern Swedish navy.

Fred Hocker, PhD, Director of Research at the Vasa Museum. He was formerly the Yamini Associate Professor of Nautical Archaeology at Texas A&M and a senior researcher at the National Museum of Denmark, and has been a visiting fellow at the MacDonald Institute of Archaeology, Cambridge University. He has conducted shipwreck excavations in the United States, Turkey and Denmark, and his research focuses on maritime economics and ship construction.

Patrik Höglund, Phd-researcher in history and maritime archaeologist at the Swedish Maritime and Transport Museums. His research has mainly focused on conditions and social interaction aboard Early-modern ships.

Johan Rönnby, PhD, Professor of Maritime Archaeology at Södertörn University. Director for the Maritime Archaeological Research Institute, MARIS. His research has focused on different shipwrecks in the Baltic Sea, but have also concerned lake dwellings, harbours and prehistoric landscapes under water, coastal landscapes and human cultural and social interaction with water.

Ingvar Sjöblom, PhD, Assistant Professor. Director of Studies, War studies, advanced level, Swedish Defence University. Sjöbloms research focus on naval officers during the 16th century, naval warfare and artillery from medieval to modern period. He is specialised on operations, tactics and interdisciplinary research between history, archaeology and war studies.

Kekke Stadin, PhD, Professor of History at Södertörn University. Most of her studies focus on cultural history and gender history in early modern Sweden. Her later publications deal with masculinity, men's fashion and clothing from the renaissance until the present day.

Sabine Sten, PhD, Professor in osteoarchaeology at Uppsala University, Campus Gotland. Her current research interests are marine osteo–archaeology, covering both human and animal skeletal remains. Sten's studies involve material from shipwrecks but also coastal material from Gotska Sandön in the Baltic Sea.

Rolf Fabricius Warming, Cand.mag. (Prehistoric Archaeology) and MA (Maritime Archaeology), Director of the Society for Combat Archaeology. His research efforts have mainly focused on historical weaponry, conflicts and warships. He is currently involved in the projects *"Gribshunden* (1495)" and "Mars Makalös (1564)" as an independent researcher, and is leading the experimental archaeology project "The Viking Shield" in collaboration with Trelleborg Viking Fortress (National Museum of Denmark).

Figures and Tables

Figures

Tables

Södertörn Archaeological Studies

1. Bolin, Hans (red.), *The interplay of past and present: Papers from a session held at the 9th annual EAA meeting in St Petersburg 2003*, 2004.

2. Edberg, Rune, *Vikingaskeppet Ormen Friskes undergång: Ett drama i det kalla krigets skugga*, 2004.

3. Ej utgiven.

4. Burström, Mats (red.), *Arkeologi och mångkultur: Rapport från Svenskt arkeologmöte 2006*, 2006.

5. Cassel, Kerstin, *Det gemensamma rummet: Migrationer, myter och möten*, 2008.

6. Burström, Mats (red.), *Samtidsarkeologi – varför gräva i det nära förflutna? Rapport från en session vid konferensen IX Nordic TAG i Århus 2007*, 2008.

7. Burström, Mats (red.), *Arkeologi i förorten: Berättelser från norra Botkyrka*, 2008.

8. Arnshav, Mirja, *"Yngre vrak" – Samtidsarkeologiska perspektiv på ett nytt kulturarv*, 2011.

9. McWilliams, Anna, *An Archaeology of the Iron Curtain: Material and Metaphor*, 2013.

10. Eriksson, Niklas, *Urbanism Under Sail: An Archaeology of Fluit Ships in Early Modern Everyday Life*, 2014.

11. Arnshav, Mirja & McWilliams, Anna, *Stalins ubåtar: En arkeologisk undersökning av vraken efter S7 och SC-305*, 2015.

12. Gustafsson Gillbrand, Patrik, *Stenbruk: Stenartefakter, råmaterial och mobilitet i östra Mellansverige under tidig- och mellanmesolitikum*, 2018.

13. Henriksson, Mikael, *Arkeologiska förväntningar i mötet med ett landskap: Stenålderns Blekinge ur ett kunskapsperspektiv*, 2019.

14. Törnqvist, Oscar, *Röster från ingenmansland – En identitetsarkeologi i ett maritimt mellanrum*, 2019.

15. Rönnby, Johan (ed.), *On War on Board Archaeological and Historical perspectives on Early Modern Maritime Violence and Warfare*, 2019.